Mamma Mia, Americans "Invade" Italy!

True Stories of the Americana in Italy

STEPHANIE CHANCE

WestBow·
PRESS
A DIVISION OF THOMAS NELSON
& ZONDERVAN

WestBow Press books may be ordered through booksellers or by contacting:

WestBow Press
A Division of Thomas Nelson & Zondervan
1663 Liberty Drive
Bloomington, IN 47403
www.westbowpress.com
1 (866) 928-1240

ISBN: 978-1-4908-3697-3 (sc)
ISBN: 978-1-4908-3698-0 (hc)
ISBN: 978-1-4908-3696-6 (e)

Library of Congress Control Number: 2014908527

Printed in the United States of America.

WestBow Press rev. date: 05/21/2014

CONTENTS

Dedicated to:

Tony Filaci, the Sicilian—I love you dearly!

Dwight A. Brannon, the scholarly attorney—you taught me more than ten thousand days in an university! I'm forever thankful.

1

THE VELCRO GIRDLE

Racing through the airport like a caravan camel, my large backpack controls the mobility of my wavering body as I haphazardly pull two bulging pieces of luggage tagged with huge pink circles that dangle back and forth with the printed name Stephani Chance. This is absolutely normal behavior for me.

It's a beautiful day here in Dallas, Texas, and I'm excited to start another Italy adventure with the Americans. I love taking them to the many fairy-tale places that are off the tourist paths and allowing them to experience Italy as the locals do.

I'm already thinking of Tony and Nino standing outside the international-arrivals doors at the Roma airport, eagerly awaiting our arrival and ready to begin our two weeks of magical, fairy-tale bliss. However, my exciting thoughts of enchanted adventures come to a hair-raising halt as I realize something is wrong with one of my passengers. Gladys is walking slowly, right in front of me, and seems to be breathing hard. She's pulling her luggage toward the international terminal while I motion for the other twelve people in our group to go ahead of us. I can't imagine why Gladys is walking so slowly, huffing and puffing like she's just run a marathon. We've walked only a short distance, and there haven't been any hills to climb or cobblestone streets, just a flat concourse in the Dallas/Fort Worth Airport.

Just a few months earlier, Gladys had been in my store, Decorate Ornate, signing up for this Italy tour, excitedly telling the whole store of customers how physically fit she was. I remember our conversation clearly, and the diet cola she accidentally spilled all over a beautiful designer pillow as she childishly reenacted an outrageous acrobatic maneuver with her marshmallow, spongelike arms.

"Stephani, I want to see all I can in Italy, and I can assure you that there will be no lounging around or sleeping in for me. This is a once-in-a-lifetime experience for me, and my body is trained like a wild tiger, ready to let loose and run like the wind."

Looking at her in hopes she wouldn't display any more acrobatic techniques, I explained in great detail the daily adventures: "Gladys, every morning after a delicious breakfast, we hop aboard our Mercedes-Benz coach and zoom off to the most unbelievable, fairy-tale sites in the world. We go to villages that are frozen in time—places that are truly out of storybooks. The minute our feet hit the cobblestones and we walk inside these fairy tales, experiencing them one page at a time, you will think you are in a real storybook, with walled gates. I can try to describe a few of the places we'll go, but words can't come close to describing the beauty and magnificence of what you will see in Italy.

"Every single region of Italy is different and beautiful. Most of the people who go on our tours—some twice a year—have been traveling with us for years; they never get tired of Italy. And Gladys, you say you are in perfect health and can run like a tiger. Wow, you will pass me up for sure on the cobblestones."

Before I finish my sentence, Gladys interrupts me. "Stephani, I can assure you that I'm very athletic. I jog every morning. I do acrobatics, and with my new spandex body girdle, I'm ready to roll."

Thinking back to her words leaves me wondering what happened. Is this the same Gladys? Is this the same lady who was in my store signing up for this Italy tour? I look down at Gladys now as she cautiously grips her luggage and says, sounding exhausted, "I'm prepared for the worst possible situation. I've purchased a security-proof, spandex body girdle to keep my euros safe, and of course, full protection is guaranteed against any potential serial rapists on the prowl. You can never be too cautious while visiting these foreign countries such as Italy, girls." I flash a surprised look to the others in our group as we now stand in line with them.

"Gladys, are you okay today?" I ask with growing concern.

"I've never felt better. I feel like a racehorse ready to go. However, I must admit that with my new girdle on now, I'm a little restricted in the movement department. Oh, but girls, you are sure going to wish you had my girdle on when those Italian Romeos start flirting. And then, well, you know, they have the reputation of being the world's best lovers." Gladys gives us a serious wink. Her eyelids are highlighted in bright, neon blue eye shadow with green eyeliner magnified through her designer, cat-eye-rimmed glasses.

Before responding to such nonsense, Sandra Crow from Bogota, Texas, roars with laughter and announces to everyone in the long line that we're now standing in, "Gladys, I don't think you have anything to worry about with that kind of contraption enveloping your body. I've not heard of any serial rapists in Italy. Have you, Stephani?" Sandra rolls her dark black eyes, looking toward me with a big grin.

In a split second, right in front of the long line of people who are already stripping off their extra apparel, preparing to go through the rigorous, international-security check, Gladys releases her luggage from her tightly gripped hands as though they were hot frying pans. Right in front of us, Gladys plummets over like a folded piece of paper, sending her flocked curls upside down and polishing the tile floor. Before I can swallow my assortment of M&M's, Gladys springs right back up, almost hitting her head on my stomach with her shoes now dangling in her hands.

"Good golly, Miss Molly," shouts Sandra, who is shocked beyond her wildest imagination.

Acting as though nothing just happened, Gladys grabs her luggage and proceeds a few more steps toward the international conveyor belt. She stands in a way that reminds me of a dog sniffing the air while its head hangs out of the car window. However, needless to say, Gladys is in the airport awaiting her turn to place her luggage on the belt and her personal items in the little basket. The rest of my group stare at each other, and then someone says, laughing, "Okay, this might be a good time to say, 'Mamma Mia!'"

My adrenaline is exploding throughout my body, having witnessed such bizarre behavior from Gladys, and I'm wondering what's going to happen next. Stepping in front of Gladys to get a better view of her spring-loaded body, I'm absolutely flabbergasted at the rainstorm pouring from her. Perspiration is dripping profusely from her Cabbage Patch face, reminding me of a melting snowman, and now she's smiling as though a professional photographer is ready to snap her photo.

"Stephani, in all my years of nursing, I've never seen anything like this," Mayrene said repeatedly, along with others in the line. "I'm a registered nurse, and I've never witnessed such a sight. I can't believe how she bends. I mean, how …? She is as wide as she is tall, and … I am speechless. Did you see how she bent over? I thought she was doing some kind of exercise, but she was grabbing her slip-on sandals. I could never do that without bending my legs.

After placing our carry-on luggage and personal items on the conveyer belt, we step forward with passports in hand, and one by one we go through the enclosed radar detector. All of us pass through with flying colors. There is no difficulty at all until Gladys. No sooner do I place my shoes back on my feet than Gladys steps inside the radar-detector passage. Suddenly, the red lights start flashing and the loud alarm sounds.

"Madam, can you please step back and walk through again with your passport in clear view?" Gladys nods at the airline attendant, and then in a split second, we all once again watch in shock.

Backing up like a car jammed into reverse and then shifting back into forward, Gladys speedily rushes through the security detector like a shoplifter fleeing the police. I don't know if Gladys thinks "speed" will fool the security system or what, but her legs can no doubt run.

Again, the lights go to flashing and the alarm shrieks with deafening tones. "Madam, please come here. Stretch out your legs and arms," the security worker demands, pointing his long electronic wand toward her sweaty body.

Surprisingly, Gladys looks as though she's been selected for a game show prize and excitedly reaches for the end of her silky white blouse. In a matter of seconds, we watch with open mouths as Gladys pulls her blouse upward at the speed of light, over her flesh-colored body girdle and up over her red-flocked curls.

"Don't worry sir, I have all of my credentials right here, safe and sound," Gladys says to the airline attendant, pointing to her breasts underneath the Velcro girdle.

"Stop! Please put your blouse back on," shouts the stuttering officer, while flashing his eyes toward the security camera above his head. I'm sure he's hoping the camera is recording this rare event that's happening before his very eyes.

"Oh, sir—no, ah, look—my passport is right here," Gladys declares as she brings her stubby fingers toward her padded, protected breasts and pulls the Velcro tabs outward. Immediately like a magic show, her two enormous marshmallow breasts pop out like a jack-in-the-box, and then, at the speed of sound, plunge downward in a fast, dangling kind of way.

"This cannot be happening," I say aloud with my hands over my mouth. "What kind of person does such a thing?" I look at Sandra, who is speechless and appears to be in shock along with the rest of the people in line.

Well, all I can say at this point is "Mamma Mia!" Getting through international security at the Dallas Airport was quite a show, and I'm sure they will never forget Gladys, because we're all still asking ourselves, "Did we really see what we think we saw?" And yes, sadly, we did—both of them.

2

GLADYS' BIRTHDAY PARTY

After the ordeal with Gladys at the airport in Dallas–Fort Worth, and arriving in Italy, my inner dialogue questions, *Could this woman possibly embarrass us any more? Well, needless to say, the answer is yes.*

With Gladys walking along with our group, we've made four steps away from our fabulous overnight stay here in the heart of Roma, Italy. It's Gladys's birthday, and we are celebrating at a restaurant called Canova on Piazza del Popolo. Canova restaurant is renowned as a celebrity rendezvous, with movie stars and television personalities.

"I can't believe I'm actually in Italy. This is my lifetime dream coming true," Barbara exclaims as she aims her camera at the striking marble statues while we continue slowly toward Piazza del Popolo.

"Oh, just wait until you see the famous Trevi Fountain, the Pantheon, the Spanish Steps, Piazza Novana, the Vatican, the Sistine Chapel, the Catacombs, the Mamertine Prison, where the apostles Peter and Paul were imprisoned before their deaths, and of course, the many hidden jewels," I recite without pausing in a vain attempt to contain my urge to jump up and down from the excitement and adrenaline surging throughout my body.

Before continuing, I notice Gladys holding her hands up like the drum major of some kind of marching band, signaling the group to stop at once. She is wheezing and perspiring like an unbridled sprinkler, and I see that Tony is already on his mobile phone, waving his hand high in the air and repeating the mantra, "Mamma Mia, Mamma Mia."

"Stefania, we must send the *signora* in a taxi. Mamma Mia Madonna! Where did you find this Americana?" Tony asks for the hundredth time.

Gladys appears as if every organ in her body has sprung a leak. Within seconds, the little taxi arrives on skidding brakes, sending out a burning, rubbery smell that engulfs our lovely Italian air. The aroma of burning rubber filling our nostrils is overwhelming, but before we can complain, we gasp at the sight of Tony forcibly pressing Gladys into the backseat of the little taxi. Watching him push her protruding hips, which seem to linger outside the little door, leaves the taxi driver very impatient, perhaps because he does not want to see his meter rest so idly.

"Signora, can you please press in more?" Tony asks and then says, "Stefania, you must go to the other side and pull the signora's arm."

"Have you lost your mind? There is no way she will fit in this tiny-tot car," I retort, passing my purse to Louise as I traipse around to the other side of the little taxi.

"Stefania, hurry! She will fit, but you must hurry and pull," Tony pleads with anguish, pushing on Gladys's ample buttocks. "Mamma Mia" replays from Tony's mouth like a broken record. The taxi driver has grabbed Gladys by the collar with the intention of helping her move in toward the middle. Sadly—or should I say, embarrassingly—her hips are a span wider than the comparatively minuscule entrance of the toylike taxi, leaving no apparent way for her entire body to fit inside.

Having gripped Gladys's spongy marshmallow of an arm tightly, I tug and pull with all my strength while Tony thrusts and rams from the other side of the car. In a bleak moment, we hear a dreadful ear-piercing sound of ripping fabric, and then shrieks as the driver's body crashes backward and slams into the steering wheel, with Gladys's fabric collar clutched tightly in his hand. With the comedy act rolling at full speed, the cartoonish spectacle entices the small crowd of local Romans, who are gathered on the sidewalk, to join in. They whoop with excitement as if hyping up their very own soccer team while Tony gives her extended hip one more forcible push with his leather shoe and finally manages to slam the miniature door shut.

Suddenly, I sense a heavy force as the pint-size taxi lifts up and tilts toward me. Before I understand the situation, Gladys's body rolls back against the door that Tony just shut. Now the little taxi is rocking back and forth, leaving us in a frozen stupor. Slamming the door shut on my side, I inform Gladys that we will meet her in a few minutes, but before I can complete my sentence, the taxi driver slams the gas pedal and peels out with that familiar fragrance of burning rubber.

We walkers arrive at our destination just as the taxi hurls around Piazza del Popolo with Gladys molded to the backseat. No sooner have we taken seats at our superb table in Canova's restaurant than Gladys announces that she must go to the toilet.

Tick tock. Tick tock. Tick tock. Where is Gladys? She's been gone to the toilet for a long time, and this is her birthday party. Finally she returns, sweaty and completely exhausted, but not one of us dares to ask why.

Hours later, after feasting on delicious Italian foods, singing and dancing, we make our way back down the straight and narrow street of Via del Corso. I veer off to the left, directly toward the famous Trevi Fountain, which is a picturesque masterpiece of magnificence under the glowing light of the moon. The Americans are lingering along with me, trekking at slow speed, stopping and peering through the shop windows, all except for Gladys, who did not accompany us. Gladys said she was ready for bed and none of us should be out strolling the streets at night in a foreign country. Therefore, Tony called a cab for Gladys.

We are within feet of the Trevi Fountain, and most entertainingly, the Americans giggle like schoolchildren at the young and the old, who are all suctioned tightly lip to lip with their lover or their gelato. We can smell from a distance the chestnuts being roasted by an old man across from the Trevi Fountain. He stands up and gazes into the fire in anticipation of the next batch of chestnuts to scoop into the little brown bags resting at his side.

"He's always here in this exact spot, year after year," I say to everyone, feeling the urge to snap his photo again.

"Wow, what a masterpiece before us," Sandra dreams aloud in her lovely Southern drawl. "The Trevi Fountain is just as spectacular as I remember it from last year. I sure wish Lanny were here to see this with me. I'm telling you now, Lanny is going to love this place when he comes to Italy with us," she continues as Tony reaches for her right cheek, giving it a soft squeeze and a slight twist at the end.

"Mamma Mia, Sandra. When do we see this husband of yours?" Tony asks with a laugh.

"One day you will," Sandra replies calmly before jetting off across the cobblestones in search of late-night gelato.

We are in heaven right now. The air is brisk, the chestnuts are roasting, and an orchestra of many exotic instruments fills in the space as the Americans bombard the Trevi Fountain with camera flashes while giggling and acting as though they have reverted to their childhoods. The Trevi Fountain is frozen in time, along with everything else here in Italy. It looks the same as it did in the old American movies, generations ago.

Looking up, I see Karen approaching me with a towering cone of chocolate gelato already dripping onto her hands, too absorbed in her camera to pay attention to the chocolaty masterpiece melting onto her designer sleeves.

"Stefania, I wonder what Gladys is doing right now. She's probably going to bed, no?" Karen asks aloud and then mumbles her own answer to herself, wrapping her tongue around the gelato.

"This should be an interesting night," Sandra Crow responds while licking her own gelato and changing the subject. Gladys is her roommate for the duration of this tour.

"Oh, she will be fine," John says. "She seems like a nice lady—just a little out of shape, I suppose. She was probably a chain smoker in her prime." He laughs and snaps a photo of a statuesque Italian woman while fibbing to his wife, "Oh, honey, I'm getting the perfect photo of the Trevi Fountain now."

Only a few minutes have passed since we left Canova's and watched Gladys hoist herself inside the large van with a flashing taxi sign on top. Tony is at ease now, knowing that he saw with his own eyes Gladys getting into the taxi van and the door slamming shut. He is chuckling and savoring a towering gelato as he expresses his concern for Gladys. "Stefania, I feel much better now that Gladys is on her way to bed for a good night's sleep," he says. "Mamma Mia, she must be very tired from the flight. Do you think that's the problem?"

Before answering Tony, Sandra says, "Well, I hope that's all that is ailing her, but we'll see by tomorrow morning, I guess. You do know that Stephani assigned her as my roommate?"

Looking out my window this morning, I see the brilliant sunbeams tickling the ancient cobblestone street. While strapping my shoes on for an adventurous day in Roma, I hear Sandra pounding on my door, desperation racing through her voice.

"Open the door. Oh, you will never believe what I've been through with that crazy Gladys," Sandra cries hysterically. She rambles on and on as I open the door and watch her fly right past me into the room.

"I've had *no* sleep. That crazy Gladys is afraid of the dark, but oh no, that is just the start of it. The lights had to stay on all night. Every fifteen minutes, she gets up to go to the bathroom with that ear-piercing Velcro ripping from that blasted body girdle. Gladys would not take the darn thing off. Unbelievable! I have never seen anything like this in my entire life. Now listen to this, Stephani. That blasted body girdle has Velcro over the crotch area. Can you believe such a garment is even on the market?" Sandra asks while wrapping her arms around the bed pillow.

"Listen to what Gladys told me last night," she goes on. "To use the toilet, she has to pull the Velcro tab up." Sandra jumps off the bed. "I'm telling you the truth. Gladys is nuts. For her to use the toilet, she has to pull the Velcro tab up. Now, how crazy is that?" Sandra asks in a state of hysteria before starting up again.

"Oh yes, that crazy woman is wrapped tighter than an ancient Egyptian mummy. She is wearing the tightest body girdle I have ever seen in my entire life. I'm telling you, the contraption has pull-out Velcro tabs over her breasts, crotch, and buttocks. Oh, there's more. Underneath the Velcro is where she keeps her euros. She stuffed herself full of euros, and God only knows what other things she has underneath it all. She's been trying to find your room number, but thank God the innkeeper protected you until this morning." Sandra tries to catch her breath while springing back on top of the bed.

There is a loud knocking on my door. Sandra and I stand frozen inside my room as loud, ear-piercing bellowing bounces violently off the door.

"Stefania, help me! I've lost all of my euros. They were hidden underneath my girdle and now they're all gone. My euros are down the drain, every last one of them, down the drain," Gladys cries out, sobbing and wailing like a bad opera singer.

I open the door hesitantly, and feeling light-headed, I watch in disbelief as Gladys springs into my room. With the door still open, I see Tony rounding the corner in hot pursuit, shouting, "Mamma Mia, Madonna! *Basta*, enough, stop."

My head is spinning and I feel faint as Tony gets closer to the door. He looks like a cartoon character with both of his hands swirling in the early morning air. As though we are in a movie from the wildest imagination ever known to any producer, Tony flies through my open door, passing right in front of me while speaking Italian words not known to any of us.

"Mamma Mia! What kind of signore are you? Where did you find this one, Stefania?" Tony asks in English, appearing to be exhausted from his near-fatal hysteria.

I now have all three of them, Sandra, Gladys and Tony, captured inside my room. Wide-eyed, we stare at Gladys as she continues rambling hysterically, and for a flashing moment, I envision a real, animated, Cabbage Patch doll right in front of me. But no, it's just Gladys.

"I remember now what happened to my euros. It happened last night while in the restaurant. I went to the toilet, and while sitting down, I reached for the Velcro flap to pull it up," Gladys says hysterically between sobs. "I forgot my euros were hidden inside the crotch area underneath the Velcro." She sobs even louder. "I hid them inside the crotch area underneath the Velcro so they'd be safe. Oh, help me."

I reach for a tissue and offer it to her, but she refuses and continues on, saying, "While on the toilet, I totally forgot about the euros when I pulled the Velcro tab up. Oh, how could I have forgotten them? I hid them in the perfect place. I cannot believe I did it, flushing them down the toilet at my very own birthday party last night. I had them safely hidden in my crotch area underneath the Velcro, securing them so tightly," Gladys echoes over and over, now sobbing louder.

Finally, as she pauses to blow her nose, I take advantage of the chance to blurt out the obvious: "What are you talking about, Gladys? What do you mean you lost all of your euros in your crotch and flushed them down the toilet?"

"Mamma Mia, Madonna," shouts Tony as he sees Gladys yank her elastic pants down in hot pursuit to show us her body girdle and the Velcro flap covering her crotch area.

"You must get my euros out of the toilet," Gladys pleads in agony, blubbering and crying like a newborn *bambino*. "I had my partial stash of euros right here. They were right here in my crotch area. They were safe and secure, but when I sat down on the toilet last night, I pulled the flap up and totally forgot that my euros were underneath the Velcro." Gladys cries louder and louder, hysterically pointing to her crotch, which is, thankfully, covered with the Velcro flap.

"This is absolutely unbelievable," I say, looking at Tony, who is stuck on the same mantra of Mamma Mias.

"Okay, Gladys, I think I understand what happened now. You were seated on the toilet, and when you pulled your Velcro tab from your crotch area, it released and sent your stash of euros plummeting down through the Roman ..." Though I say this with a straight face, I am fighting the urge to explode into laughter at any second.

In between sobs and wiping her red nose on her sleeve, she yanks her yellow polyester pants down again in an attempt to show us one more time how her body girdle operated with the lift-up tabs of Velcro. Before she can send Tony into a massive heart attack, I grab her polyester pants and holler, "No, Gladys, we completely understand."

There is more to this true and unbelievable odyssey with Gladys, but I choose to withhold some details—not that they would come off as credible in the first place. In all of my fourteen years of taking the Americans to Italy twice a year, I have never experienced anyone like Gladys, thank God. She unequivocally receives the prize as the most peculiar person I've ever met or taken to Italy.

After all these years, Sandra and I still laugh and talk about this episode, still struggling to believe it really happened. But yes, the anecdote is completely factual, except for the woman's name. I did change her name to Gladys.

3

TONY FILACI, THE SICILIAN

People say to me, "I can't imagine how you spent your entire career as a paralegal, working in the long box on countless court cases, right beside one of the most talented attorneys in East Texas. Then, in a moment's notice, you're traveling all over Italy and other foreign countries, searching for castle doors and rare relics for your very own import store you named Decorate Ornate. And, if that's not the craziest thing, you are now nestled in the tiny oil-boom town of Gladewater, Texas, which is officially tagged the Antique Capital of East Texas.

"Not only that, but you also design, plan, and take fun-loving groups of Americans to Italy twice a year. Not just any tour, they say—no, they're nothing like the large commercial tours where people are packed like sardines inside a huge double-decker bus. They say your tours are magically fascinating, alluring, and mysteriously seductive, leaving the Americans to go back with you, time and time again. You zigzag around tiny, narrow roads in a beautiful Mercedes-Benz coach with your microphone in hand, entertaining groups of Americans, along with a gorgeous bronze love magnet who drives the magical coach.

"Interestingly strange, these travelers say that once inside the coach, there is no remedy for the hysterical laughter that will indeed possess you. And the places you go are truly fairy-tale adventures, leaving them begging to see more and more. They say when the Americans return home, they are somehow never the same. They are never satisfied until they return to Italy with you, stepping back into the fairy-tale storybook they left behind from the previous adventures.

"They do also say the places you go in Italy are not the usual touristy places like the other tour groups advertise in the colorful brochures mailed out in massive bundles. The Americans talk of going to magical, off-the-beaten-path places with your very own mysterious protector of a man, Tony Filaci, the Sicilian who is, without a doubt, the breath and air of Italy. He's a replica of an *Americano* movie star, they say. Mamma Mia, Stefania, please tell us more of this life you're living."

Tony Filaci is everything you have ever thought of when thinking of Italy. He's the spicy Italian-Romeo kind of man who's full of life and laughter. He's a sizzling slice of mozzarella cheese, stretched wide and flavorful over the beautiful regions of Italy while firmly caressing the beautiful body of his beloved homeland, Sicily. He's the breath and air of adventurous fun, always ready to stop the coach when the Americans holler, "Stop the bus" to let them jump out and run to something magnificently fabulous. He's the key that opens closed doors. He's the voice that translates many languages into English. He's the friend who bounces in, unannounced, and receives the royal treatment. He's the laughter that makes the party. He's the connection who will introduce you to the personal taste and life of Italy, and ... by all means, let's not forget the legs. The three enticing legs of Sicily are interwoven tightly into Tony's soul, producing a Sicilian character of the most unusual kind.

One would surely assume the proper name for Sicily would be Tony Filaci, for they seem to be one and the same. Not for his long legs—no, that would be silly—but for his inner being, his soul, his superstitious beliefs, stitched so tightly throughout every organ, every heartbeat, never altering. His animated demeanor is comically funny, appearing to be Hollywood performances to the Americans but no, this is Sicily. This is Tony Filaci.

Long before Tony's arrival, his long legs were known as the *Trinacria*, an alternative name for Sicily and a synonym for its national symbol, the Triskelion, which also appears on the flag of Sicily. I have a flag hanging in my store, waving high above the ceiling in red and yellow colors, with the Triskelion looking down upon everyone who enters. This is proudly placed in honor of Tony.

Sicilian-Italian dialect flows from his mouth, leaving you mesmerized by his powerful poise of strength, along with his enormous love for family and food. Tony is Sicily, the Old World of Sicily. You cannot change his beliefs, his sayings, his upbringing, his heritage, his bloodline. No, he is Sicilian.

When supping at the table with Tony, you will hear the pop of his olive-kissed lips, swishing and whooshing, letting the exquisite wine linger in his mouth, giving you the happy approval of its magnificent taste. Tony says you must use your nose, eyes, and mouth to taste the wine. "Do not be intimidated by the wine. Take your time with the wine. Allow the bouquet to explode within your mouth before you swallow," he repeatedly says to the Americans, hoping they understand his love affair with the liquid red like the Americans have with iced tea.

Finding the words to describe such a rare individual as Tony Filaci is hard—very hard. What words can describe such a powerful and wonderful man? Tony is a man who flows like the fine wine flows throughout his country of Italy, and of course his beloved homeland, Sicily. Everywhere we go throughout Europe, Tony is known to all the locals. His mother tongue is Sicilian, but his linguistic skills span many languages. And without a doubt, one language the Americans love is the Italian he sings. Tony has a mesmerizing voice, sending the *Americana* straight up to the heavenly clouds every time.

The Americans fall head over heels in love with Tony. Not in the romantic way—ideally not, since he is married to a Welsh-born beauty who resembles an American movie star. Nonetheless, they want to be near him throughout the tour, just like a little bambino wanting the mamma. They lean on every word that flows from his liquid red lips. Within minutes, they feel as though they are kindred spirits from long ago, surely from the old Sicilian world of the Godfather, they say. They giggle uncontrollably like little children as his dialect says, "We'll be there *mead-e-ott-e-ly*"—meaning "immediately." They act as though they understand every single word spewing from his mouth, and it leaves all of them begging for more.

The Americans meet Tony for the first time at the Italian airport, and within minutes of stepping into the magical coach, they're saying he's the Italian version of Rodney Dangerfield, except for the connections he has to the old world of Sicily. And not by coincidence but by a higher power, Tony is my extended Sicilian papa, assuming the role of my deceased papa years ago. When they say Tony reminds them of the late Rodney Dangerfield, an American movie star we all loved, it's not his looks or silliness—no, not at all. It's his fun-loving, happy character that draws everyone to him. Everyone wants to be around Tony. There's something about his intriguing, mysterious Sicilian soul that brings comfort and protection, and most certainly a sense of knowing without a doubt that you are highly favored and blessed to be in his spicy Italian presence. One thing you will surely catch from Tony is his laughter, his optimism about a beautiful day, and his delightful spirit—highly contagious, bringing out the best in all.

4

NINO, OUR LITTLE BAMBINO

Did I mention our sun-kissed Romeo of a driver who guides our motor coach throughout Italy with Tony sitting behind him? He's not just a driver; he's family. Nino is Sicilian by birth and Neapolitan by marriage.

"Nino, our little bambino," we say all the time to Nino. I want to say thanks to a dear friend, Jacquelina Narrell, in Dallas, who tagged Nino with the special endearment while on one of the many Italy tours with us. Every time Jacquelina comes within sight of Nino, a sudden urge sends her voice box into a mega-star performance, talking like a baby, repeating over and over to him this silly phrase, "Nino, you're my little bambino. You make me want to drink a cup of cappuccino, my little bambino." Afterward, we all break out in roaring laughter as Nino's face lights up with blinking tones of reds.

Nino is unaware of and totally innocent about his gorgeous face, it seems. Time and time again, when the American women encounter his olive face for the first time, a strange, magnetizing force seems to be at work. It's extremely amusing to witness such a show. Getting off the plane, the American ladies excitedly blaze through the double doors, pulling their colorful luggage as if their pants are on fire. The minute they spot Tony and Nino standing amongst the flock of people holding up signs that welcome foreigners to their magnificent country, they spin into a funny, shufflelike dance resembling animated puppets, their arms flying up, waving hysterically as though Elvis Presley himself was standing there. Their echoing accents, mixed with Tony's roaring laughter, ricochet like flashes of lightning throughout the airport. What a sight to see. And I, making my way from the luggage carousel, rolling my bright pink-and-purple luggage through the double doors, eventually get to Tony and Nino's open arms. I hear Tony asking the big question, "Mamma Mia, Stefania, what a beautiful group of Americans, but"—he explodes with laughter—"which one will it be this time?" On nearly every tour, we have at least one American who does something unbelievably strange, causing Tony and Nino to say, "Mamma Mia, Stefania, where did you find this one?" Therefore, with raised eyebrows and a big smile, Tony inspects each American's face, hoping to detect a slight clue as they happily hug and make introductions.

Nino, who always stands close beside Tony, stands out like a freshly baked chocolate pie adorned with golden meringue on top of his perfectly round, glazed head. The Americans go crazy over Nino. Surely it's his gorgeous face, with the ruby-red blush, painted perfectly by God's own hands, along with his sexy smile as he flashes his perfectly polished white teeth. Then again who knows: it could be his European stance, standing so proper with his Italian man-bag strapped perfectly around his lean body.

Whatever it is, there is definitely something supernatural going on within or around his aura. I've witnessed it time and time again. It must be some kind of supernatural force, engulfing their senses and clouding their minds; it's like a magical vapor, taking control of their voices and minds. Strangely, the vapor animates their arms and legs, commanding them to take every opportunity to run and embrace Nino wherever he may be, at any given moment.

And at the end of our tours, Nino is totally exhausted. His face hurts from the puppet's wide-stretched grin. His cheeks have been squeezed and twisted at every given opportunity. It doesn't matter that Nino is busy or in the middle of eating his pasta. The Americans pay no attention to what he is doing or that he's glued to Tony's right side; they just plow through to him, aggressively and robotically, grabbing his face as though it were play dough. Then, like a grand finale, they pat the top of his golden glazed head as though he were a little puppy dog.

Sadly for the Americans, though, Nino is married to a gorgeous Neapolitan beauty named Assunta—meaning "the Madonna"—whom we call Susy and love dearly. The minute Nino laid eyes on Susy, his mind was totally consumed with her beauty. Nino was hopelessly in love, longing to be with her and to hear her voice. He has one hand on the steering wheel and the other one clutching his mobile phone, holding it tightly to his ear and intently listening to Susy's angelic voice.

Nino is oblivious to any other woman in sight, only longing to be with his love, his Susy.

The magical love potions within the brain's neurotransmitters exploded throughout Nino's body as Susy permeated his love-struck head. Shortly thereafter, the incredible occurred. Nino and Susy married in a fairy-tale setting in Napoli—which I was honored to attend—along with Tony and his beautiful Welsh-born wife, Pat. Now that the years have come and gone, Nino and Susy are the proud parents of a beautiful bambino, a little boy they named Jacopo, which is Jacob in English.

5

THE PASSION OF CHRIST—
MATERA, ITALY

As we round a tight curve, far from civilization, there appears an eerie Gothic church—surely from Dracula's day—hauntingly perched on a picturesque hillside and almost engulfed by scarlet poppies amid towering Italian cypress trees. Several feet below, I spot petite, toylike dogs with pearly coats gallivanting toward us as they meander along the rolling hills as though an artist meticulously painted the wonders of another world. The sight intrigues me with its ghostly panorama. Leaning forward in my front seat, I brace myself as though someone has slapped me hard in the back. My heart acrobatically flip-flops. I have never seen Dracula's castle—not here in southern Italy—and this is my fourteenth year to bring Americans to Italy, twice each year. I realize this is not Count Dracula's castle in Transylvania—modern Romania, but it reminds me of Dracula's humble abode.

Momentarily, I forget about the sixteen Americans seated behind me, singing to the Italian tunes that are ricocheting through the stereo speakers. Many of them are pretending to play the piano while some blow on invisible horns. The foreign lyrics bounce through the vibrating speakers and ricochet from one side of the coach to the other. It appears that everyone is inebriated, totally doused in the liquid red, but they're not. No, they're submerged in roaring laughter and the beauty that's surrounding us.

Silvery leaves on low-hanging branches swish and sway with a magical grace, choreographed to dazzle the Americans' wide-stretched eyes. The ripe fruit on the olive trees clasp tightly to its nourishing branches as a swirl of cool air tosses them amongst the silvery foliage. A few feet away, luscious green vineyards gently roll up and down like the rise and fall of a camel's fur back. As our Mercedes-Benz coach approaches the edge of the timeworn Roman road, we catch glimpses of the legendary purplish-black grapes theatrically dangling like juicy, bite-sized trapeze artists, swooshing as though an invisible hand is swirling them in the cool Italian air. I marvel at how the heavy clusters of grapes cling so tightly, never breaking from the vine or crashing into the dirt. From afar, variegated shades of red and pink roses explode into full color as the sun smiles down upon their delicate perfumed petals. Beautiful rosebushes burst into bloom at the end of every row of grapes, guarding the luscious fruits from the hungry appetites and flapping wings of feathered friends. And with the rub of a genie's bottle, a flurry of fragrances roll upon me—basil and oregano—dancing through the air, or perhaps it is merely the enchantment of the most beautiful country in the world altering my consciousness.

Adrenaline has exploded throughout my body, and my heart is racing like an Italian Lamborghini revving up for takeoff. From the front passenger seat inside our coach, I can see something unbelievably strange. The dogs trot along behind a man holding something that resembles a tall stick. If I didn't know better, I would say it's one of the patriarch saints.

They are so unusual, I think to myself, grabbing my camera to capture this beautiful sight. I'm witnessing a real-life reenactment of the biblical days of Moses and his tall staff, herding the people out of Egypt, except there are no people, just tiny white pooches in a picturesque storybook setting. And, this particular scene before me right now has Dracula's castle in the background with Casper, the friendly ghost, about to appear any second.

Intrigued, I lean in to get a closer look, but my intentional restraint, the seat belt, refuses to cooperate. Excited, I clench the microphone in my left hand and feel the erupting force of exhilaration bubbling upward. Before I ease back into my seat, I bring the microphone to my red-painted lips and blurt out, "Look at the tiny dogs strolling down from Dracula's castle."

Adrenaline rushes through my body, gushing like Niagara Falls, and without thought, my thunderous voice breaks the sound barrier with a southern accent, interrupting the Italian music that was bouncing out through the same connected power source as my microphone. Over all the commotion oscillating through the coach, I hear the passengers'

24

harmonic shout ricocheting back to me like a church choir singing in perfect harmony, alerting me to the fact that they are not dogs.

"They are sheep. Yes, woolly white sheep following a shepherd boy," someone shouts, peeling their eyes away from the coach window.

"Look at them. I've never seen a real shepherd boy, not in real life," Louise shouts in an alarming tone, drawing her hands back to her chest as though Saint Peter is standing in front of her with the woolly white sheep.

Turning my head around to look toward Tony, my mouth drops open. Tony is gripping the back of Nino's seat, appearing to be an animated Sicilian marionette. His eyes are bulging, in and out, like a cartoon character plugged into an electrical outlet.

Unknowingly, I tighten my grip on the microphone still in my left hand and watch Tony's eyes slowly dance their way to a rapid blinking performance. He is no doubt a Sicilian replica of the famous American actor Rodney Dangerfield.

"Mamma Mia! They have sheep in America, do they not, Stefania?" Tony asks with dilated eyes that cause Nino, my olive-kissed driver, to flash his black-licorice eyes toward the rearview mirror, hoping to get a better view of Tony's animated outburst, which ends with an orchestrated dance of twirling arms.

"*Si, si,*" I respond slowly while clicking my camera along with the other Americans glued to the window. They too hope to capture this picture-perfect moment of experiencing Italy, ogling a real shepherd boy with a flock of little sheep.

We are on a secluded road, staring at a flock of woolly white sheep who follow a modern-day shepherd as though caught in biblical times. It is a fairy-tale moment for all of us—well, at least for us Americans on board my September Italy tour. Of course, Tony and Nino were born and raised in this fairy-tale world of Italy; in fact, they were born and raised in the Old World of Sicily. For them, seeing all of this enchantment, castles howling out spine-tingling vibes, so it seems, with real shepherd boys leading flocks of woolly white sheep up and down hilltop mountains surrounded by medieval walls enveloping a whole village, is normal. Nonetheless, for us, the Americans, everything here seems fairy tale. Even the brooms are fairy tale. In fact, the brooms are identical to the witches' brooms in the storybooks we read as children.

We are close to Italy's Basilicata region, heading toward a city called Little Jerusalem—or at least that's what the Italians call this magnificent creation of a city that resembles a biblical storybook.

As we bump along, clicking our cameras, Nino taps his left hand against the leather steering wheel while singing to the Italian tunes reverberating through the stereo speakers. I am seated within inches of Nino in the front passenger seat. The microphone still dangles in my left hand, and for now, I am silent—which is rare. However, the words dancing within my head are overwhelming. Looking through the windshield, I see silvery olive trees on the left and right sides. They are riding up and down like flowing waves in perfect symmetrical harmony. Behind them, I see ceramic roof tiles in rustic reds with tall, Italian cypress trees lining the long driveway. Oh, it is truly picturesque, just like Renaissance oil paintings portraying the Old World of Italy, a world so different from America.

Within seconds, my vocal cords' brief siesta abruptly ends with the tap of Nino's leather shoe slamming hard on the brakes. The sudden urgency magnetizes his fingers around the leather steering wheel as though he were holding down a team of wild horses. Simultaneously, his seat bucks and rocks. He appears to be a bobble-head doll, bouncing up and down as though riding a bucking bull. The wheels of the coach slowly skid toward the side of the road, causing loose gravel to pop and crackle wildly underneath the rubber tires and hot metal. We hear loud fireworks resonating, sounding as though a thousand pieces of buttery popcorn are exploding inside a microwave when the radioactivity zaps and strikes each kernel of corn.

Startled, Harry George, from Houston, gasps, firing out what seems like sixty minutes of precious Italian air. The other passengers follow along, exhaling strange hiccupping jingles that suspend the musical choir in midnote.

Looking through the windshield, wide-eyed and feeling as though my hair is standing up straight, I, along with the jolted Americans, witness a long stream of men robed in white, clustered together in tight sequence. In the rush of applause spontaneously rolling toward the front of the coach—like an unexpected tsunami in the Gulf of Mexico—they feel, too, the Israelites' serendipity at the Red Sea—the parting of waters—the pleasant surprise of good fortune, God's favor in an unexpected moment. Yes, we are experiencing a serendipitous moment.

Before us, flocks of monks are marching across the road with musical instruments as if a vehicle has no place here. Behind them, trotting along as a group of penguins in symmetrical harmony, we see black-and-white-robed nuns, singing and bouncing amid the honking of horns and clanging symbols. Ah, it's an *Italiano* moment, a very special moment indeed.

Comparing Italy with America is really quite easy. For one, the food is always pasta, and it begins with an eye-popping array of colorful enticements. Meals start with *l'antipasto*, meaning "before the meal." L'antipasto includes my favorites, such as bruschetta, mozzarella cheese, and olives, along with the liquid gold olive oil—oven-baked bread, and much more. The antipasto is just the beginning of this orchestrated dance of a feast; however, no sooner do we say, "We are full" than out comes *il primo* or "first course," which is always pasta or a delicious soup. *Il secondo*—"second course"—is the main course, such as a wide variety of meat or fish. *Il contorno*—"side dish"—is vegetables such as my favorite, *melanzane* (eggplant), or *insalata mista* (mixed salad). Finally comes *il dolce*, or "dessert," which might include the all-time favorite, tiramisu, or perhaps creamy swirls of gelato, fresh fruit, or another favorite, which is probably my number one, the lemony baba rum cake.

And of course, let's not forget siesta, the sacred nap. Oh, yes, every day the Italians take a siesta, from 1:00 to 4:00 p.m. I hate the sacred siesta because for one, the little shops slam shut at the sacred tick tock of one o'clock. Americans are not accustomed to a ritual nap. Ha! That's almost funny. Americans barely take the time to eat lunch, much less sleep for three hours—plus, one more hour to eat the garlicky pasta and swallow the liquid red. That's unheard of in America.

In Italy, the celebrations are many—too many to count, one after another in this amazing country. Just like now, out in the middle of nowhere, I see flickering red candles below a tiny, chapel-like shrine with beautiful gold and blue shimmering mosaics depicting the iridescent glory of the old wooden Madonna holding baby Jesus. I love the biblical storybook presence that hovers all around us throughout Italy. It's everywhere, not just in churches. In Italy, we see and feel God's omnipresence. It is beautifully showcased on every street corner and flowing hilltop. We see reliquaries filled with sacred ex-votos. We see Madonna and baby Jesus wrapped with the beaded rosary. We see the crucifix dangling around the necks of biblical saints. We see large and small crucifixes, sprouting up in the rolling vineyards, in fields of wheat and tobacco, and in meadows of ruby-red poppies and yellow-kissed sunflowers. We see beautiful shrines in various sizes, adorned with real flowers and glowing candles.

The sheep and shepherd boy are now miles behind us, and we are slowly approaching another towering castle that appears to be from a Cinderella storybook. The liquid blue Mediterranean is the backdrop for this fairy-tale castle. It doesn't look real; it looks like a painted masterpiece for a movie prop, perhaps a fabled movie with Cinderella and Prince Charming stepping out of their magical pumpkin carriage.

Allen, my olive-kissed Romeo, has his dark black eyes pressed against the coach window. He is absorbing every detail of the castle's breathtaking beauty. Looking back at him, I snap the camera and capture this picture-perfect moment. *Where else in this amazing world can one capture fairy-tale photos, one after another, throughout the whole country?* I ask myself as I turn back around in my seat and see more spine-tingling beauty that can be found only in Italy.

In no time at all, Nino brings the coach to a smooth stop. Stepping off, we see our dear friend Maria standing tall with shuffling feet and waving arms. Maria's face is naturally enhanced by the liquid gold, painted by nothing more than the splash of cool water. Her thick hair resembles a pony's tail—black and coarse and deeply rooted, always styled to perfection. However, in a matter of seconds, a swish of wind turbulently slaps across her long black locks, causing her hair to dance and fly. We watch and wave as Maria swings and jerks her head, excitedly waving at the same time. Maria is a local resident of this ancient region and a licensed tour guide. She will be taking us on an exclusive and personal tour of this ancient city. She is not only a guide, but an actress. She played a role in a blockbuster movie filmed right here in Matera.

"*Buongiorno, Stefania!*" Maria shouts, grabbing me, hugging me, kissing me twice, and then reaching for the Americans, kissing them twice on each cheek, all the while wearing a wide smile. Maria is eagerly anticipating the surprise that will soon grab and yank the Americans' eyes and hearts. It's guaranteed, and Maria knows that once the Americans look upon the soon-to-be city, they will explode with emotions. It happens every time with Americans, because for one, there is no place like this in the United States or the world. And in 1993, UNESCO declared Matera a World Heritage Site.

"Andiamo—let's go!" I say to my gathered flock of Americans, who are strapping on their cameras, preparing for the hundreds of photos that are sure to be taken. In a slow, childlike way, we walk the sidewalks and pass the embellished gelato shops that display towering swirls of rainbow-colored ice cream. Many of the Americans stop dead in their tracks, clicking their cameras at the hypnotizing array of gelato adorned with soft, colorful swirls and fluffy white cream.

Within minutes, we race across the flat streets while tiny toylike cars zoom in front of us as though we are invisible. The Americans are laughing and talking amongst themselves while flashing their eyes toward the locally made sugary concoctions piled high in the colorful window displays. Feet away, we smell the alluring aroma of baking breads, causing our mouths to explode as though a water sprinkler jetted off on a hot summer's day.

"Oh, don't worry, you will have plenty of time to shop and taste everything fabulously created here in this region," I explain, "however, let's carry on. Just a few more twists and turns to Little Jerusalem." I jump up and down with excitement, knowing that within minutes they will be speechless. In less than five minutes, we pop out to open air with a high ledge to our left side. This is the place I've anticipated seeing, the old city of Matera, "Little Jerusalem," a prehistoric settlement that is the most unbelievable place I've ever seen.

"Get your cameras ready," I shout, feeling my adrenaline skyrocket to the moon and back. "Come on. Are you ready to see the most unbelievable city in the world? When you get to the ledge, look down."

"Welcome to the city of I Sassi of Matera, better known as Little Jerusalem. There is nothing comparable to this city," I say again, standing in front of the Americans. I watch them gasp with emotions that are erupting like a massive volcano. We stand in awe—hypnotizing awe—looking down over the ancient city of Matera, a city of cavelike dwellings from the dinosaur age.

We might as well be on Pluto or Mars. It probably wouldn't be much different from what we are seeing right now. We are looking out over a time capsule, taking us back before the biblical days, at an ancient city built of natural caves with rock mountains surrounding the valley. I wonder how old this city is. The countless natural caves in Matera were the first houses of the neolithic inhabitants of the region; they transformed the natural landscape into new shapes of architecture that are cave houses. And this conglomerate of cavelike houses, one on top of the other and all in shades of white, is absolutely unbelievable to human eyes. In fact, it takes a few minutes for my eyes to adjust to the realization that an entire city is below.

"Andiamao! Let's go. Shall we stroll along, go downhill amongst the city and walk the zigzagging paths? Shall we taste the oven-baked breads and pastas with the locals?" Maria suggests, dancing around in her long blue-striped skirt with brown leather sandals displaying her red-painted toes. "I'm sure Stefania has told you many things about Matera, also called the Sassi, meaning 'stone,' or the City of Stone, and now, my friends, you are going to experience it. Matera is a maze of caves, which are the residents' houses, churches, and shops, dating back to the dinosaurs." Maria laughs, turning her head upward to inhale the mouthwatering aromas of baking breads floating throughout the air.

"Do you see the zigzagging steps and stone facades carved from the massive slopes of whitish tufa stone? The Sassi are houses dug into the tufa rock, and the houses are nothing more than little grottoes, caves in the white rock. These amazing streets of the Sassi are on the rooftops of other houses," Maria says, pointing toward them while nodding to one of the locals who is flashing his bedroom eyes at our friend Gloria from Dallas, who used to be shy and reserved but seems to have recovered from her awkward bashfulness.

Trying to act as though Romeo and Gloria are not making a love connection, Maria clears her throat for the hundredth time and jerks her left leg up and down, as though a spider is crawling in her leather-strapped sandal. In a brief second, Maria yanks her shoulder bag off the nearby table with the good intentions of grabbing it as she leads us down the rocky steps. However, when she stumbles over a flowerpot, she sends her bag flying over the mountainous, clifflike ledge.

"Mamma Mia!" Maria shouts sharply, jolting Romeo and Gloria back to reality and causing them to jump as though a dart has pierced them in the back. Like a ping-pong ball ricocheting back to Maria, we hear a loud Italian voice echoing in slow waves, "Mamma Mia, today is my lucky day." Without thought of falling, Maria stretches her body over the ledge and shouts out, "It's me, Alessandria. I will meet you at the table with Mamma in twenty minutes or so. Bring my *borsa* [purse] with you."

Feeling relieved, Maria stretches her olive-kissed face into a sweeping wide smile and says to the Americans, "Excuse me, I'm so sorry, let me explain … I mean, where were we? Ah, yes, there is indeed a great similarity between the look of the Sassi and that of the ancient sites in and around Jerusalem. And, I must ask, did Stefania tell you that Matera, where you are standing right now, was used to portray Jerusalem in Mel Gibson's movie *The Passion of the Christ* and the movie *The Gospel According to St. Matthew,* along with being the set for many other films, such as *King David* and *The Nativity Story*? And, did Stefania tell you I was featured in *The Passion of the Christ*? I was one of the actresses in the movie."

6

The Coliseum

It's late May, and the red and pink geraniums are exploding with vibrant blooms, hanging gracefully over the baroque iron balconies that I love so much in Italy. Driving past a lovely pink villa splashed with waterfalls of fuchsia bougainvillea, bright yellow hibiscuses, and towering green palm trees, we click our cameras again. Nino and Tony have gathered us from the Roma airport and in no time at all, I'm telling everyone to get their cameras ready again for the picture-perfect photo, of the Coliseum, which is to our left. It seems as though I was just here with the Americans, but that was months ago on my September/October Italy tour. With me bringing two different groups to Italy, twice a year, and then returning to Italy again, in between the tours for buying trips for my store, Decorate Ornate—yes, it does seem like I was just here. Nonetheless, I'm now here with a whole new group of Americans for another fabulous and fun adventure.

Before ending my sentence, I hear screams of exhilaration explode behind me, sounding as though the Americans have just won the largest lottery ever known to humanity. Stretching my neck backward, I see the ecstatic flock of Americans flashing their cameras at the magnificent Coliseum. "Oohs" and "aahs" are rolling out, and the excitement is high. Speaking the word *Coliseum* through the microphone stirs a whirlwind of emotions entangled with the pure excitement of being in the eternal city of Rome.

"Just imagine the history inside this Coliseum. Let me take you back in time," I say, stretching the cord of my microphone out too far, watching it disconnect and go flying through the air right across Tony's nose. Within seconds of the loud thump, we hear Tony spilling out words in Sicilian dialect, sounding as though he's saying, "*Minghia.*" Then like an echoing choir, everyone else in the coach sounds out "Min … ghia" as well, thinking they have just absorbed their first Italian word.

Drawing attention away from Tony, I ask the Americans, "Can you see through the open arches of the massive arena? Ah, then let your imagination take you back to the days of the gladiators. Allow your mind to visualize the happenings as I take you inside." Excitedly, I continue. "I can almost hear the roar of exotic lions, the clank of plated armor, and the crashing blades hitting one another as the gladiators file out of the open gates into the huge arena. The applauding crowd cheers as the emperor comes forward, raising his arm and shouting, 'Let the games begin.' Instantaneously, raging excitement accelerates throughout the crowd." I swallow hard. "In a moment's notice, the blades crash against one another, sending arms, legs, heads, and fingers flying through the blood-filled arena. The audience goes crazy, screaming with excitement and sipping the liquid red from their ornate goblets."

Nino brings the coach to a snail's crawl as I continue with my imagining of what it was like inside the Coliseum. "It is early morning and the sand is already soaked from the bloodshed of the exotic animals and humans. No mercy has been shown, not today. The morning festivities have satisfied the emperor's appetite for blood and death. Already, just a few minutes before noon, many gladiators have fought to their death. The exotic wild animals, such as the magnificently created striped horse, loudly announced as 'zebras' from the southern parts of Africa, along with a large array of magnified cats announced as 'exotic tigers' from the deepest jungles, all leap hungrily across the arena, and have fought to their death." My hands swirl as I talk.

"Mamma Mia! Stefania, why do you tell the Americana such horrible things?" Tony asks, knowing it's useless to try to stop me.

I continue as if he hadn't interrupted. "Before the batting eyelashes of the aristocrats crash down, another large array of paraded humans are forced into the arena. The crowds shout with excitement, knowing the midday executions are about to start. I see barebacked slaves with bent shoulders and too many slashes across their backs, shackled with heavy chains, along with common criminals too beaten to claim their innocence.

"Not far behind them, barely able to walk with the heavy chains shackled around their bruised legs, I see prisoners, now slaves, who were snatched from their own countries, and a gathered flock of strange people

33

of all ages calling themselves Christians who have refused to bow and worship the Roman gods. Some of them have done nothing wrong other than petty offenses such as stealing a cluster of grapes from a nearby Tuscan vineyard to satisfy their hunger. Whatever their case may be, they are now part of the entertainment for today's festivities. One by one, they are paraded out to the cheering spectators who are not satisfied until they see more blood.

"The sound of music blasts out from the shiny brass trumpets, pumping the spectators up to an adrenaline-high frenzy. The crowds grow louder, cheering and ready for the games to begin. The silk-laced Nubian slaves make their way to their masters, serving platters piled high with pastries. The loud clank of goblets rings out as the liquid red splashes into the air. The enthusiasm is high, knowing the gladiators are coming soon as they make their way through the underground tunnels. They are running like warriors through the dark, torchlighted tunnels, and the loud clanks of heavy metal echoes throughout the bottom floor. Seconds later, the ironclad slaves pull on the thick ropes below the top floor, forcing the pulleys to go around and around, opening the hidden doors and bringing up more of the exotic animals. Before the crowd finishes their liquid red, the bloody dead are raked up like piles of loose leaves. Afterward, they're carted off through the opened door, causing the crowd to cheer louder."

"Mamma Mia! What's the matter with you, Stefania?" Tony subpoenas with hands swirling above his head.

"With too much blood on the floor, the intermission begins and the pulleys start. The servants are huffing and puffing as they pull and tug the enormous, thick ropes around the pulleys. Amazingly, as they pull hard on the pulleys, which lifts the floor up on one end, the designed mechanism attached to the floor allows gallons upon gallons of blood to drain into the open vats. The blood collected will be used for dyeing their fabrics. The Romans never waste anything that can be used for profit," I explain, stretching the microphone cord to its maximum length again, which restricts me from going beyond Tony's seat. Not realizing the distance of the cord, I once again feel the release of tension as it springs out of the socket, hitting Nino.

"*Minghia!*" shouts Nino, rubbing the top of his bronze-glazed head.

Never stopping to reconnect the cord, I keep talking, but in a louder tone. "From the imperial box, the emperor sips the liquid red from his ruby-studded cup, all the while nodding for the two little Nubian slaves to wave the colorful peacock feathers back and forth. Just a little ways from the men, I see Lady Peggy Suelina sitting with the other aristocratic women, all of them lavishly pampered by the small hands of their regally dressed slaves. Up toward the top seats, I see two Jewish slaves wearing metal collars around their slim olive necks with inscriptions shouting out to me, 'Capture Me and Return Me to My Master, Lady Connie Jolena, and You Will Receive Great Reward.'"

I give the passengers a quick wink as I surprisingly tag their names with a little twist to the aristocratic women of my imagination. Lady Peggy Suelina is Peggy Sue Garmon from Gilmer, Texas; Lady Jacquelina is Jacque Gibbs from Liberty City, Texas; Lady Janie Jantzlena is Janie Jantz from Edmond, Oklahoma; Lady Lanatana is Lana Niemann from Gladewater, Texas; and Lady Connie Jolena is Connie Jo Robinson from Huntsville, Texas. All of them are regular travelers with us.

Knowing the Romans brought back thousands of Jewish slaves, I continue the history that is frozen in my mind, allowing it to spill out like running water. "A young Jewish girl named Martha, who was purchased by the highest bidder at the open market here in Rome last week, stands over Lady Jacquelina, waving back and forth the long, colorful peacock feathers in an effort to keep the still morning air moving around her new master.

"'Ah ... yes, indeed. Money well spent for the perfect little gift for me,' Lady Jacquelina says, tilting her head slightly toward the morning air, now coming from the peacock feathers held in little Martha's hands. Turning her head in the opposite direction, from the peacock feathers, Lady Jacquelina nods with approval as her two Nubian slaves serve her, in perfect harmony, from two tall platters of blood-red oranges from Sicily that were soaked in pure, rich honey, with thick slices of *al cioccolato dolci*—chocolate sweets—drizzled abundantly over them. Afterward, they present her with an imperial glass of Prosecco, which is a light, effervescent, white wine, and happens to be Italy's answer to bubbly champagne. Reaping the benefits of the cool breeze from Martha's peacock fan, the two Nubian slaves stand close to their lady, allowing the warm air to brush against their dark black skin."

I continue my story. "Young Martha is obediently laboring over Lady Jacquelina. She waves the long peacock feathers back and forth in hopes of keeping her new mistress satisfied and not giving the woman a reason to return her to the slave market for an exchange—something routinely done if they decided they didn't like their new slave in the first day or so. Can't you feel the pain and humiliation little Martha feels? Just imagine being snatched from Jerusalem, stripped from your family and your homeland, and not being accustomed to the horrible pagan entertainment before you right now," I say, pain dancing across my distraught face.

"Mamma Mia, Stefania, why do you say such horrible things to the *Americana*, our people, right now? Tony says. "Mamma Mia, you make them very sad right now. Look at them. They are disturbed. You must talk about nice things. Let's talk about the nice food we shall eat tonight, something nice, Stefania." Tony rolls his eyes, reminding me again of Rodney Dangerfield.

"I must tell them the truths of this Coliseum. Do you want to know the truths?" I ask our spellbound group.

"Mamma Mia!" rolls out from Tony's mouth again, his hands twirling above his head. Nonetheless, I continue where I left off. "Amongst the ladies of upper class is Janie Jantz. Oh dear, I do mean to say Lady Janie Jantzlena, who is elegantly perched on her fluffed, burgundy velvet cushion, with tassels dangling from the vibrant purple threads. She is popping plump Toscana grapes with honey-rolled figs into her mouth, along with a boundless supply of the liquid red. While excitedly chomping and smacking with the eagerness of a hungry hyena, Lady Jantzlena's eyes catch a glimpse of the wealthy and exquisitely radiant Lana Niemann— now Lady Lanatana—who is an aristocratic rival of hers after making off with her last Romeo lover. Resisting the inclination to kick Lady Lanatana to the lions, Lady Jantzlena weighs the consequences, the embarrassment of enacting such a tantrum. She then turns to her left, flashing her long lashes of a pony's tail in a seductive wink to her newfound beau, Tom Antonio, a highly sophisticated engineer in his short silk toga, seated a few rows over among the other aristocratic Romans." I say this breathlessly, batting my black lashes, Cinderella-like.

"As the screaming crowds cheer for Gladiator Maximo, who enters the arena as a celebrity star, Lady Jacquelina shouts, 'Fill the arena with Maximo's blood. Let the pulleys tilt up the arena floor and drain every ounce of his blood into my golden cup.' Lady Jacquelina stretches her face wide, flashing her gorgeous blue eyes toward Lady Lanatana and Peggy Suelina, feeling a sudden stillness of wind that causes her temper to soar. Can you see the aristocrats, the wealthy ladies flaunting their powers?" I ask the Americans, who are seated behind me as I continue with the animation of characters flying throughout my mind.

"'Martha, keep the air moving faster, you stupid little slave,' Lady Jacquelina shouts as her right hand slaps hard against Martha's olive, Jewish face. 'Do not ever stop fanning me, you stupid little Jew. Do you want me to take you back to the slave market for an exchange, perhaps get a more obedient slave?' Lady Jacquelina roars out to little Martha, who is trembling now." I take a quick breath.

"'Yes, my lady,' pouts young Martha, who feels the burning sting from the strong slap across her sweaty bronzed face. The thought of standing at the arena for hours upon hours all day as she waves the peacock feathers back and forth brings instant pain to Martha's small, stretched arms, not to mention that now her red face is stinging as if a bumblebee had kissed her face. Little Martha's Jewish status is lower than her master's dog, and it shows today as she rubs her face with one hand while continuing the fanning of peacock feathers with her other hand.

"There are fifty thousand spectators eager to see blood and death, the entertainment of games inside the arena," I say as the ecstatic Americans continue to flash their cameras toward the magnificent Coliseum.

"Can you feel the excitement, the taste of death, and the agony and pain from the illustration I just painted for you?" I ask them again while they look toward the Coliseum with grief-stricken faces.

"Can you hear the clink of fine crystal, filled with the liquid red? Can you hear the pumping hearts, beating loudly as the chains rattle beneath the Coliseum floor? Can you hear the chomping and crunching of the plump purple grapes? Do you see the ruby-red juice, spurting and spraying all around, dripping from the corners of their overstuffed mouths? Do you see the haughtiness of the aristocratic women with their long, waggling, sharp tongues, speaking boastfully?" I ask them. They stare at the Coliseum through the coach windows.

"It's a sin, those dirty courtesans from Venice. Let the lions rip them apart. They are nothing but filthy harlots from northern Italy, thinking they will come to Rome and sleep with our men. Ha! Devour them. All of them, one bite at a time," I shout, bringing my right hand toward my heart, showing disgust as though the courtesans are among us.

"Mamma Mia, Stefania," Tony interrupts. "What is the matter with you? I cannot believe what you say to these people. Why do you bring the Venetians and the courtesans to our ears? The people are sad, very sad— me, too. Very nice, what you did to us," he declares once again, rolling his Rodney-Dangerfield eyes, which are now protruding like those of an animated cartoon character.

"I, for one, cannot walk through the Coliseum without visualizing the daily horrors that the Romans called entertainment and the extravagant lifestyles of the emperors," I explain as Tony throws his arms up, rolling his eyes once again. "I can visualize the aristocratic women giggling and drinking the liquid red as they whisper their innermost secrets to one another. Tomorrow, we shall go inside and see the Coliseum. We will see the underground tunnels where they kept the animals. You will see everything tomorrow."

"Mamma Mia, Stefania, why do you tell them so much? We have the guide tomorrow. Do you remember? No, you do not remember. And Stefania, I do not believe the Christians were killed inside the Coliseum. They were killed at the Circus Maximus, where they held the chariot races. Why must you tell the Americana these horrible things? You bring sadness to their ears, Mamma Mia. You must talk nice to people. What's the matter with you? They have come to Italy for a holiday, not a funeral." Tony swirls his hands over his head as though wishing to throw salt over his shoulder to get rid of the bad luck of the horrible things I say to the people.

"Stefania, please explain the meaning of the Arch of Constantine before we get to it," shouts Jacque Gibbs, who loves the history of Christianity.

"*Va bene*, okay," I say and start up again.

"Ah, yes, the Arch of Constantine was erected to commemorate Constantine's victory over Maxentius at the Battle of Milvian Bridge in 312, and if you will look over there, it's just west of the Coliseum. There are two arches out there: the Arch of Titus and the Arch of Constantine. The Arch of Constantine dwarfs the nearby Arch of Titus," I point to the arch, but it's too late; Nino has to continue with the flow of traffic.

"Can you visualize what Rome was like before Christianity was legalized?" I ask my delightful group while Nino drives slowly in front of things they've only seen in history books. Tomorrow, they can feel and touch everything we're seeing right now, but since our overnight home for the next few nights is just around the corner, I want Nino to drive around and show them from a distance.

"In a few minutes you'll look upon the magnificent Arch of Constantine again, and then immediately to the right stands the greatest symbol of the Roman Empire, the Coliseum." The sighs of thrills roll throughout our coach as I continue to speak through the microphone, asking Nino to drive around once again. In the soft background, I hear Tony reciting his mantras of Mamma Mias. "In the history-making year 312 AD, Emperor Constantine defeated his rival and enemy Maxentius," I say, holding up one of my favorite tapestries of the early crusaders with the cross imprinted upon their shields.

"The night before the bloody battle, Constantine had a dream of a perfectly drawn cross in the star-studded sky, and interpreted it as a sign he would win the battle under the sign of the cross. Therefore, Constantine had the cross painted on his soldiers' shields.

"From history, we know that Constantine's mother, Helena, was a devout Christian as were his sisters. As a mother, I can surely imagine her prayers for the defeat of Maxentius, a mother's urgent plea for God to intercede and give victory to her son and the Christian people. His mother, Saint Helena, had a great mission to the Holy Land. She located the many relics, such as the original cross Jesus was crucified on, the nails, the spine (the thorns), and the holy stairs belonging to Pilate's residence, which are the steps that Jesus walked on the day he was sentenced to death. All are in Rome, except for the 'spine'— the thorn—and it's in another region, close to Bari, Italy. And if you want to go, we will climb on our knees the wooden walnut steps, which are covered in glass to protect the stains from Jesus' blood. Oh, there is so much to tell you," I say, holding my microphone closely to my red painted lips.

"After total victory in defeating Maxentius, Constantine became sole emperor and instantly legalized Christianity throughout the Roman Empire. Can you imagine awaking the next morning to the realization that the Roman pagans are no longer allowed to worship all their thousands of idols and pagan gods and may no longer amuse themselves with the unmerciful torture of Christians? I sometimes wonder what they did with all the beautiful, exotic animals held in cages beneath the Coliseum floor of the arena, which you will see tomorrow. I'm sure they carried on with the games, just not the killing of Christians.

"Constantine's victory meant immediately prohibiting the killings of Christians. Can you imagine how the attitudes toward Christianity changed overnight, no longer satisfying the hungry lions' appetite with live Christians and no more crucifying them alive? No more burning them alive and no more gladiators ripping them apart as the Romans cheered them on for more entertainment? You must remember the era of Rome, the history. Rome was a kingdom of warriors, trained to fight and kill. Rome was a nation of warriors, building the Roman Empire by conquering neighboring countries, such as Israel. Remember, the Coliseum was finished in 80 AD, and legalized Christianity didn't come to Rome until Constantine's victory in 312 AD," I explain.

"Do you know where the apostle Paul, as in Saint Paul, was imprisoned? Right here in Rome, in the Mamertine Prison. And tomorrow, while strolling through the Roman Forum, you will go inside. And what about the horrible torture of Christians, such as Rome's most notorious emperor, Nero? He crucified the apostle Peter and tortured thousands of Christians, used them as human torches dipped in hot wax, pierced with sharp, spherelike poles, and elevated high above to illuminate his elaborate garden parties. Imagine the nights of Nero's lavish parties, the dark skies illuminated by the flaming torches of real human beings. And in mockery of God's word, Nero reportedly spoke to the burning Christians who were illuminating his elaborate parties, saying to them, 'Now you are the light of the world.'"

"Mamma Mia, Stefania, the people are seriously depressed. Why do you feel the need to tell them such things?" Tony asks, his hands swirling and dancing in the air.

Before I can answer Tony, someone hollers out, "Stefania, do you know that Nero used the skins of animals to sew up many of the Christians inside of them and then feed them to the hungry lions?"

"Yes, and can you imagine all of the persecuted Christians awakening to the news that Christianity was now legalized? That meant no more hiding and no more digging in the catacombs. Another thing Constantine did: he ordered the construction of the original Saint Peter's Basilica on the site of the apostle Peter's martyrdom," I finish, reaching for my bottled water.

"Mamma Mia, Stefania, the people will hear all of this from the guide tomorrow morning. You are telling them too much. Mamma Mia! Let the people relax and enjoy their view."

"*Va bene*, okay," I say to Tony, as another thought comes to mind. But before I start, someone hollers out, "What is a CAT-er-comb?"

"Mamma Mia!" Tony says, his eyes bugging out. "What do they say? A what?"

"Mrs. Johnson is asking what a catacomb is," I answer Tony.

"*Mille grazie*, a thousand thanks, Stefania. Now you have the Americana confused. They do not know the catacombs?" Tony asks, shaking his head, not believing his ears.

"Ah, yes," I reply, knowing Mrs. Johnson probably misunderstood the pronunciation. I mean, even Tony says I chop my words in half, not pronouncing them correctly, not like Pat, his English, Welsh-born wife. Tony says the English language is quite dismantled by the time I finish with a sentence, dragging the words out like a stretched accordion—you know, the Texas drawl that branded me in Dallas with the first slap into this world.

"My mother is to blame for such an accent," I tell Tony with a childlike laugh. "It was she who placed me with Ms. Croketta, the proper English and etiquette guru from New York City. I started voice and piano lessons when I was a little girl as well as lessons with my favorite tap and ballet teacher, Mrs. Billie Wood. Oh yes, being groomed and trained at the hands of Ms. Croketta did affect me. Ms. Croketta, God bless her little soul, was a redheaded, sophisticated, mink-shouldered, wine-drinking dwarf. At my young age, it was extremely alarming to be left alone with someone cloned from my fairy-tale storybooks. It wasn't her height that scared me—no, not at all—she was adorable. It was her stern, no-smile seriousness. She spoke with a distinct New York City accent, integrated with a fiery breath of alcohol, blazing out like a prehistoric dragon," I explain to Tony, who is repeating, over and over, "Mamma Mia."

"Ms. Croketta always met me at the door, hanging her head out the small opening, appearing to be a stand-up happy doll glued to a tightly fitted designer skirt and jacket with skyrocketing, fuchsia stilettos pumping her up just below my chin. The minute the door slammed shut, my mother accelerated her latest Ford Mustang, her pageantry hand waving to the wind. I can still see Ms. Croketta as though it were yesterday, taking tiny steps toward her green velvet winged-back chair, stepping upon her matching footstool, and effortlessly climbing to the edge of the chair. Just like a car making a perfect U-turn, Ms. Croketta would swirl her doll-sized body around, kind of like a cat chasing its tail. Nonetheless, she always ended up in the perfect position, staring directly toward me with her gigantic, crystal wineglass filled with the liquid red."

"Mamma Mia, Stefania," Tony echoes himself like a broken record, discombobulated by my story.

"After two sips and a quick swirl, her cartoonish dialect instructed the solo recital to begin, With me reciting the lyrics from *The Sound of Music,* starting with Do-Re-Mi-Fa-Sol-La-Ti-Do. Afterward, she instructed me to play the piano, singing the highest notes in Italian operetta. I am sure it would have been heavenly, that is, if … I had been able to sing. I suppose the money was appreciated, because Ms. Croketta boasted to my mother that I was most certainly her first student with such classical potential. 'Oh, she is such an aspiring operetta singer. Someday, my little student will be famously known,' she would say to my mother, lying through her teeth. Even as a small child, I thought it enchantingly curious, forcing my voice to glass-breaking explosions. Sometimes you think you've found a true prodigy, when it's really just an opportunity to gain light—a larger bank account, a status quo, or a quick laugh, even … fantasy. You know, a wishful diamond in the rough, but no— nothing more than a synthetic gem, cubic zirconia, blasting out glass shards, painfully piercing to the ears."

"Mamma Mia, Stefania, what does this have to do with the Americana and the catacombs? Stefania, you must not talk too much. The Americana is very confused, and so am I," Tony says, and then asks Nino, "Who is this Signora Croketta?"

"Oh well, back to the Catacombs," I say, wondering why I started telling Tony about Ms. Croketta in the first place.

"It's pronounced 'Cata-combs.' Ha, just wait until we go beyond the city walls of Rome tomorrow to visit the underground burial chambers, which are called ... catacombs. The catacombs are where the Christian saints and martyrs were laid to rest. Just remember the time and era. The Christians were being persecuted. They had no place to bury their dead and no place to go but underground, unless they took the risk of being in public, to be seen and killed. You will see the famous *Appia* road tomorrow; it's the road that leads to the catacombs," I say hurriedly before Tony decides to start up again, but out of the corner of my eye, I see him reaching toward me.

"Stefania, can I have the microphone, please?"

"Si, yes," I say, handing the microphone to Tony.

"Stefania is telling you the truth, and I will tell you another truth, *va bene*—okay? Since Stefania refuses to stop talking, I will tell you about the oldest road in Rome. The best-preserved road in Rome is *Via Appia*, which was built in 312 BC. Stefania is talking about this road. Yes, we will go there tomorrow. However, do you know what happened on this road? Ah, let me tell you ..." Tony turns around in his seat to look at the people.

"While imprisoned in Rome, Saint Peter escaped the Mamertine Prison and fled on the road, Via Appia, or as we say, the Appia Way. While fleeing on the Appia Way, he met Jesus. When Saint Peter met Christ, he said to him, 'Lord, where are you going?' And Jesus replied to the apostle Peter, 'I am going to be crucified anew.' Tomorrow, I will show you the church that was built to commemorate the apostle Peter meeting Jesus on the Appia road. The name of the church is Domine QuoVadis."

Tony is full of history, and I'm hoping he will continue sharing his vast knowledge, but no, he stops and turns to me with a smile. With stretched arm, he hands me the microphone and says, "Con-ta-new—continue."

With no refusal, I start up again. "On Via Appia, underneath the cobbled pavements, are the winding tunnels called ..." I wait a few seconds, and everyone shouts out, "Catacombs."

"*Brava*! That's where the early Christians buried their dead as you now know, and tomorrow we are going to the most famous catacomb of all. Well, at least it is to me. We are going to the Catacombs of San Sebastian, the catacombs where the apostoles Peter and Paul were taken after being martyred. According to Roman law, no one could be buried within the city walls of Rome, so they were taken to the underground tunnels, the catacombs. And yes, tomorrow, we'll have a professional guide in the catacombs, so I will stop now."

"Mamma Mia, I don't believe," Tony laughingly says while everyone else roars with laughter.

"Oh, let me say just a few more things about tomorrow in the catacombs."

"Mamma Mia, I knew you can't be finished," Tony says as everyone laughs again.

"Well, I forgot to tell them something very important," I say in my defense. "Tomorrow, do not be surprised if you hear some of the guides saying things such as, 'The Christians probably never hid in the catacombs, even though they were highly persecuted and killed.' And, if you ask them why they think such a thing, they will reply, 'We know they met and prayed down here in the catacombs with the dead, but the smell of the dead would be too horrible. How they could stay hidden down there—we don't believe, absolutely not—not with that kind of odor.'"

With a roll of my eyes, I give the Americans a look of total disagreement and then say, "Of course, they hid down there. But many of the Roman guides who are licensed are determined to pound it through the tourists' heads that the Christians were not killed or tortured in the Coliseum. One licensed guide was telling the long line of tourists at the entrance of the Coliseum this very thing: 'Do not believe that the Romans killed or tortured the Christians in this Coliseum. No, that is all Hollywood. Yes, it's all make-believe, just like Hollywood. The Christians were killed and tortured but not in the Coliseum. They did a lot of the public killings and torture of Christians at the Circus of Maxentius, the racetrack for chariot races—you know, over there.'"

I feel the need to reiterate the time line of history, but no, everyone already knows that Titus sacked the city of Jerusalem and the Temple was burned down. They know millions of Jews died during the revolt, and they already know that thousands of Jews were taken captive and deported to Italy, where they were forced to build the Coliseum in Rome. The evidence is still there. They will see the Arch of Titus and the story carved out by the slaves' own hands.

I give another show of rolling eyes and say, "Remember, the Coliseum was finished in 80 AD, and legalized Christianity didn't come to Rome until Constantine's victory in 312 AD—so yes, absolutely, it is true."

I feel the urge to go into full story line again, using my descriptive historical truths, but I restrain myself. That is, until I hear Dr. John—or should I say, Mr. PhD in Roman/Jewish History—speak up and give the historical truths.

"Well, of course they killed the Christians in the Coliseum, and of course history tells us that the persecutions were very serious," Dr. John says passionately. "It didn't matter whether you were a Christian or a Roman citizen in those days. The Romans were unmerciful when it came to anyone breaking their laws. And of course Pope Benedict XIV dedicated the Coliseum to the memory of the Christian martyrs killed in the arena."

I start up again. "Tomorrow, you will hear the Roman guide say alarming things. I was told many times, 'There is no need to make the tourist feel badly when entering the Coliseum; therefore, we tell the tourist that no killings happened inside the Coliseum.' That is the most ridiculous thing I've ever heard. Why would you discredit the history of something that actually happened to justify someone feeling better? That is the same thing as Americans saying they never killed the Indians, they never took their land, and they never had African slaves. Of course the Americans did these things, but do we try to deny it with some other outlandish, untrue story? That is why it's called history, whether we like it or not." My internal thermostat is rising at an alarming rate.

"Mamma Mia, Stefania, you must calm down. What's the matter with you?" Tony asks while motioning for me to have a chocolate cookie, which he knows brings a smile to my face every time.

I take a cookie with pleasure, and jump back into a conversation that is now going on toward the back of the coach.

"Remember, the early Christians dug an estimated three hundred and seventy-five miles or more of tunnels, many layers thick, up and down, and going for miles and miles. Once we go down into the catacombs, you will understand the hardships they suffered, such as hiding from their persecutors there with the dead. We'll walk through the San Sebastian Catacombs tomorrow, and you'll see for yourselves the endless tunnels and the many symbols on the tufa stone." I feel the need for the Americans to understand the hardships.

"Stephani, where was the cross back then?" Janie asks, sitting almost on the edge of her seat.

"Remember, it was a pagan world in Rome. Thousands of idols were worshipped every day until 313 AD, when Emperor Constantine legalized Christianity. The cross was seldom seen before the legalization of Christianity. The cross was disguised by symbols such as the dove, the anchor, and the fish, just to name a few. The dove is a symbol of the Holy Spirit. The Christians had their own sign language to communicate with each other. Just wait until you see them with your own eyes tomorrow. It's amazing to read the epithets on the Christian tombs versus the epithets on the pagan tombs."

"Mamma Mia, Stefania, why do you keep talking on and on? The people are fed up with so much information," Tony repeats like an automated message, along with his animated arms in an orchestrated performance through the air once again.

"Oh, Tony, we want to hear more," pleads Dr. Isaac, who is sitting directly behind me, snapping another photo.

"Shall I continue on?" I ask. The group immediately responds with rolling waves of 'yes' that ricochet forward and slap me in the face, justifying my continuation. "Cremation was a pagan ritual, not a Christian practice, and tomorrow you will see the pagan burial sites with the old cremation urns. Christian martyrs were taken to the catacombs, wrapped in cloth like Jesus Christ, and laid in the tufa stone. As long as the air didn't reach the tufa stone, it was very soft, and easy to cut. Tomorrow, we'll go from the warm air to the cool air, down below the ground. You will see and touch hundreds of niches hollowed out in the tufa walls where the Christian martyrs were laid. And I can't wait for you to see the many symbols carved in the tufa stone as well. When we drive outside the city walls of Rome tomorrow and park outside the San Sebastian Catacombs, you will never believe what's behind the doors."

Before I get the last sentence out of my mouth, they start again, clicking their cameras. Turning my head, I understand why. We are right beside an ancient Egyptian pyramid. Who would have thought a pyramid would be in the city of Rome?

"Stop, stop," screams Barbara from Shreveport, Louisiana, who is a loyal customer of Decorate Ornate and a first-time participant on our Italy tours. No sooner have my eyes scanned up than her inflated, pear-shaped body springs out of her seat and slides across the aisle, landing perfectly in the lap of tiny Sally from the fun state of Florida. Having no idea that Nino must swerve to miss a zooming scooter that darted out of nowhere, Barbara gets an extra punch of speed, which guarantees her arrival on the other side of the coach in milliseconds. Before Sally can catch her breath, Barbara's weight sends Sally into a hyperventilating frenzy, zapping all oxygen from her lungs. If I hadn't seen this with my own eyes, I wouldn't believe it had really happened. Sitting in Sally's lap, Barbara clicks her camera three times, hoping she captured the long-gone pyramid, before springing back up and taking a few steps to her seat across the aisle. All of this excitement to click a perfect photo.

7

LOVE IS IN THE AIR FOR JAMES HANSON!

"Tomorrow we have the whole day with a professional Roman guide who will explain the Coliseum and much more," I say to the Americans as Nino brakes right in front of our beautiful night's stay. It's just feet away from the ancient Coliseum and a hop skip to the Basilica of Saint Peter in Chains. Bursting with energy, I feel as though I could run to the Trevi Fountain in minutes. Rome is so energizing. I love the beautiful basilicas, the marble statues, the angels, the hundreds of shrines with glowing candles, and of course, the lighted Madonna on every corner.

Leading the way toward Via del Corso, I shout, "Andiamo, let's go."

Immediately, James Hanson, a tall, good-looking, and fun-loving American from Longview, Texas, who signed up for this tour while shopping in Decorate Ornate, walks a few steps in front of me and says, "Stefania, I'm going with you. Who wants to go rest when we can be out having fun with you? I can't imagine why anyone would want to go rest when in Rome."

After inching down the street, stopping, looking, and jetting in and out of wonderful shops, James abruptly stops in front of me in a skidding halt.

"James, you just left skid marks on the cobblestones," I laughingly say as he yanks me to a sudden stop, pointing to the shop across the street.

"What in the world do you see?" Before I finish my sentence, James peels out, magnetically drawn toward a beautifully decorated shop with an alluring window. Out of curiosity and the fact that James is with me in a country he's never been to, I decide to approach the shop. I see a mannequin in European underwear. Not just any underwear. It's more like half of a regular piece of American underwear. It's the typical European Speedo underwear, except this one has David's manhood beaming in full force with "David"—as in Michelangelo's *David*—printed on the front.

To the left stands another mannequin with the same full exposure, except this one is female, blazing in full color.

"Mamma Mia," I shout, having seen these many times here in Italy but never having an American—one of mine—actually stop to buy one.

"Oh, Stefania, I must get these, one for me and one for Nino," James blurts out, yanking the sliver of fabric downward, stripping them both off the mannequins. Feeling as though I'm watching an action-packed movie right before my eyes, I stay tuned to see more. James is now darting over to the hysterical shopkeeper, who is experiencing a major meltdown while pointing to the neatly stacked assortment of underwear on the nearby table. Too infuriated to move, the shopkeeper manages to raise his one finger back and forth, shouting, "*Basta*. Stop!"

The Americana ladies in our group are giggling like teenagers as they eye James while gathering up piles of Italian shirts for themselves. Glancing to the other side, I see a mountainous heap of white T-shirts almost oscillating up and down. It appears as though they are suspended in the air by a magical force. But before my eyes flash away from the tall pile of shirts, I hear roaring laughter from behind them. To improve my panorama, I extend my neck like a turtle and inch closer. I spot a statuesque, olive-kissed girl with a small face and a beak nose of a colorful toucan, eluding her boss, I suppose. She's seized by a fit of uproarious laughter.

For some regrettable reason, I feel the need to explain Jamess' strange behavior to the Roman shopkeeper. But in doing so, I create a catastrophic world event in the little shop.

James pays for the two slivers of underwear and yells loudly, "I'll be next door. Don't leave me," with his underwear in tow.

"We'll be right behind you," I say, swinging my hand into the air. When I bring my hand downward, somehow it catches hold of a Roman soldier, dangling far too low from the ceiling. The fabric from my sleeve attaches to the heavy Roman soldier, and before I know what's happening, I bring down a whole array of brilliantly colored Murano vases that were neatly stacked in a creative, pyramid-shaped display. The crashing thunder ricochets throughout the little shop, leaving me paralyzed, scared, and wondering what just happened. I watch in disbelief as the shopkeeper drops to the floor in hopes of saving just one of the brilliantly colored vases, shouting at the same time, "Mamma Mia, Madonna. Get out. Get out," plus a few other choice words I choose not to repeat in Italian or English.

"Oh no, I'm so sorry! I will pay for them. Yes, absolutely, I will pay for them," I say tearfully and repeatedly, as though I'm a record player on endless playback. My words are useless, completely void to his ears. And because of my adrenaline rush, I somehow, along with the others, arrive much sooner than planned at the Trevi Fountain.

Days later, we are in the storybook village of Verona, home to Romeo and Juliet, the Capulets and the Montagues. Being in this storybook setting, with the medieval wall surrounding the village and Juliet's house just around the corner, brings out the romantic feelings that Shakespeare described hundreds of years ago. I've tried to put the naked underwear and broken Murano vases out of my mind. However, James, who is seated next to me along with his two nude purchases he got in Rome, brings a grand finale to our farewell dinner.

All twelve of us are seated at a long wooden table, covered lavishly with ceramic pottery and antique gold Murano glasses, filled with the region's finest liquid-red. Everyone is talking about the amazing arena, similar to the Coliseum, built by the Romans in 100 AD.

"Oh, Stefania, it is unbelievable the way they built things then," Helen says. "For me, seeing Verona's opera and sitting on the stone seats inside the two-thousand-year-old arena, well, nothing can beat that for me. No, you can't show me anything that will ever come close to its beauty." The liquid red slowly disappears as she talks.

"Well, I will say, I'm in love with the rolling vineyards and gorgeous landscape outside the village walls. These vineyards surrounding us right now produce many of the Veneto wines," Peggy Sue explains, with a slight nod of her head, motioning for the young server to fill her glass once again.

"Tony, is this one of the local *Soave* wines you told us about?" Dr. Clark asks, swirling his tongue around the rim of his wineglass as though he will never get another drop.

"Mamma Mia," Tony says, motioning for the server to refill his glass. "Si, si, this is the local Soave [white] and here come the others: *Valpolicella* [red], *Bardolino* [red wine of Lake Garda], *Amarone* [a red wine made with the same grapes as *Valpolicella*, but using a special processing method called *recioto*], and Prosecco, Italy's sparkling wine. Si, si, very nice, but where is my favorite one, the *Brunello di Montalcino*?" Tony curls his nose at the large selection before him.

With all of the commotion from the abundance of wines, I reach for another ruby-red tomato sprinkled with the liquid gold. As I swallow my last bite of pasta, James leans over and whispers in my ear, "Stefania, I must give Nino his gift, and now is the perfect time."

Before I can process his words, I see James out of the corner of my eye, wiggling around in his chair, pulling and tugging as though he's taking his pants off. Sure enough, James slips on his female, blazing-bush underwear, and in a matter of seconds, like a bottle rocket, he shoots up out of his chair with lightning speed and flies around the table to Nino. Before any of us can grasp James's ascension and his speedy sprint around the table, he has yanked Nino up from his chair. Like magic, James stands with his female underwear on over his jeans with Nino standing by his side. Now, appearing in front of all of us, there's a "stand-up" altered Barbie doll, with Ken-Nino standing by his side. However, in Nino's defense, he has no clue what's happening to him. He does not see the imprinted underwear on James at first, but as James yanks the other pair of underwear out of the bag, flipping them in front of Nino's jeans, we gasp with mouths full of pasta at the flashing, full-color underwear of David's manhood, flaming right in front of our eyes.

Flashing like a blinking red light, Nino's gorgeous face imitates a vibrant and dynamic light show as he snatches the underwear from James, frenetically tossing it high in the air. In a matter of seconds, the minuscule sliver of fabric makes a landing, collapsing into a puddled blotch of color. Simultaneously, we hear the familiar Sicilian word, alongside a mantra of "Mamma Mias" as Tony throws his hands up, whirling them around faster than I can devour my garlicky pasta.

He repeats "Mamma Mia" over and over with his cloth bib tucked neatly into his open-buttoned shirt. In between the chants, Tony slurps the long pasta, and it jets down his throat in rocket speed. Nervous laughter spills from Nino's mouth as he gyrates from the table and scurries frantically, tossing about the same Sicilian words as Tony.

We sit, dumbfounded, all except for Tony, who is an animated cartoon character with eyes bugging in and out and his hands dancing in the air. Finally, the familiar Italian words spring from Tony's mouth, *"Va bene,* okay. *Buon appetite.* Enjoy your meal, my friends."

Moments later, I realize the obvious. James fell passionately, head over heels, for Nino. Mamma Mia!

8

MAMMA MIA! WHAT IS A NUMBER TWO?

As Nino drives away from the walled, medieval village of Assisi, home of Saint Francis, I notice Vicki from Los Angeles. She is seated a few seats behind Tony, thrusting her Pekingese-like face against the slightly tinted window. Her lips, freshly painted, grope the glass like a suction cup. I assume she longs to stay in Assisi as it gradually fades into the distance from the high hill on which it so majestically sits.

"Look at Vicki," I suggest to Tony, and he twirls around, stretching his neck for a better view.

"Mamma Mia, what's the matter with her?" Tony motions for Dr. Jones to have a look as well.

"She's in deep thought, perhaps appreciating the last memories of Assisi's astounding beauty, in the same way that she savors every nibble of the Italian cuisine. Did you notice how abundantly she serves herself the liquid red and then douses her bread with a strong hand of the liquid gold?" I ask Tony while looking at Vicki.

"She's probably yearning to return to the arms of her Italian lover, the one she left behind in Assisi. I'm only speculating from what I saw last night, but she was zapped silly over Giuseppe, the sweet man who lives with his mamma. I might be overdramatizing, but she was accompanied to the old castle, hand in hand, through the cobblestone streets last night. And, judging from what I saw of her this morning, I would say something zapped her. She all but skipped to the breakfast table this morning with her blood-red orange juice in hand. When I said good morning, her voice cracked with emotions, and her tongue frequently swirled over her lips, moistening them as though exhausted from ... well, last night. But, who knows, she could be longing for a few more stolen moments of solitude, a little more time for herself. Or perhaps she possesses a strong genetic connection with the kindred spirit of Saint Francis, who was a kind, gentle saint, always contributing to the impoverished and assisting the elderly." I say all this to Tony with an air of being a Hollywood gossip columnist for the Toscana newspaper.

"Mamma Mia, Stefania! Why must you talk with me like I'm a stupid? You talk to me like a bambino. Do you think I not know who Saint Francis is?" Tony defends in his theatrical demeanor.

Giving Tony a trivial smirk, I continue speculating. "What is she thinking, gazing through the window, oblivious to everyone?" Before I turn around in my seat, she extracts her rosy, painted lips from the window, leaving a perfect imprint. In her left hand, I observe as she kisses a small tarnished key, or at least that's what it appears to be from my position. It's discernibly a lover's gift, given her entire aspect of intense thoughts, in an internal torment of emotions, I presume. At first, she appears jovial, and then she slips back into the melancholy expression of a lonely puppy. Her eyes protrude—far from her Pekingese face. I feel driven to pet her, console her, and perhaps hold her for a brief moment, but the urge quickly passes when her eyes light up, twinkling and dancing with elation. Strange and awkward, she seems. Finally, I decide it must be her repressed emotions, thinking of her lover and then thinking of his absence. They bubble up, and then in a fast halt, the lid slams down with reality.

As I amuse myself by observing her whimsical behavior, I flinch at the abrupt voice of Misery, the strange name that Tony gave to Connie from the sunny state of California. Connie is a free-spirited artist who looks identical to Kathy Bates, the famous actress in the film *Misery*. The slight distinguishing factor between the two of them is the eclectic plethora of hats that Connie always seems to be wearing. In fact, at the moment she is sporting a floral turquoise hat, parked lopsided amongst a head full of wiry salt-and-pepper hair. She has a unique humor and tremendous talent. Seated a few rows behind Tony, she's bellowing out tunes unknown by anyone. The lyrics are funny and eccentric, such as those from the song she is currently sharing with us: "My Dog Has Fleas."

Now we are engrossed. We didn't expect anyone to burst out into song, and now hysterical laughter reverberates within the coach. We are chanting—at the top of our lungs—"My Dog Has Fleas."

"Mamma Mia! She's starting up again," Tony says with a wide grin spanning the entirety of his Sicilian face, then repeating, over and over, "My Dog Has Fleas."

When Tony first met Connie at the airport in Roma, he immediately tagged her with the name Misery. Laughingly, Connie admitted, "Oh well, everyone thinks I'm Kathy Bates, but no, I'm an artist." Glancing over to Nino, our beloved driver, Connie flashes her pale lashes, attempting to wink, but resembles more of struggle against a trapped speck of dust. Nervously, Connie blurts, "Before leaving Italy, I will paint that handsome hunk of a man," points to Nino, and then says, "Oh yes, I will depict Nino in the Toscana moonlight and highlight his bare, sun-kissed body with my acrylic paints." She gave Nino a quick wink with her left eye again, along with an impulsive whack across his perfectly shaped torso, leaving us speechless.

I remember so well how she gravitated close to Tony, and how Nino's face illuminated with flashing tones of red, unaware of what he was doing to deserve such special treatment from Misery. Then, of course, followed Tony's whirling of hands in the air as he repeated his chants of Mamma Mia and saying with projecting eyes, "Mamma Mia, Stefania. Where did you find this one?"

I already miss the serenity and beauty of Assisi as it slowly blends with the horizon. Watching the monks these past few days has been magically fascinating for all of us. Seeing them in their long black and brown robes with their toes protruding from their flapping sandals fills me with a nostalgia from the medieval times. I love seeing them walk the cobbled streets, up and down, in their Gothic glory; it tantalizes my creative energies, causing me to snap photo after photo. I'm in love with the medieval villas and the way of life here in Umbria. I love the iron-forged balconies displaying the geraniums in vivid, rainbow colors and the beautiful medieval churches.

Assisi is a village with joyful chimes, charming us in a magical and glorious kind of way. The view invites us to stand longer on our tiny balconies overlooking the storybook setting of ceramic roof tiles and listening to the musical chimes bouncing from rooftop to rooftop. We hear church bells dinging and donging in their morning routine, along with the chorus of nuns and monks chanting their own melodies. The

Umbria region of Italy features many hilltop villages, but there is a special enchantment about Assisi.

"Stephani, will we hear the heavenly chimes of angelic church bells ringing throughout the rolling hills tomorrow morning?" Alice from Dallas, asks, peering behind at the fading hills of Assisi.

"Ah, yes, we'll awake to the magnetic aromas of freshly baked breads along with celestial ding-dongs replacing our alarm clocks," I reply with a gentle laugh.

"Well, I can't imagine it being any better than Assisi." Alice continues to look back toward Assisi.

Allowing the microphone to dangle in my left hand just a few inches from Nino, our adorable driver, I feel as though I'm in a dream, a fairy-tale dream. I've been silent for minutes now, clicking my camera and trying to capture the rolling beauty of this region, but I know photos cannot do justice to the magnificence of God's creation here.

Assisi is now miles behind us, and our coach is vibrating with the beat of the Italian music. Looking backward, I see an ecstatic group of Americans hysterically laughing and singing. They remind me of a group of hilarious lunatics, fluttering their hands to the beat of the music while whooping out peculiar sounds. Tony, who is comically animated, trumpets out the exact sound of a braying donkey to the rhythm of the melody, and like a breath of fresh air, uncontrollable laughter vibrates throughout the coach once again.

Nino has stopped the coach. The laughter behind me is still loud; the music continues vibrating down the aisle; and many of them are singing while jumping, up and down, like spring-loaded, Energizer bunnies. They are hilarious, imitating someone playing the drums, the horn, the saxophone, the piano, and so on. They are not even aware that Nino has stopped the coach.

Opening the coach door, Nino hops out and allows his friend Nando to take over the driver's seat. We hate to see our adorable Nino go, but he's on his way to Napoli for the greatest event of his life. Nino is getting married tomorrow. Yes, tomorrow evening we will be in Napoli for Nino and Susy's storybook wedding overlooking the gorgeous cobalt Mediterranean. This colossal Italian extravaganza will be a wedding ceremony directly out of the fairy-tale storybooks.

There will be a huge array of Neapolitan chefs in tall, pristinely white hats and fitted suits, all of them presenting mountainous heaps of mouthwatering delicacies at two in the afternoon. Tony will be the sole judge of the tasting before the guests arrive at this celebrity-style wedding, determining each flavor in a bite or two. The grand circling of tables will be adorned in extravagant fabrics, presenting an unbelievable variety of foods, all specialties from Napoli.

Tomorrow is the prelude of Nino's fairy tale, with locals arriving to mingle and savor the vast supply of the liquid reds and the vast abundance of foods. All of this will be majestically displayed underneath huge white canopies overlooking the Mediterranean's pristine waters. This dramatized setting has already started; the contracted professionals are already preparing the white-pointed tents high above the bay of Napoli, right next to the infamous volcano Vesuvius.

The wedding ceremony begins at four, and then comes another taste. Oh yes, there is the gastronomy, the music, and much more. At the stroke of midnight, another momentous event will begin inside the palace. A ten-course meal with exquisite music and a renowned celebrity, an operetta singer, will sing at each table, serenading the guests with her angelic tones. After the huge extravaganza comes more dancing, singing, and eating until you nearly explode. And if you think that's all, well, no. When the clock strikes early morning, Nino and Susy will be presented as man and wife. They will appear as two bronzed beauties underneath another magnificently created castlelike arbor, enclosed with thousands of fresh flowers hovering around them. If that's not enough to blow an American away, then I'm sure the towering wedding cake debut will.

I become excited just imagining the wedding tomorrow. But living in the present, I'm giggling with our wonderful group of Americans, who are singing their hearts out to the Italian music.

Nando, our new driver, exits onto the *autostrada*, leading us straight toward Rome. Glancing over, I watch Nando stretch and relax back in the driver's seat as we resume with the singing of "My Dog Has Fleas." Nando is bamboozled with such a song but continues to smile and tap his fingers on the steering wheel as we sing together. Looking at Tony, who is seated right behind Nando, I start to laugh. Tony has started braying like a donkey again.

We have been driving for twenty minutes or so, all thirteen Americans happily singing at the top of their lungs, along with Tony and our borrowed driver, Nando, who doesn't speak English. I think we've sung the flea song to death, so we suddenly jump from Misery's song to the Italian CD with all of my favorite songs.

Immediately, all of us begin to sing our adopted Italia song, *"Tu Vuo' Fa L'Americano."* I'm pretending to play the piano across the dashboard, and Tony is belting out the lyrics with both hands dancing over his head. Nando has one hand over his heart while squeezing his eyes shut, as if he were singing a heartfelt love song to his sweetheart.

Amidst the laughter and performance to the beating music rebounding through the speakers, I feel an abrupt tapping from behind. Mr. Brown inclines himself over my shoulder. I feel his breath and hear his urgent plea. "Stephani, I must go to the toilet, *now.*" Unable to understand him, I reduce the volume and ask him to repeat himself, and he does so without pausing.

"Oh, dear, we just left Assisi a few minutes ago," I say, "and there's no place to stop on the autostrada for at least thirty minutes."

Before I finish my sentence, Mr. Brown makes an abrupt U-turn in the narrow aisle. I turn and watch as he wiggles back to his seat, in a fidgety kind of way, past Tony. Before Tony can turn around to see what the problem is, Mr. Brown plops into his seat next to his aristocratic, pale, and extremely thin wife.

"Mamma Mia! What's the matter with you?" Tony asks Mr. Brown with protruding eyes. Mr. Brown cannot reply. His mouth is clenched tightly, and he appears to be holding his breath while in horrific pain.

Within seconds, Mr. Brown shoots up out of his seat like a firing rocket, lifts his legs high into the air, and crisscrosses them like some sort of twisted pretzel. At the speed of light, he releases them just enough to force his way back to the front of the coach. Like a rerun with added animation, his obvious, urgent, and sweating pain compels him to forcefully tap my shoulder. This time, bursting from his mouth in agony, his trembling voice bellows, "Stephani, I must do a *number two!*"

"Mamma Mia! What is a number two? I do not understand what a number two is, Stefania," Tony says, alarmed, and then he mumbles,

"This must be a joke. Perhaps Stefania is putting him up to performing for us."

Turning around to face Mr. Brown, I watch in disbelief. He darts back down the aisle, bouncing up and down like a Russian ballerina. His legs are locked together while he holds both hands over his tightly squeezed buttocks as though a colony of fire ants were ambushing and stinging him at full force. I flutter an eyelid, and before it flashes again, he has plunged into his seat, sweat cascading from his brow.

Alarmed by such animation, Tony swiftly leans toward me with ballooning eyes, inquiring in his thunderous Sicilian manner, "What's the matter with him, Stefania? Is this an Americana performance called a number two? Mamma Mia, he has gone mad."

I lean back toward Tony and whisper, "He must do a *number two*, and he needs to do it now."

"Mamma Mia, what do you mean a number two, Stefania? What's a number two?" Tony demands loudly, alerting the entire group to the dire situation in progress. Immediately, turning toward Mr. Brown, Tony demands, "What is a number two? I do not understand. What is this bloody number two?"

Unable to keep still long enough to reply, Mr. Brown shoots up again like a bolt of lightning as his twisted body ricochets uncontrollably. Given the magnificence of his performance, I understand the alarming pains that are surely punching and boxing from within his stomach as he twists and jerks. Then, as if a sizzling branding iron scorches his buttocks, he takes off again in a fast, dancing rhythm, sprinting toward the front of the bus as though seeking an exit through the windshield. Right before plunging straight through, he turns around, jets back in the opposite direction, and, tightly holding his buttocks, dances in a ballerina style while hollering hysterically, "Stephani, I've got to do a number two *now!*"

In the midst of trying to explain to Tony the meaning of a number two, a thunderous explosion blasts through Mr. Brown's pants, transmitting the worst aroma ever known to the medical doctor himself, who is frozen in disbelief in his seat. With ballooning eyes, the doctor's demeanor becomes wildly animated.

Having a weak stomach, I immediately grab my scarf and tie it around my nose as the horrible stench engulfs the entire coach. Within seconds,

I'm in a gagging frenzy along with Nando, who understands nothing. The engulfing odor consumes all the clean oxygen within seconds, and I don't need to explain the happenings of a number two.

Like a programmed robot, Nando continues chanting "Mamma Mia" while frantically groping for the button on his left side, which allows the driver's window to go down. Nando hangs his head out the window like a dog sniffing fresh air. I can tell by his flashing red face that he is under the illusion that the repugnant odor will dissipate into the fresh air outside.

"Basta, Basta. Stop, stop," shouts Tony. "Stop the bus." Tony makes Nando turn the wheel to the right, bringing the coach to a skidding halt on the autostrada's narrow shoulder. Looking to the left, I see the oncoming traffic, which is now bumper to bumper. We hear cars and scooters sounding their horns with one hand while twirling the other hand through the air and shouting words too offensive to repeat. Immediately, Nando presses the button for the door to open, and Mr. Brown flies out of the coach like a caged animal with Tony at his heels.

Mr. Brown runs toward the back bumper of the coach, but stops abruptly as though an invisible wall is in front of him when he sees the drivers of bumper-to-bumper cars and scooters staring at him. When Tony reaches to grab him, he turns around in a sharp U-turn, running back in the opposite direction.

I see him now, jetting past my passenger window, holding his sagging, loaded pants, with Tony chasing behind him hollering, "Basta, stop! What's the matter with you? Mamma Mia."

The cars and scooters are now at a standstill, with people watching the show as though they've arrived at a drive-in theater. If I were not sitting inside the coach, I would faint and hit the floor. I've never in my entire life seen or experienced anything like this. It's more animated than a Disney production performing at its cartoonish peak.

I can't imagine what comes over Tony, but within a split second, he catches Mr. Brown and pulls him down as though tackling a football player, Mr. Brown kicking and hollering all the while. Before my eyelashes flip down, Tony tugs and pulls on Mr. Brown's pants, and his pants and underwear go flying off as if he were a magician. Now Mr. Brown is completely exposed to the heavy traffic from the waist down, and people are whooping and hollering hysterically at his expense.

60

In a matter of seconds, it's like an electrical jolt goes through Mr. Brown, and he instantly springs back up and takes off running again, with Tony chasing him. The two grown men, now covered in chocolate brown, run back and forth from one end of the coach to the other.

Tony finally grabs the back of Mr. Brown's white designer shirt, ripping it off as though he needed to perform CPR. Mr. Brown is now completely exposed, totally naked to the heavy traffic, which prompts the onlookers to holler and honk even more. We are all witnesses to the naked Mr. Brown running as though a flaming torch is blazing his buttocks with fire.

On impulse, Nando jerks the gear into reverse, and squashes his Italian leather shoe all the way down on the gas pedal. Nando is trying to camouflage Mr. Brown's fudge-covered body as the tires burn rubber, spinning the coach backward in a whiplashing maneuver. Heavy clouds of black smoke mushroom up from the burning pavement as small pebbles pop and fly.

No sooner is the coach headed backward than Mr. Brown makes an abrupt U-turn at the end of the coach and then flies back toward the front. Nando jerks the gear into drive, and away we fly, zooming forward as Mr. Brown and Tony run alongside the coach.

Nando is giving his all with the coach, trying to keep Mr. Brown concealed from the heavy traffic. Back and forth, we go, spinning the hot rubber tires. After too many of these "whiplash" tactics to try to hide Mr. Brown with the motor coach, we break out laughing hysterically, all the while holding our noses.

Losing count of the many times Nando pushes the gear into reverse and then forward, we finally get the hang of the forward and backward rhythm inside the coach while Mr. Brown continues to run, back and forth, outside. Mere inches behind Mr. Brown, Tony is running behind him, shouting.

People in the heavy pile-up of traffic are chanting and hollering louder and louder as they watch the most entertaining show they've ever seen in their lives, I'm sure of it. The thought occurs to me that they are watching an R-rated movie with no censors, along with Nando ramming the gears, trying his best to block the man's naked body with the coach. I hope no children are viewing this free show. Nevertheless, the gathered flock of Italians are laughing and relishing Tony's vocabulary and Mr. Brown's complete nakedness.

After hours, it seems, but probably just minutes, Nando presses the passenger button that rolls my window down, and now we hear what Tony is hollering at Mr. Brown.

"Why did you rubbish all over yourself? What kind of Americana are you? Basta, enough, stop running. You must get this rubbish off of you."

I watch in disbelief, my scarf still wrapped around my nose, as Tony yells himself into a near state of cardiac distress. We all hear loud and clear the word *rubbish*, which is probably an English word that Tony claimed from his beautiful wife, Pat, who was born and raised in Wells, England.

Here we are, all seated in the smelly coach, wide-eyed and mortified to the point of hysterical laughter. Well, most of us. Seated in the back of the coach, the doctor reprimands all of us as though we were out-of-control children. He blurts out in a stern voice, "For goodness' sake, give this poor man a little dignity." He turns his head toward the back window in hopes of not losing his dignified pose by accidentally joining us in uncontrollable laughter.

Racing for the coach's door in a state of hysteria, Mr. Brown attempts to leap inside the coach, but Tony grabs his foot and wrestles him back out, kicking and squealing like a terrified pig. Tony ventures to wipe Mr. Brown down with his ripped off shirt, but he slides away and plunges back into the coach. Immediately the laughter stops and we all cover our noses as Mr. Brown slides in toward his wife. Just like a professional baseball player sliding in for a home run, Mr. Brown plunges down in his seat right beside his mortified wife.

The flock of spectators, backed up for miles on the autostrada, have raised their hands in victory, shouting, "Brava, Brava," along with a few other words."

We sit in complete silence, except for Tony, who also entered the coach and shouts, "Andiamo, let's go," alerting Nando to jerk the gear into drive, plunging us forward while burning rubber squeals on the pavement underneath our smoking tires.

I press my scarf tighter around my nose and breathe a sigh of relief, knowing we're heading to the nearest trattoria—a store that I hope has a shower.

Turning around and looking directly at Mr. Brown, Tony says, "Mamma Mia, what's the matter with you? I do not understand why you did such a thing. Do you know how to say *toilet*? This is unbelievable that you rubbish all over the place. You must not eat anything until you get back to America. No, you must drink liquids, nothing but liquids. Mamma Mia!"

Tony turns back toward the front, and sweat drips profusely from his brow like a sprung water leak. He's breathing hard through his flaring nostrils. Tony throws his hands up in the air and continues his mantra of Mamma Mias like a broken record. He looks as though he's just escaped a mud-wrestling match as the tainted goop plops from his elevated elbows.

9

THE CONFESSION

The sun is shining brightly this morning, and Mrs. Brown looks happy and content, sipping her cappuccino with the evidence of *cornetto* crumbs sprinkled sparsely on the white linen cloth adorning the elegant breakfast table. Right beside her, appearing as refined as white sugar, sits her husband, Mr. Brown, who is enjoying a mouthful of Toscana peach marmalade along with a huge, freshly baked cornetto—croissant.

"Buongiorno. Good morning. How are you this morning?" I say, walking past the breakfast table, making my way to the towering tables of heavenly baked cornettos and hot fudge delights.

"Stephani, can I please have a word with you after breakfast?" Mrs. Brown asks with utmost seriousness on her frail, thin face.

"Yes, absolutely," I say with a smile, though my internal dialogue cries, *Oh no, what now?*

After consuming too many homemade pastries, along with two glasses of blood-red orange juice, I excuse myself from the breakfast table and sling my camera over my shoulder. I head to the coach, feeling excitement race throughout my body. Today is going to be another fun-filled adventure of fairy-tale bliss, ideally without anyone needing to do a number two.

"Stephani, can I talk to you before Mr. Brown comes out?" Mrs. Brown asks, looking beyond the corner to make sure Mr. Brown is not following behind.

"Yes, absolutely; is everything okay?" I ask, and then think to myself, *How could something like this happen to such a distinguished, wonderful man as Mr. Brown?*

"Stephani, I must confess the truth of yesterday's eventful occurrence with Mr. Brown," Mrs. Brown says with a serious face. "I will never tell Mr. Brown what happened. Well, not here. Not now. I will wait until we get home, back in America. He will probably laugh. Do you think he will laugh, Stephani?"

"Yes! Oh, yes indeed. Well, no, I mean, yes, well ... I don't know." I am very confused about yesterday's tragic event with Mr. Brown. I have no idea what happened to him unless something from another planet stole his body for a few hours, replacing it with someone else.

"Please understand it was a terrible mistake. I can't believe this happened to him." Mrs. Brown continues, looking perplexed before starting up again. "You see, yesterday, late evening, Mr. Brown had a craving for a chocolate candy bar. He was so persistent. I told him to go look inside my purse for the candy bar that I had nibbled on earlier in the—" She stopped, looked around to make sure it was safe and then whispered with a slight grin, "It was a chocolate laxative—he ate the whole bar!"

10

THE DAY OF THE DEAD

I'm here in Italy with sixteen Americans, plus Tony and Nino this morning. I can already tell this is going to be a fun group, especially with Zelma Rocklin on board. Zelma is a unique woman from upstate New York who reminds me of Barbara Walters in a serious kind of way. Zelma, or on a more professional level, Dr. Rocklin, found Decorate Ornate on the Internet while searching for a certain gold-carved chair. After I'd talked with her on the telephone for more than an hour, she purchased the ornate chair, along with this Italy tour we're now on. I know nothing about Dr. Rocklin, other than that she's a medical doctor, loves European furniture, and is married to a man who chooses to spend his time hitting golf balls when not sipping tea with his socialite mother and her entourage of "Stepford wives." I did detect a little bit of hostility when she mentioned the Stepford wives during our phone conversation, along with the mental image of her rolling her eyes.

Before us right now is a tiny blue Fiat, bouncing along, jiggling over potholes, with a little dog sniffing the Italian air from the half-open car window. We're walking on the cobblestones, watching the locals load carts of beautiful chrysanthemums and armloads of red candles.

"Stefania, what's the occasion for all of this beauty?" shouts Dr. Rocklin, clicking her camera.

"It's a very special day in Italy. One of the most bizarre celebrations of all. The Italians know today as the Day of the Dead," I explain as they flash looks of surprise and shock.

"Very funny, Stefania. Now really, where are they taking all of those flowers and carts of candles?" Dr. Rocklin demands, giving me the urge to salute her in a military sort of way.

"I'm not joking. Today is the official day the Italians visit the dead as though they are still alive in the tombs. It's a celebration of love and remembrance of their loved ones. And all the beautiful flowers and candles you see are going to the cemetery. Let's follow along with them." I nod, hoping they will join in with my spontaneous suggestion.

"Stefania, have you lost your mind this morning? We don't know anyone in the cemetery," Dr. Rocklin shoots back while grabbing a potted chrysanthemum from the little nearby cart, slowly examining it for duty inspection.

"Oh, don't worry, we'll join in and have some fun." I wear a big smile while walking toward the wooden cart loaded with the beautiful chrysanthemums.

"*Grazie.* Thank you," I say to the curvy signora, simultaneously pulling out my euros and handing them to her. Just like Follow the Leader, everyone proceeds to do the same, buying a little potted chrysanthemum along with a few candles.

We tote our chrysanthemums along with the wax candles, and bypass local shops and old medieval churches. We are a happy flock of Americans, joining the celebration of the Day of the Dead as though we've come from across the world to reminisce and pay homage to our dear loved ones. We pass and cross ourselves at the locals, and they return the gesture with a wide-eyed stare. Passing them on the tiny streets prompts me to draw the curtain closed on my stretched smile. I change my facial expression to show a more serious one, which seems more appropriate right now.

Rounding the narrow corner on ancient cobblestones, we come face-to-face with a flock of local sisters. They are adorned in long, white nunnery dresses, singing beautiful Italian hymns.

A spell has seemingly been cast upon us, and we drop our heads as though looking for a lost treasure on the street. Somberly and quietly, we follow the locals, rounding the twists and turns of the narrow, cobbled streets. We are passing many little shops that give me the urge to dash inside, but I don't. We round another corner and see Tony and Nino sitting on an old bench. They seem to blend in with the locals.

"Cover your face with the mums," I say as we come within feet of them.

"Look at them, wrapping their tongues around those towering piles of gelato," Sandra says, walking right past them with a huge grin stretched across her sweet face.

Whew, that was close, I say to myself, gasping and giggling aloud as we stroll past them, hidden by the crowd. I didn't want Tony and Nino to see us following the locals. They would think I'd lost my mind, taking the Americans to such an event.

We continue following the locals out through the medieval entrance gate that leads down into the rolling valley. I'm already feeling excitement rise within me. Spiraling downward through the olive trees and vineyards, I see the old medieval monastery rising from the valley like a picturesque oil painting from long ago. What words can describe such a sight before us? We're looking at Tuscan hills saturated with gorgeous vineyards. Before us right now is what you see in the paintings of Tuscany. There are no words to describe this fairy-tale beauty. It looks unreal, just like a painted canvas.

Amongst this beauty, I click my camera toward the ancient monastery to the left of us that reminds me of a rising angel spreading its wings. Unable to resist, the Americans join me, clicking their cameras at the ancient beauty.

"Wow, I can't wait to see inside the church," whispers Margie from Little Rock, Arkansas. "Oh, this is just like being in a movie from long ago—you know, the fairy-tale books with magical people jumping out of nowhere at any given moment. I cannot believe this place. I feel as though I'm in a living storybook."

"We're not going inside the church right now." The locals in front of us dart across the road, headed toward the medieval cemetery's gate. Following behind them like a marching band, our anticipation explodes upon seeing the wonderment of floral and marble beauty. Some of the Americans on this tour have never seen Italian cemeteries. Now, since they are with me and I've made such a big deal about them, they are eagerly anticipating the introduction.

Words cannot describe Italian cemeteries. They are so different from American cemeteries. The Italian cemeteries are floral masterpieces filled with colorful flowers and gorgeous, mausoleums that are styled like medieval houses, not to mention the towering marble angels and tall Gothic crucifixes.

Following the locals who are ahead of us and scattering inside the flower-filled cemetery, we feel like little children going through an enchanting storybook. Within minutes after we slip through the iron gates, I rush to the tallest, white-marble angel, towering every bit of twelve feet tall. I reach for its spanning wing, stretched out as though rippling in the wind. It's soaring high, almost ready to fly. I feel its coolness; the touch of marble is cold. The lifelike marble angels are everywhere, fluttering around, kneeling down and kissing the tombs inside this flower-filled sanctuary.

The tombs are on top of the ground, one after another, each one with its own photo and candle. The scent of lavender floats through the air with a hint of fresh-cut roses nearby. It's a glorious setting, filled with hundreds of flowers.

Below the angel, I see an old tomb with a framed photo of an olive-kissed man. His hair is tightly curled with black ringlets, and his happy face smiles directly toward me. He makes me laugh, beaming with such happiness. I think it's his bushy, black eyebrows and thick-lashed eyes, accented with the distinct nose of a standard poodle, all perfectly coordinated together, that make me laugh. His eyes are framed with the largest set of black-rimmed glasses I've ever seen on a man. I immediately think of an Italian version of Elton John, singing, "Benny and the Jets," with his huge round, sequin glasses.

Totally embracing the moment, I position the beautiful mums below his framed face and say as though it's the right thing to do, "*Ciao*," all the while clicking my camera. I cross myself without thought, feeling it's the respectful thing to do, and then read the Italian words sketched in the marble below his face. When I glance up, our eyes meet. Without hesitation, I rub the thick glass that's protecting his sweet face with my scarf and flash him back a smile. Before drawing my wide-stretched smile back to normal position, I see out of the corner of my eyes a gathered flock of locals staring at me with raised eyebrows.

"*Come stai*? How are you?"

"Mamma Mia, Madonna," they shout together as one *signorina* drops her potted chrysanthemum, simultaneously bursting into tears.

In puzzlement, I watch the *signorina* jet off like a soaring eagle, running hysterically toward the forged-iron gate. I'm too shocked to move, and for once, speechless. I want to explain why I'm sitting here, gazing into this man's eyes and placing chrysanthemums below his face, but I don't.

The crying signorina has disappeared among the vineyards, and I feel the urgent need to explain why I'm perched on their loved one's tomb. I try to speak, but my words are not being heard. They are talking amongst themselves, pointing at me, and the longer they chatter, the louder they get. I can clearly see they have assumed something terribly upsetting, and I'm sure it seems strange for me to be sitting here smiling at their loved one as though we're deeply in love, not to mention placing a beautiful bundle of flowers below his smiling face.

I start to explain my love for Italian cemeteries but the lengthy Italian words have escaped from my mind. The more I say, the more ridiculously insane it sounds. Nevertheless, I shuffle myself around on top of the marble tomb, stretch my face to a wide smile, and start up again.

"I bring the Americans here because the cemeteries are so beautiful and different from American cemeteries. The cemeteries here look nothing like American cemeteries, nothing at all," I say, pointing up to the towering marble angel.

"The beauty here intrigues me, along with the gorgeous marble angels, the Gothic crucifixes, the huge abundance of floral beauty, and the glowing candles flickering like diamonds in the wind. And this particular man, who is staring at me from his framed photo, just happened to grab my attention as I entered through the old, forged-iron gate," I say with all the sincerity I can muster, pointing to his smiling face in the round photo frame.

"And with his comical and oh-so-European Elton John glasses, along with his distinct nose of a standard poodle, I ran to him. First I saw the towering marble angel, and instantly my legs magnetized to this tomb. You see, I love the Carrara marble. In fact, we take the Americans to Carrara, Italy, when we're close to the region. I always tell the Americans that the Carrara marble is the most expensive marble quarried in the world. And oh, the pink flowers mixed in with the red roses really got my attention as well."

In the awkward situation I find myself in right now, I ramble on and on, chattering with no direction at all. Before I get the last words out, the locals start up again, flashing their dilated eyes at me. The more they talk amongst themselves, the more I understand. And within minutes, reality hits me hard.

"Oh Mamma Mia, they think I'm the mistress. That's why they're acting this way," I say aloud in English, knowing they do not understand a word I'm saying. The minute I get the last word out of my mouth, I draw my smile closed and sheepishly twist about in a quick swirl on the white marble tomb. I'm hoping to make a fast getaway on the other side, but feeling their eyes on me, and remembering the hysterical signorina, I turn back around. I now face them, surrounded by raised eyebrows and suspicious minds. Paralyzed with shock, I hear them repeating to one another so many untrue statements.

"Mamma Mia Madonna. She's the lover of Roberto."

"Si, si, yes, she is here to celebrate Roberto's life."

"Where are Roberto's bambinos? Surely they have many bambinos."

"She is no Americana. No, she is surely one of those desperate Moroccan *prostituta*. Si, si, yes, she is a Moroccan *puttana*. But no, she speaks like the Americana, but with a strange twist. She sounds like the Americana in the western movies, like John Wayne but with a strange drawl," says the superior one.

They repeat their hair-raising verdict, one after another. They are convinced that I am Roberto's lover, mistress, the mother of his many bambinos, who are surely dangling in some secret place in Italy. I want to talk, but the only thing I say is, *"Come si dice?*—What do you say?" Then, like a ricochet coming back to me, they reply, *"Come si dice?"*

On impulse, I grab my potted mums from underneath Roberto's smiling face and leap across the tomb in the opposite direction from the flock of Italians and run as though my pants were on fire. The closest place to go is toward a creamy-white medieval mausoleum. It looks like a "mini-me" Gothic church, and at this point, I'm willing to spend time with whoever is resting peacefully inside this lovely house. Not sparing a minute, I push open the beautiful Gothic iron doors and race inside. The heavy doors slam behind me, and when I look up, I see another gathered group of Italians who have jumped with surprise. Immediately, all six of them stampede past me, screaming and shouting, arms in midair, *"Babbo, Babbo!* Papa, Papa."

I try to move out of their way and they leave me in a twirling spin, wondering what just happened. No doubt, they *were* celebrating their loved ones inside these marble tombs, all six of the group inside this tiny, candle-glowing house. But why they shouted "*Babbo, Babbo*" and ran like crazy, I do not know.

Looking up from my dizzy state, I see pure white Carrarra marble tombs, two on each side of me, with a beautiful altar toward the front. The glowing candles on the left tomb are reflected in an old tarnished, oval-framed photo. Inside the frame is a beautiful signora with long black hair and big round eyes. She is smiling with pale pink lips … and a gold crucifix hangs from her neck. Without thought, I stretch my potted mums toward her framed face, cross myself with a semi-bowed head, and turn toward the heavy door. I pull it open and run like a racehorse to the finish line, which is the forged-iron gate.

"Mamma Mia, Madonna. The Day of the Dead is unbelievable with you, Stefania," Tony declares, shaking his head while all the Americans talk at once, trying to tell him what I did in the cemetery. Finally, I regain my breath, and praying my heart will slow down, I laughingly say, "We can never come back here again, not to this village. They think I'm Roberto's lover, and I don't have a clue why those people in the little house took off running."

The Americans will forever remember the Day of the Dead celebration in Italy.

11

OOPS! THE DOOR IS GONE!

This morning we have said our farewells to our dear friends in the storybook village of Orvieto, Italy, and loaded all of our purchased wares into the already packed coach. Minutes before stepping inside the coach, I see flapping wings of a startled pigeon fly by me. No doubt he enjoyed his morning slumber before all of us loud Americans piled laughingly inside the coach. I take one last look at the fabulous Duomo, which is considered one of the greatest of all of Italy's Romanesque-Gothic cathedrals. I glance back at the ceramics hanging everywhere around the fairy-tale shops and remember the famous Orvieto Classico wine inside the corner shop. I raise my hands in the morning air, waving goodbye to our surrounded friends, and then turn to get inside our coach.

Winding down the thousand-foot hilltop village of Orvieto, I look over and see Nando driving. I should be seeing Nino sitting there, but I don't. I know Nino will be back in his driver's seat soon and Nando will be off to the vineyards, but for some strange reason, I feel the urge to sing, "Nino, our little bambino." But, knowing Nando will think I'm completely crazy, I force myself to stay quiet. Looking straight ahead now, I see rolling hills of vineyards and olive trees. There are no words to describe the beauty before me. It looks like a painted masterpiece of Tuscany, but it's not. We are nestled in the region of Umbria, smacked magically amongst the rolling hills.

Behind me, I hear the clicking of cameras and a chorus of American words expressing their own verbal enchantment. It doesn't look real to these American eyes, because there is nothing comparable to this in their country. Orvieto is one of the Etruscan villages that existed centuries before Christ, and some even believe it was once considered an "Etruscan Mecca."

Heading back to Assisi for the next four nights, we decide to stop at one of our favorite places to buy olive oil and the famous chocolate liqueurs. Like always, we park toward the back of the building. But today for some strange reason, Nando shoves the gears into reverse and plows the coach beneath the branches of a towering tree. Within seconds, we have cleared the coach and are racing toward the family warehouse, which is stocked full of gorgeous ceramics, wines, chocolates, and more.

"Mamma Mia, you must be careful with the bus. Nino will be extremely upset if you disturb the paint," Tony spouts to Nando, who looks confused, wondering why Tony is saying such a thing when he's only parked underneath a tree. Swinging his head of black curls as though they were annoying him, Nando follows Tony, hoping to get a taste of the delicious chocolate liqueur before the Americans slurp it all down.

More than two hours go by, and we are saturated with strong helpings of creamy liqueurs and the endless supply of the liquid reds. However, I see no reason to rush this wonderful experience. Looking over the towering bottles of chocolate liqueur I hold tightly in my arms, I see Larry Dale from Houston, squeezing through the narrow aisle.

"Just a few more, please," he pleads, holding out both hands as though he were a small child from a poor third-world country. I have to walk past him to get to the checkout counter, so I imagine myself invisible, hoping to not stop and chat in my heavily loaded predicament.

"Oh, Stefania, these are the most delicious olives I've ever tasted," Larry says. "After you free yourself from all those bottles in your arms, would you grab ten or so sacks from the checkout counter so I can fill them up with olives? There is no reason to purchase these olives when they have so many of them growing out there on the trees. Oh, just one more thing to ask of you: as soon as you get back with the sacks, I'll open the jars and fill them up." Larry opens another jar of olives and tosses the lid on the floor.

So much for my being invisible, I think to myself, and then reply, "You can buy all the filled bottles you need; they are for sale."

How insane he must be, thinking I'm going to ask for free olives when these people are in business to make a living. They are always so kind, giving us abundant samplings of everything they have for sale before we buy. They are open for business, and ideally to make a small profit, not to give it all away to a man who happens to be a wealthy millionaire many times over. Perhaps we should go to the olive groves tomorrow and let Larry see the hard work and time it takes to produce the taste of one small olive. And, if he thinks picking the olives off the trees is all it takes to get the taste he's experiencing now, well, he is sadly mistaken. You cannot pick an olive and eat it from the tree without suffering a very bad taste.

Feeling embarrassed by Larry's gluttony, his going back for eight more handfuls of the same olives and leaving too many empty olive jars on their counter, I must act. I run my purchases to the coach and head back inside. Grabbing a large basket, I fill it with the remaining jars of olives, and hand over my euros at the checkout counter. Like all Italian storekeepers, they place the many jars of olives in a nice box and wrap it up with beautiful paper, tied with a bow. I feel excited now. Excited to give Larry something he will truly love, and excited to repay our dear Italian friends for their generosity. The scale seems to be a little more balanced now.

I am a strong believer in the Bible scripture that says, "We reap what we sow," also referred to as karma. I would never intentionally cheat someone out of anything, because it would come back around.

After spending too many euros inside this Willy Wonka–like chocolate liqueur paradise, we all pile back into the coach. Laughing and buzzing with an all-time high from the abundance of chocolate liqueur and liquid reds, we express how fabulously blessed we are to not have a care in the world other than asking, "When is our next taste?"

I am feeling so high right now that I'm floating in the heavenly realms of chocolate paradise. I consumed every glass of various flavors of the chocolate liqueur, along with the lemony liqueur that was placed in my hands.

"Stefania, you must taste this one," they had insisted. "Do you like? Ah, yes, try this one; it has the taste of mint with a little twist of creamy chocolate liqueur. Oh, Stefania, you must taste the chocolate amaretto, oh please. And Stefania, this is the best one, we do believe. Try it; it is chocolate liqueur with red hot peppers. Do you like the taste? Ah, yes, now you need the liquid red to cool the tongue."

Once we are all safely inside the coach, Nando presses the button to close the open door, and for no reason other than watching the door close, everyone breaks out in roaring laughter.

"It's the chocolate liqueur," I say to Nando as he presses the gas pedal for takeoff.

Like a comedy cartoon, the coach shoots forward with a jerk, ripping the passenger door completely off our beautiful, Mercedes-Benz coach. Unbeknown to Nando, when he first opened the door on arrival, the robotic door pushed back into a low-hanging branch and attached itself to the hinge of the door as it closed.

"Mamma Mia, Madonna!" Tony hollers hysterically, his eyes bugging out like a cartoon character in shock. "Basta. Stop!" Tony looks back toward the dangling door, which is now swinging back and forth from the large tree limb.

The mantras of "Mamma Mias" continue to pour from Tony's mouth as his arms dance and swirl over his head. He appears to be conducting an orchestra, totally animated with his Rodney Dangerfield eyes bulging. And when everyone on the right side looks out their window and sees the door dangling from the tree limb, uncontrollable laughter explodes within the coach. This is better than any cartoon for sure.

I fall out of my seat from too much laughter. Nando shoves the gear into reverse, hoping to rescue the door, but sadly, it is too high in the air, swaying back and forth as though it were a swing.

"Andiamo, let's go," Tony says, urging me to hop out the door-less opening and clear the way for him to leap outside for his inspection. Nando has already skyrocketed out of the driver's door and raced around to our side. Words cannot describe this cartoon scene. "Did this really just happen to our new Mercedes-Benz coach?" I say aloud.

Nando looks like a bouncing chimpanzee, jumping up and down, trying to grab hold of the dangling door. However, he is too short to reach it. Before Tony can open his mouth to give an order, Nando zips around the back of the coach and climbs to the top. The passengers inside hear loud metal steps above their heads. It sounds as though the roof of the coach will cave in, but just when I become alarmed, Nando takes a dive toward the door in midair.

It's a miracle, a real miracle. Nando is swinging back and forth, high in the air, and holding on to the dangling door. We immediately give a hand of applause for his heroic jump, but in a matter of seconds, the tree limb snaps and breaks, sending Nando and the door plummeting straight toward the ground.

Thankfully, Nando and the door survive the hard landing. Nando springs up and pulls the heavy door back to the coach. He places it in the outside coach compartment and staggers back to his driver's seat.

By this time, I am seated in the passenger seat in the front of the coach with no door. I stare through the windshield pretending to be serious, but laughter is still vibrating throughout the coach. Glancing over to see Nando behind the wheel, I realize he is totally stressed out. His face is fire-truck red, and the sweat dripping off his face proves beyond a reasonable doubt that he is close to some kind of breakdown.

Breathing in and out at a rapid rate, Nando hits the gas pedal, which alerts the tires to peal forward. In a matter of minutes, buckled tightly in my seat, I feel the Toscana wind slapping my ponytail, whipping it around and around, like a spinning wheel.

"Stefania, we are in crisis. We have a big *problema*," Tony shouts for me to hear.

"No, you are joking," I say sarcastically, too afraid to turn my head around for fear of being suctioned out the door-less opening.

"Mamma Mia, Stefania. I do not believe the luck we have with Nando. Mamma Mia, he must go *immediatamente*, immediately. Yes, yes, the bad luck he brings to us is too much. I've already called Nino. I told him to forget the errand; you must come to us now, I said. Oh yes, I told Nino the door was ripped completely off by a bloody tree limb. Stefania, tell me how this could happen. Mamma Mia! I do not understand why this Nando pushed the coach under a tree. Why didn't he push it in the open lot like a normal driver? And Stefania, you must prepare the people to be careful going to their rooms. Oh yes, until we get rid of this Nando, the luck he is bringing to us, oh, Mamma Mia!" Tony's eyes are dilating and he pauses for a brief second before starting up again.

"Here we are with no door on the passenger side of the coach, and it's Sunday. Mamma Mia Madonna!" Tony articulates in Italian while seated in his usual seat behind the driver, knowing there are no mechanics working today, not in Italy on God's faithful day of rest.

"We cannot continue like this—no, we must find someone to repair the bloody door," Tony says aloud while pulling out his mobile phone and hurriedly pressing the little buttons, then starting with a tone of S-O-S in progress.

In a matter of seconds, Tony connects to the next dot, who will, no doubt, correct the damage we've suffered. And of course, we have no magic genie hidden in a bottle, but we do have Tony Filaci, and that's all we need to make our crooked paths go perfectly straight.

Speaking in his Italian dialect, Tony directs Nando where to go and then relays the message in English that we're in hot pursuit of an emergency reattachment.

Nando is staying on the right side of the road, trying to shield me from the passing cars. However, he feels the need to pass a tiny Fiat. As Nando zooms around the Fiat, I'm side by side with the driver. I could literally stretch my leg over and kick the side of his window with my foot. Nevertheless, the sudden urge to do so quickly slips away as the little Fiat zooms ahead, leaving me engulfed in lung-exploding exhaust fumes.

Before realizing what has happened, Nando exits the autostrada and brings the coach to a sudden stop. And just like magic, right beside my door-less opening, stand two qualified mechanics, eager and ready for the emergency reattachment of our door.

12

MAMMA MIA, TONY DOES THE SPLITS!

As he steps off the motor coach on a beautiful Tuscan morning, both of Tony's legs speedily divert in opposite directions, similar to a cheerleader doing the splits, leaving him agonizing in severe pain and wondering if he will ever walk again. Blame it on gravity, overweight, or maybe slippery cobblestone streets, only God knows, but Tony is out of commission for the next few months.

This horrible bout of fate leaves him hopping around on crutches, leaving me to wonder how or if he'll make it to our upcoming tour. Tony is not one to be restrained for weeks at a time, and I can't imagine how Pat, his beautiful, Welsh-born wife, will remain sane while keeping him confined. I can already see Pat fearlessly rendering doctor's orders to Tony as he lounges in his big fluffy chair, reclined just enough for him to bask in the breathtaking sunlight colors reflecting off the magnificent Italian Riviera. I can hear Tony's voice roaring in his Sicilian dialect, "Pat, Pat, Pat! Where are you, Pat?" This is going to be a stressful situation for Pat.

Nevertheless, Tony will certainly be pampered in their priceless piece of Toscana paradise, towering majestically over the Italian Riviera. Just imagine their lifestyle, surrounded by the shimmering turquoise Mediterranean waters highlighting their charming villa, with Tony's entourage of exotic parrots singing operetta in Italian. And let's not forget to mention that they have every exotic plant known to humanity; one of Pat's acclaimed hobbies is pinching plants. Yes, taking plants! The two of them, along with their beautiful daughters, Giada and Clairessa, are happily living a fairy-tale dream on their very own piece of priceless Italian Rivera. And just a few feet below their villa, where the spectacular blue and turquoise waters splash against the sand, you will see such celebrities as Prince Charles and his wife, Camilla, docking their yacht and walking amongst the locals.

The alarming thought of not having Tony on our Italy tour is consuming my mind. But before I have time to contemplate my missing link, the phone rings.

"Stefania, come stai? How are you, Stefania?" Tony asks, not giving me time to answer before he continues. "I have very bad news to tell you. I must have knee surgery. You must not worry though; Nino will meet you at the *airporta*." Tony does not realize my heart is beating too fast and I feel faint.

I can't believe the news. I am lost without Tony, totally lost. Tony is my right arm, my partner, my Sicilian papa, and my magical fairy who waves his hands in the Italian air, making everything wonderful. His Sicilian/Italian dialect makes closed doors open, crooked paths straight, and padlocks open freely, and brings tons of hysterical laughter to all of us.

Italy awaits his commands, his wisdom, and his direction. I'm lost without his smiling presence, totally lost. We're like Sonny and Cher, a strange but funny team. We're always finishing each other's sentences and bringing flavorful animation to all of the Americans.

Suddenly I think about crowning Tony on the coach. *What will we do about the crowning?* I think to myself, glancing over to the bag of red wax lips lying on my desk. I always crown Tony with a silly hat of some sort and place huge red wax lips on his mouth. Afterward, I present him to the passengers, ridiculously disguised. Just imagine Rodney Dangerfield with huge red lips, and you will see Tony. This sends our passengers into hysterical laughter. Mamma Mia, it makes me laugh just thinking about it. Even though Nino is driving the coach, he's never forgotten. He receives an adornment of honor too.

This event has brought nearby drivers on the autostrade—highways—to instant laughter. Nino is gorgeous in his aristocratic, royal hat or perhaps a Texas cowboy hat on his olive-toned head. The best part of the ceremony is when I place the hat on top of his head and watch his gorgeous face stretch to a wide, puppet-painted smile. At that very second, I plunge a set of red wax lips in his opened mouth.

"Don't worry about a thing, Stefania, everything will be fine, *va bene?* Okay?" Tony says to me again.

"Si, si. Tony, this is terrible news, just terrible."

"Stefania, you must not worry about a thing. You will be okay. *Va bene?"*

I feel myself sinking into a deep, depressive state of mind.

13

No Tony

It's a beautiful, cool spring morning here in Italy, and I've brought a rather large group of Americans for another magical adventure. However, there's no Tony with us. Ever since his legs speedily diverted in a painful cheerleading split weeks ago, Tony has been convalescing at his home, way above the turquoise blue waters of the Italian Riviera. In talking with Pat via the telephone, I get the weekly reports on Tony's recovery. Pat says she is sustaining her sanity quite well, thanks to her brilliant idea.

In her proper English accent, Pat explains how she seductively secured Tony in his chaise longue, with both legs locked and suspended high in the cool Riviera sea breeze. This guaranteed there was no chance of him getting up or escaping his paradisiacal surroundings—not with the locking mechanism that secured his legs, which now dangled high above him. There was absolutely no hope of Tony standing up without the turn of the key, which brought a big smile to Pat's gorgeous face as she laughed with every detail over the mobile phone. I'd already heard reports of Tony trying to bribe his two daughters, Giada and Clairessa, with heavenly delights if they would unlock the mechanism suspending his legs from the high rafters of their picturesque portico.

"It's the perfect convalescing remedy," Pat says through the mobile phone lines. Pat keeps an eye on Tony while she tends to her massive supply of exotic plants and flowers, which surround him. Just as the evening sun begins to slumber, Pat serves Tony a delicious small bowl of clear chicken broth, just enough to entice his appetite and stir his enormous love for Italian cuisine. Adding a little splash of variety to his lounging life these days, Pat mixes it up occasionally by giving him a small bowl of beef broth—the clear liquid broth that is—Mamma Mia!— guaranteeing her beloved Tony a quick recovery and without a doubt, a much slimmer physique for our upcoming tour.

Feeling the need to get away from the tempting bribes, Tony and Pat's beautiful daughter Giada hops aboard with us, all twenty Americans, along with Nino. I am definitely going to miss Tony on this tour, but with Giada in tow, this will be another memorable adventure.

We're heading to the famous Cinque Terre, the area with five fairy-tale villages dating back thousands of years and overlooking the colorful and breathtaking Italian Riviera. The only way to see the Cinque Terre is by boat, train, or on foot. There are no cars to get from one village to the other.

The cameras have already started clicking as we spiral through the gorgeous mountains, passing the famous Carrara marble, which takes my breath away, time and time again. Clutching the microphone in my left hand, and with Nino concentrating on the tiny cars zipping around us, I feel the need to tell everyone about the beautiful famous marble before us. Of course, I mention Michelangelo's breathtaking *David,* the famous *David* made of this marble, as in David and Goliath of the Bible. You would think everyone would surely know from their childhood days the Bible story of David and Goliath, but sadly, I have found they do not.

Looking through the coach's windshield is nearly too much for my heart to take. In Italy, the beauty of God's creation is spectacular. I've passed this area a hundred times, and it still takes my breath away. How does one possibly describe such wonderment and beauty? You can't; no words can possibly do it justice. That's why I bring Americans to Italy, twice a year, every late May and late September. You have to come and experience it for yourself.

How can you describe a fairy-tale village perched on top of a soaring mountaintop, surrounded by a medieval wall? How do you explain to an American the feelings of going inside these village gates? How can you describe things you've never seen in America? How do you tell an American who has never stepped off American soil that in Italy, people still live as though they're frozen in time? That life in Italy is more than work? It is about family, friends, food, and the sacred grape, the liquid red and the liquid gold. It's about God, giving thanks to him, and celebrating life. The Italians work enough to live; they don't live to work and accumulate. They celebrate at any opportunity. Throughout Italy, amongst the hundreds of villages, you will always find some kind of celebration going on, and always, the smell of wood-burning ovens cooking mouthwatering dishes.

Clutching the microphone in my left hand, my body rumbles like a volcano, exploding within and spewing out the words without thinking.

"Hurry—look to the left. Do you see the snow-covered mountains?" It sounds like an orchestra of cameras clicking as I continue, "It's not snow; this is the famous Carrara marble that Michelangelo used to carve the many sculptures. Can anyone tell me what Michelangelo carved from this marble?"

Immediately, shouts from behind me bounce upward. "*David*!"

"Yes, *David*, the masterpiece of the great Florence Renaissance era carved somewhere around 1501 and 1504."

Zooming beside the majestic walls of marble, I feel their excitement and eagerness to hear more, and that's all it takes for me to continue talking through the microphone.

"The statue represents the biblical hero David." Hearing my own words, I'm electrified, wanting to say more about my love for Michelangelo's incredible talents and his love for the Jewish people.

Before I start my next sentence, someone seated a few seats behind me shouts out with a long southern accent, "Stefania, tell us about the Sistine Chapel. Tell us how Mickey-Angie-Low stood on his head for fourteen years to paint the Sistine Chapel."

Not sure who spoke, I turn around in my seat and observe Laurie from Florida, who jumps out of her seat and claps her hands over and over before jumping back to her seat as though she's an animated wind-up jumping doll.

"Oh, no, Michelangelo did *not* stand on his head to paint the Sistine Chapel," I say in Michelangelo's defense. "No. He designed his own, one-of-a-kind, ever-in-history, freestanding trapezelike scaffolding."

"It took Michelangelo four and a half years to paint the Sistine Chapel, not fourteen years. Mamma Mia," I say laughingly as Nino turns his head toward me with a slight smile, seeming to understand every English word spoken.

"Stephani, tell us about the Sistine Chapel in Rome," Dr. Landrow says while sticking his thumb up in the air. I presume he's giving me a thumbs-up for the go-ahead.

"Well, Vatican City, home of the pope, was built centuries ago in Rome. *Sistine* is a derivation of the name Sixtus. Pope Sixtus IV had Giovanni de Dolci erect the chapel. And it is a replica of King Solomon's Temple in the Bible. You can read the dimensions in the Old Testament. In the sixteenth century, Pope Julius II asked Michelangelo to paint the ceiling, which he didn't want to do, but who could say no to the pope and still have a neck in those days? You must remember Michelangelo was a sculptor, not a painter. Nonetheless, he left Florence and came to Rome under strict instructions from the pope.

"As I said earlier, he spent more than four years painting the ceiling of the Sistine Chapel. Twenty years later, Michelangelo was called back to the Sistine Chapel again by Pope Paul III to paint the *Last Judgment* on the altar wall of the Sistine Chapel. This is a gigantic painting showing we are all judged by God. It shows the separation of the good souls from the bad souls in vivid color. This was another huge task for Michelangelo, taking him four years to complete," I say, reaching for my sunglasses on the dashboard.

"All of this Vatican wonderment is protected by a surrounding wall, and happens to be the tiniest country in the world. It's truly amazing that the Vatican, so small of a country, stands so majestically, along with Saint Peter's Basilica, behind a medieval wall. They have their own postage stamps, along with their own everything. They are their own country in Rome. It's amazing to me." I hope they are realizing the wonderment that such a teeny-weeny country is known throughout the world.

"It would take days for me to start from the beginning, but I'll hit the high points. The Vatican is home to Saint Peter's Basilica; the apostle Peter lies directly below the high altar underneath the magnificent ninety-five-foot canopy." I stretch my arms open to emphasize the size of the canopy. "Can you grasp the magnitude of such a magnificent creation of art? The bronze canopy is gorgeous. It's Bernini's masterpiece, and his first work in Saint Peter's. Can you really comprehend that the ancient tomb of Saint Peter, the *apostle Peter,* lies directly below the altar?"

I want to release all the stored history within my brain and explain the importance of the mosaic floors in the Sistine Chapel. I want to tell them how my eyes have observed the Stars of David and the Seal of Solomon, which are inside the Sistine Chapel. I want to explain in detail the amazing truths of the Sistine Chapel. I want to explain the deeper truths of why the Sistine Chapel is a replica of King Solomon's Temple, described in the Old Testament of the Bible. I want to tell them about the partition in the Sistine Chapel where they can walk through to the other section. I want to tell them to walk all the way to the back of the Sistine Chapel, sit down, and view the whole ceiling before exiting. Walking through that section, I can imagine the high priest going behind the veil. That is where the Ark of the Covenant was placed, behind the veil, in the Holy of Holies in King Solomon's Temple. Would they remember the three things placed inside the Ark of the Covenant? The Bible tells of Aaron's rod, a gold pot of manna, and the Ten Commandments on stone tablets.

"When you walk into the Sistine Chapel, you will see the partition toward the middle. That's where the veil hung in King Solomon's Temple. Just imagine, behind the veil is where the high priest would enter once a year to ask for forgiveness for the people. It was called, the Day of Atonement. Once the priest entered behind the veil, he was in the holy presence of God. The word *veil* in Hebrew means 'a screen, divider, or separator that hides.' What was this curtain hiding? Essentially, it was shielding a holy God from sinful man. Whoever entered into the Holy of Holies was entering the very presence of God. Anyone except for the high priest who entered the Holy of Holies would die. And, if there was any sin in the priest's life as he entered behind the veil, the Holy of Holies, he would surely die. Can you imagine waiting outside the veil, wondering if the priest would drop dead? To be on the safe side, someone would tie a rope around the priest's ankle, just in case he had sinned in his life. Imagine, waiting and listening for a loud thump outside the veil as his body hit the ground—and then dragging and pulling his lifeless body out by the roped ankle while his own robe brushed the floor."

I would love to explain the meaning of the Arch of Titus in Rome, which was erected to honor Titus, the destroyer of Jerusalem, and how the Jews were brought from Jerusalem to Rome as slaves after the Romans sacked the Holy Temple. I want to tell them to look carefully while in the Roman Forum tomorrow, for they will see the carvings on the Arch of Titus portraying the triumphant victory of the Romans and the defeated Jews, along with the sack of the Holy of Holies and the Jews, now slaves, bringing all the treasures back to Rome. During the four years of war, the Romans took more than 97,000 prisoners.

Literally thousands of them were crucified in various positions daily. Thousands of them were forced to become gladiators and were killed in the arena, fighting wild animals or fellow gladiators. Many of them were burned alive for Nero's entertainment, and the little girls and women became market-sold slaves to the Romans. It was common for the upper-class Roman children to receive a Jewish slave for a present.

I remember telling another group of Americans about little Martha, taken from Israel and sold as a slave in Rome. I told them how little Martha waved the peacock feathers back and forth in the hot Coliseum, hour after hour, laboring over her spoiled mistress who, no doubt, lounged in her satin-cushion seat, consuming platters of honey-soaked figs and gallons of the liquid red throughout the day's eventful entertainment. Not only were the Jews brought to Rome, but at the Roman slave market, you could purchase Nubian slaves. They were highly profitable to the Romans, especially jeweled with dangling brass and exotic silk outfits, playing their flutes for entertainment.

Most of the Jewish prisoners were brought to Rome, where they were forced to build the Coliseum. Every time I look upon and walk through the Arch of Titus in the Roman Forum, I think of the many Jews, the sack of the Holy Temple, and the promise God gave to his people: the temple will be restored! I would love to speak of these truths right now, but we are not in Rome or the Vatican today.

14

GIADA FILACI BRINGS EXCITEMENT

We are all excited that Giada hopped aboard to stand in her papa's place to help Nino and me with the twenty Americans. With Giada and Nino on board together, it's going to be a fun time. To describe Giada Filaci is like describing the magnificent blue Mediterranean. What words can describe something as fantastically wonderful and beautiful as she is? Giada is a breath of fresh air that brings people of all kinds to a new world of excitement. She gives them a volt of her energized self, causing them to jump and dance at any given moment in her presence. Giada never meets a stranger. She loves people and is a favorite friend to all the Americans. Everyone wants to bundle up Giada and ship her back to America. However, with Giada being such a free-loving spirit, she truly belongs to the magnificent wonders of Italy. I can't imagine Italy without Giada's beautiful, smiling face popping up all over. Giada is everything a woman wishes to be, and more. She is gorgeous and vivacious; she can dance the tango on a cold, rainy night; she can parachute at any given moment from a soaring mountaintop; and she can sing the greatest love songs while making the most amazing tiramisu.

Within minutes of our arrival at the Cinque Terre, Giada walks to the front of the coach and grabs the microphone to say, "Okay, everybody, you do as I do, okay, everybody?" Immediately she swings her body in a fast-moving motion, twisting and turning up and down, bellowing a loud, strange sound similar to an agonizing holler but with a few skipping beats in between. Her left palm flies to her head, with spreading fingers. Roaring laughter spills out throughout the coach, giving Giada more confidence to continue her animated dance, but in a faster mode. Within minutes, the whole group is imitating her hilarious singing dance, with Nino joining in at the wheel.

Getting off the coach, still laughing, singing, and having fun, we look ahead and gasp at the beauty before us.

"Wow, I can't believe the gorgeous colors, and the flowers cascading down the legendary iron balconies," shouts Janie, pointing toward the picturesque villas painted in a colorful array of Italian pastels.

"I've never seen anything like this before in my life, except in magazines or fairy-tale storybooks," says Mary Jane, pointing her camera toward a lemony-yellow villa with mint-green wood shutters swung open, allowing her to see two Italian lovers ripping off each other's wedding attire—in an attempt to consummate their marriage vows, I presume.

"What a sight. They're on their honeymoon, don't you think?" Mary Jane says to me with her eyes glued to her zoomed-lens camera.

"I hope so," I answer in disbelief as a ceramic flowerpot crashes to the cobblestone street below their balcony, almost hitting the little toylike Tonka truck that's pulling up for garbage pickup.

Looking away from the turquoise-blue Mediterranean, the Italian Rivera, we see colorful villas, five or more stories tall, just like a postcard or a screen saver.

"This is absolutely gorgeous—so picturesque, with the tall villas showcasing the faded green shutters and worn pastel facades. I love the colors, the Old World colors created from years of time gone by," Becky says, clicking her camera repeatedly, as though the camera is broken.

"Oh, you haven't seen anything yet. Just wait until we're in the Mediterranean, looking out from the boat," I say passionately. "In a few minutes, when you're out in the water, all I can say is get your cameras ready for a picture-perfect postcard indeed. The Cinque Terre is gorgeous and truly a fairy-tale, storybook setting. Our boat will dock at some of the most amazing villages." I am getting more excited with every word, knowing the beauty that awaits us.

Before Duane and Connie Robinson take another step toward an exploding bundle of purple flowers, Connie starts talking in her proper English accent, sounding as though she just arrived from an aristocratic bloodline in England.

"Isn't it just splendid how they harvest the grapes and tend to the vines with such a steep incline of the mountain?" Connie asks as her legs fold in a proper English-style curtsy. She calls to her beloved husband,

Duane. "Come on, Pooh-Daddy, the boat is here." We all break out with laughter at hearing her American accent changed into a studious proper English accent that only Connie Jo can do so well.

Everyone is moved with emotions while clicking their cameras at the Italian *signora* across the narrow alleyway. The two ladies are talking back and forth, floors apart, leaning over the iron balconies, talking, laughing, and putting their clothes out to dry in the Mediterranean breeze. What a beautiful site before us. The colorful boats are bobbing up and down in the mesmerizing blue Mediterranean as we stand in awe, waiting on our boat.

We see little, Tonka-toy Vespas zooming by, reminding us of cartoon-size trucks. Behind the wheels are olive-kissed Romeos. Guiding their cars through the narrow streets, they honk, and shout Italian words. In the opposite direction, I watch a signora gather bundles of freshly cut flowers in a large basket, leaving me to wonder what the occasion is. Maybe a wedding? Or could it be a funeral?

Not far from Giada, I see a storekeeper walking out to greet an early-morning shopper. They embrace, kissing twice, on the left and right sides of the face. It's a fairy-tale moment indeed. We are all standing still, trying to absorb it, to soak in our rare surroundings. "The sweetness of doing nothing. *Il dolce far niente,*" I say to them with a big smile.

Three elderly men sit on a bench, their olive-kissed toes dangling a few inches from the warm sand below. They are talking, laughing, people-watching, and feeding the little dog standing close to them. Not giving it a second thought, I break away from the laughter of our group and run straight toward the little, doll-size men with their dangling toes.

"Buongiorno Signore, come stai? Hello, how are you?" I say to them as my fingers click down on my camera rapidly, not wanting to miss their every move.

"Do you want to be in my *giornale*, the newspaper?" I ask in Italian, smiling with my bright red lips stretching to their maximum width. I'm thinking how cute they will be in my book and website: www. DecorateOrnate.com.

Bouncing up like rubber balls, they stand inches lower than me, ready for service. Not waiting for an answer, I click their photos and hop into the bed of their little toylike Vespa truck, assuming it belongs to one of them.

Immediately, the little truck tilts toward them, creating a sudden sense of panic and a loud chorus of *Mamma Mias* flowing out in a rescuing kind of way. I jump out, sending the little truck springing back up like a bucking bronco.

Thankfully, I'm not alone in this embarrassing situation. Minutes ago, Connie escaped from her beloved Pooh-Daddy for a mere moment, just in time to join me as we both leaped around the Vespa and hopped inside. Roars of Italian laughter and much chatter springs forth as the men hold the right side of the little truck up while we stare through the windshield as though we are aliens in a spaceship. Immediately, the *Mamma Mias* flow repeatedly, in a chanting, synchronized, harmonious tune.

While this is going on, a few feet away the other Americans are watching tiny cartoon-size cars zoom through the narrow streets. Every few minutes, the bells at the old church interrupt our laughter, and with the last bell ringing, we look up and see the boat coming for us.

"The Cinque Terre is a rugged portion of the Italian Riviera that is magnificent, and a UNESCO World Heritage Site. Don't confuse the Cinque Terre with the Amalfi Coast, because they're on opposite ends of Italy. There are five breathtaking villages in the Cinque Terre: Monterosso al Mare, Vernazza, Corniglia, Manarola, and Riomaggiore— plus, Giada's favorite, Portovenere," I say to everybody as we walk toward our boat. *Breathtaking,* or perhaps *intoxicating* might be the best words to describe Italy's Cinque Terre region hugging the Italian Riviera. Ah, but it is more than those two words. How can one possibly describe a place that's so fairy-tale-like? Trying to describe the gorgeous Amalfi Coast and Sorrento is equally hard. However, they are entirely different in looks, taste, and beauty.

Walking toward the approaching boat, which is surely ours, I feel a rush of excitement taking over. Within minutes, we'll experience a world wonder, the wonderment of beauty, the Cinque Terre.

"Stefania, did you say we will see five villages?" Louise from Dallas asks.

"As you wish, my dear. However, we cannot take the boat to one of them. I suppose we can dive into the liquid blue and swim to it. Ah, do not worry. You will see the five storybook places where the gorgeous

91

rocky coast and green hills meet the cobalt sea, mixed with liquid blue turquoise. The clustered mountains look as though the colorful villas were thrown hard against them, leaving them clinging for dear life, high above the gorgeous Riviera. The rolling vineyards and olive groves on the side of the high mountains are plummeting down to kiss the blue waters," I say, without taking a breath.

"The authentic cuisine will entice you to dive in for more and more until you remember, ah, we have many more villages to taste," I continue. "For romantic nourishment, the taste of the liquid red, locally grown and produced, is something you will taste as well, along with the enticing flavors of huge scoops of gelato piled higher than the Tower of Pisa. The gelato is a creamy whipped cream, swirled in a mountainous assortment of delicious flavors. I highly recommend you taste at least two flavors per village, or more.

"Just wait until you allow yourself to get lost in the enchanting tiny streets. And, if you want to be adventurous, stroll through the chestnut and oak groves with beautiful primrose and saffron-filled meadows swaddling you like a newborn bambino—not to mention the stunning olive and citrus groves popping out in rainbow-colored, terraced vineyards interspersed throughout your walk." I don't know when to stop.

"Stefania, my favorite village is the picturesque Portovenere," Giada shouts, brushing her long hair from her bare sun-glazed shoulders while she stands in line to get on our boat.

"Si, si. Yes, I know. I agree with you. Portovenere is one of Italy's most romantic places to go. I mean, come on—in Italy, every place has its magical charm and fairy-tale places, but Portovenere has the little zebra black-and-white-striped church built in 1277 that stands on the tip of the promontory that stretches toward the island of Palmaria. This little church is named after the temple and goddess of love and stands where the temple of Venus once stood."

15

CINQUE TERRE TAKES HOLD
OF THE ROBINSONS!

I yawn as though my eyes were never shut last night, but that's what happens when staying out too late, laughing and enjoying life in Italy. Nonetheless, before stepping into the bobbing boat I say, "As you know, the only way to get to the Cinque Terre is by walking the paths, taking the train, or coming by boat. Cars cannot reach it from the outside. So, is anyone up to walking the mountainous, cliff-hanging paths soaring high over the Italian Riviera's blue waters? Oh, come on, you will love the terraces on the rugged, steep landscape that makes up the cliffs overlooking the sea. That's part of its charm and fairy-tale setting. There's no visible 'modern' development either."

I continue talking as we step, one by one, onto the swinging ropelike ramp connecting to the boat.

We dock and visit the breathtaking villages that make up the world wonder of Cinque Terre. It's a magical time here today. It's a world that exists in fairy tales. It's a world I love, and the Americans are in heaven. Each clustered village is breathtaking. This is another place in Italy; one cannot possibly describe it in English words.

Before licking my last towering pile of gelato, I see Giada ahead of me, waving her arm and pointing to her watch.

"Where has the time gone today?" I ask. "It is already four in the afternoon, and our boat will arrive back here in a little while. How would you like to visit another one of the villages, such as the fairy-tale village of Portovenere, which is Giada's favorite?" Mark is standing beside me with chocolate gelato dripping from his elongated chin. Every few minutes his left hand checks to see that his neon-green sunglasses are still parked on top of his shoe-shined head. His compulsive madness gives me the urge to yank the glasses from his lustrous, egg-shaped head and throw them on the ground. Then for my own satisfaction, I want to jump up and down and crunch them into a million pieces. However, the urge to do so quickly passes when I hear someone shouting.

"Oh please, can we stay longer? I never want to leave here," says Karen from New Orleans, who has a perpetual smile, thanks to her new face-lift.

"Let's stay two more hours and then take the six p.m. boat back to Portovenere," I say to Giada, reluctant to leave this colorful treasure chest adventure.

"Si, si. Yes, yes," Giada says, nodding as she jets off to tell everyone the good news.

Minutes later, after the exciting news announcement, the Americans scatter off like little children running to the playground while a few make a sudden stop for one more towering pile of creamy gelato. I guess they took my words literally. I told them they must try the gelato, one of every flavor, in each village today. I hope the boat is strong enough to carry us to the next village.

Two hours later, looking out into the Mediterranean-blue waters, I question my decision to linger the two extra hours, and it's not because of gelato. Looking up toward the sky, I see darkening clouds rolling toward us, and a gust of wind blows my hair straight up.

"Don't worry, Stefania, everything is beautiful. We'll arrive just in time to see Portovenere one last time before heading to our villa for dinner. *Va bene,* okay, Stefania?" Giada says reassuringly. Then she breaks out singing in her beautiful Italian voice. Giada is so much fun to be with, and she's loaded with talent. Giada can sing like a bird, entertain like a celebrity comedian, and cook anything Italian, and she loves the Americans like her very own Italian family.

Loaded down with all the beautiful things purchased in the village, one by one, we swing across the rope trapeze ramp connected to the boat as it swings side to side in a fast, turbulent kind of way. If we were circus performers, the ramp would surely be the way to board the boat. However, I don't recall any of the Americans listing their occupation as circus performers on their information sheets.

A few feet from me, I see our beloved couple, Gail and Chuck Wilson from Mt. Pleasant, Texas, hesitantly await their turn to grab the hand of the smiling, olive-tone Italian who eagerly pulls each of them onto the swinging roped bridge. From where I stand, I see Gail's mesmerizing blue eyes doing the Macarena dance in full force. They grip the ropes with both hands, make their way across the swinging bridge one at a time, then magically bounce off, landing perfectly on the boat's deck. Right behind them, I see another adorable couple of ours, Janie and Tom Jantz, making their way toward the swaying ramp. Janie and Tom are regular passengers on our Italy tours too, and we've experienced some unbelievable adventures together. Today looks as it might be another one.

Stepping on, single file, they grip the ropes on each side of the freestanding ramp, which is still swinging back and forth. Side to side, high above the Mediterranean, they walk with excitement zapping throughout their bodies. Janie is a beautiful, petite lady and her dear, devoted husband, Tom, is clutching her tiny body, trying to hold her down from the high winds that could easily send her overboard. Janie seems to love the Italian experience over the blue waters as she, too, bounces off the end of the ramp, landing in a perfect curtsy, ballerina style. Tom lands a few feet behind her, speedily skidding right in front of the already transferred group of Americans, except for two.

Standing together, laughing at the comical maneuvers of each one making their way across the bridge, Gail and Chuck, Debbie and Larry, and Leigh all laugh uncontrollably as they head for the inside cabin of the boat, where they will have seats to watch from.

I try not to laugh but can't help myself as the comical husband and wife team Connie and Duane swing back and forth, side to side, in a trapeze, acrobatic-style motion. Connie is in front of Duane, gripping the rope on both sides as he heroically clutches her floral-print blouse from behind. As the high winds pick up speed, blowing furiously against Connie and Duane, we all watch in hysterical laughter as he firmly grips her stretched-out blouse, creating a movie scene that can't be real.

With the high winds pushing him backward, Duane now appears to be skiing on top of the water, with Connie as the boat. He holds tightly to Connie's blouse. As we watch, everyone comes out of the boat's cabin for a better look.

"Oh look. Surely it's going to rip right off," I say, laughing hard, with my legs crossed like a pretzel.

"Knowing Duane's character, the perfect gentleman, he will be in high hopes of heroically saving her," shouts someone from behind me.

As the wind blows harder, so does their hair. One minute nature has their hair to the left of their heads, and the next, their hair is on the right. Now it's straight up, and Duane and Connie appear to be cartoon characters holding a live, electrical wire.

"This is too much," I say to Giada, who is laughing uncontrollably along with everyone else.

I hold on to Giada's arm as laughter consumes us, and we both leap back just in time to see Connie and Duane spring off the swaying ramp, their exit sending them both skidding across the boat's painted deck. Like professional gymnasts, they land in perfect sitting positions on the wooden bench, right in front of the boat's windshield.

"I can't believe my eyes. Your blouse is still on and ...," we all seem to say in chorus, until the laughter totally consumes us.

Minutes later, we're all finally safely boarded, and everyone seems to have hurriedly scattered inside to the comforts of cozy seating within the cabin—everyone, that is, except for a few of us. Giada and I are seated on the outside deck, wanting to capture the beauty of the Cinque Terre with my camera. I've probably taken thousands of photos of the Cinque Terre throughout the years of coming here, but how can one look upon these mesmerizing villages without taking another photo and asking, "How in this world did they build villas, churches, bell towers, cemeteries, and so much more in these mountainous cliffs? It's a beautiful sight to see. So picturesque. It looks like a magical dream. How could they be so perfectly nestled together like a fairy-tale storybook in Cinderella's era?"

Bobbing up and down in the Mediterranean's blue waters is exhilarating, especially looking from the boat's view. I'm holding my camera tightly to my face, clicking the button, over and over, toward the village of Vernazza. We are leaving Vernazza, which is one of the most beautiful villages in Italy, amongst many more. The houses are stacked and clustered together in rainbow colors of apricot and yellow. They are magically suspended on the soaring cliffs facing the mesmerizing Mediterranean. I click my camera again toward the salmon-pink church, Chiesa Santa Margherita di Antiochia, nestled at the sea's edge. This is feet from the swinging bridge we used when arriving and departing.

The fairy-tale village is slowly fading away in the distance, but before I stop clicking my camera, I see more enchantment cuddling the path of

97

the coast. The beauty never stops here in the Cinque Terre. From the boat, where we are viewing this magnificently created masterpiece, my eyes follow along the staggering cliffs from behind the camera lens.

Less than ninety minutes later, we are approaching another spectacular village, Corniglia. Ah, how can I describe this stunning, picturesque artwork, painted by God's own hand? Before me, right now, is a real-life postcard from Italy. I see rolling vineyards plunging down into the Mediterranean. I see steep, terraced olive groves and terra-cotta roofs mixed in with the gorgeous colors of the Italian rainbow. I am holding my breath in star-struck awe. Corniglia is the only village of the Cinque Terre that is inaccessible from the sea. It's on a cliff some 300 feet above the gorgeous sea and appears to be something right out of a fairy-tale storybook from long ago. I keep repeating *fairy-tale storybook,* but truly, what other words can possibly describe this colorful beauty?

The steep, terracing grapevines, olive trees, and citrus trees wave proudly toward our boat. I think about the laborious task of harvesting the olives, grapes, and citrus fruits, and trekking up and down the zigzagging elevations, with hopes of not falling into the sea. The use of farming machines is useless. If there were such a machine, it would have to dangle from the air, suspended from the sky, but no, there is no such invention of a machine. The local farmers depend on gravity to take care of the large part of the harvest, along with the orange-colored netting to collect fallen fruit. And, thankfully, the farmers use a little "rack-rail car" that magically goes up the cliff-hanging mountains, carrying harvested grapes.

Silently to myself, I thank God for creating this beauty, a UNESCO World Wonder, and allowing me to bring the Americans to a country so magnificently created by his command. Feeling emotions of thankfulness and overcome by the beauty, I notice that the rolling clouds are dropping a light drizzle upon us.

"Stefania, do we stay outside?" Giada asks. I nod "yes."

"The beauty out here could never be seen from behind a windshield, don't you agree?" I ask Giada.

Smiling to ourselves, Giada and I clearly see just a few feet ahead of us, right in front of the boat's windshield, Connie and Duane sitting. Looking at them, sudden thoughts flood my mind of what a perfect couple they are indeed. They are nestled tightly together, enjoying a romantic ride in the seductive air of the Italian Riviera. The view before them is surely a fairy tale, a page out of a child's storybook. If they're looking closely, they are seeing huge clusters of grapes clinging to the mountainous cliffs that soar up, way up, and then down, to crash into the turquoise sea. The view is so colorful, ascending into the clouds. And, like magic, the village cemetery stands out like a royal crown on the soaring cliff.

Connie and Duane are holding on to each other tightly, like two burning lovers longing for each other on a seductive honeymoon night. Seated right in front of the boat's windshield, appearing as one, they are woven together as their heads recline on the boat's salted windshield. The wind is picking up speed, and the boat continues to rock up and down, like a bucking bronco. It's not scary, just fun and adventurous. Giada and I laugh loudly, holding on to the boat's rim, and I think, *Oh, what great fun—a perfect setting.*

In less than a second's notice, the rain begins to pour and the wind turns to harsh whiplashes, slapping across our wet faces. Giada and I both try to get up and run for the cabin's door, but the wind slams us back down. After a few more tries, we force ourselves up and a nice Italian gentleman opens the closed door and yanks us both inside, freeing us from the slapping winds and torrential rains. No sooner do we take our dry seats than we look ahead, and right in front of us are Connie and Duane, plastered to the outside windshield like bugs. Better yet, they appear to be glued to bright headlights on a dark summer's night. It's raining hard now, and the wind is stronger than their bodies can move.

"Mamma Mia, their heads are suctioned to the boat's windshield," Giada says loudly.

Other Italians are now standing up to get a better look and immediately join in with Giada's mantra of "Mamma Mia's, look at the human bugs plastered to the windshield."

We watch from the inside of the boat for almost an hour as though we've all arrived for a new blockbuster, action-packed movie with the hottest movie stars appearing on the big screen. However, the only screen before us right now is the boat's windshield. We watch with wide eyes, as our dear friends remain glued to the boat's windshield, until we arrive at the next village in the Cinque Terre.

We are finally arriving at the next village, but before we come to a complete stop, everyone jumps up and runs to the door. They are pushing against each other, trying to get outside the boat's cabin to inspect Connie and Duane. Making our way around the front of the boat's windshield, we come to a sudden halt. Looking at Connie and Duane brings another round of mantras of Mamma Mias. This time it's from the crowd, who look upon them as though they were Elvis Presley himself, fitted into a tiny glass box. They act as if they're viewing him, inspecting him, and at last, thanking God they didn't end up in the same condition he did.

I'm finding great difficulty in choosing the right words to describe their blackened faces. They appear as chocolate-covered raisins left out in the rain way too long. I'm not sure where the black, mudlike substance came from. Perhaps the boat's motor shot out black oil or another boat's engine discharged its oil upon them. The only thing we see of their faces is the white around their dilated eyes. In a matter of seconds, roaring laughter rolls out in a vibrating wave, bringing Connie and Duane in harmony with us.

16

Peggy Garmon, Attorney at Law in Gilmer, Texas

"Nestled in the piney woods of East Texas is a home chock-full of Italian treasures from Decorate Ornate," I say to Louise, a magazine editor on the other end of the telephone. "That's exactly how I would start off the article," I say with much excitement, all the while visualizing a beautiful glossy color spread on the front cover of her wonderful magazine.

Interrupting me, Louise asks, "Stephani, do you think she would be willing for us to feature her Toscana home in our magazine?"

"Yes, absolutely. Peggy would love that, and I can tell you exactly what to say—I mean, I can give you a descriptive story from my remembrance of her fabulous home," I rattle on in hopes she is recording every single word I'm saying for the upcoming article.

Years ago, Peggy Garmon, an East Texas attorney, walked into my store Decorate Ornate and stood in utter amazement at the towering Italian doors and beautiful architectural treasures. Even though Peggy didn't have her dream home yet, she felt a magnetic force pulling her toward a beautiful Italian door I had found at a local market in a medieval village in Tuscany. Looking up, down, and behind her, Peggy found herself in a world of fairy-tale enchantment that opened up a completely new world for her inner-design spirit.

Roaming through the mesmerizing maze inside Decorate Ornate, Peggy saw more castle doors, medieval tapestries, and hand-painted ceramics from many different regions of Italy, along with a host of other medieval treasures. Desiring to see it all, Peggy took tiny steps, one after another, slowly looking up and down as she made her way through the wonderland of gorgeous treasures. Mysteriously, Peggy felt a powerful surge magnetizing her to go deeper into the enchanting world of Decorate Ornate.

Standing in the middle of the store, Peggy saw beyond the normal East Texas design of decorating her home. She saw an Old World of medieval doors and balconies with breathtaking colors consuming her visual focus. The wheels began to turn and roll in her scholarly brain, and within a matter of seconds, she blurted out, "This is so unusual, so old, so fairy tale, I must have this door. I'm absolutely in love with this door."

Without hesitation, Peggy called for me to put a "sold" tag on the old Toscana door. And within seconds of tagging the door, a gorgeous Italian tapestry spoke sweet nothings into Peggy's ears, leaving her in a weakened state of mind. It was love at first sight, and their relationship grew strong, causing me to place another "sold" tag upon its woven threads. Afterward, at the ring of the cash register, Peggy inquired of the little sign that said, "Let's Go to Italy with Stephani!"

"Do you take groups to Italy, too?" Peggy asked as she happily tossed her check toward me.

"Oh, yes, Peggy, I take two groups to Italy twice a year, spring and fall. Do you want to go with us?"

"Yes, of course, I do," Peggy shouted back, causing her to get out another check, writing it for the full amount of the Italy tour.

The old saying goes, "All good things come to those who wait." Well, it was a good thing because Peggy's newly purchased door rested peacefully for the next two years against the wall inside her law office on Titus Street, until the perfect house came about ... and about, it did. The purchase of a fabulous house perched high upon a hill, only minutes away from her law office, started her on a road of all things Italian.

It wasn't rocket science for Peggy, because the minute she saw her new house, the wheels started to turn toward Tuscany. The new beginnings of a Toscana villa started within her mind. She visualized the beautiful castle doors throughout her home, and started by removing the closet door and replacing it with her first love—the first Italian door she purchased in Decorate Ornate. And what a huge difference it made. Peggy's broom closet instantly became the perfect "wine cellar" door. However, it didn't stop there.

Peggy hopped aboard our 2005 tour of Tuscany and Umbria, and the magnetic force completely consumed her design mentality. The thrill and excitement of zigzagging around the tiny medieval streets in Tuscany, and throughout other breathtaking regions of Italy, totally fulfilled a hidden love and passion within Peggy's soul. It was like an invisible key unlocking her hidden talents, releasing a studious array of architectural designs flooding through her mind. However, they weren't just any designs; they were Toscana designs.

I shall never forget one particular day in Italy with Peggy Garmon. Mamma Mia! With her eyes glued to the window, Peggy held on tightly as our little coach zigzagged throughout the winding, narrow roads in Tuscany. Finally, at the stop of a medieval village, Peggy found true love high above, perched on a soaring hilltop. Before us, we saw a fairy-tale village surrounded by a medieval wall with huge gates open wide. Immediately getting out of the coach, Peggy walked toward this fairy-tale-looking gate, not waiting on me or any of the rest of our group. Strangely and mysteriously, a supernatural force magnetized Peggy's body. I know this sounds ridiculous, but this is exactly what happened.

Surely it was a magnetic force that pulled her legs into fast motion, almost causing her to jog. It was like a movie in slow motion, as Peggy's legs suddenly stopped, allowing us to walk past her. Then, like a car taking off, Peggy bypassed her fellow passengers, who were already huffing and puffing toward the ballooning, hilltop beauty. I was intrigued by how Peggy shot forward, like a race car, headed for the finish line. She was excited and happy, as though she were a child running home for a big surprise.

With my own eyes, I saw a magical, magnetic force within this village, pulling Peggy inside and dramatically escalating the neurotransmitters within her scholarly, legalized brain. We all witnessed the effects of high levels of chemicals creating the rapid heartbeats within her chest, altering her entire being, and sending a blast of euphoria zapping throughout her small body. It was almost like bolts of lightning hitting under her fast-moving feet. Peggy was in ecstasy, pure jubilation, experiencing the same feelings of finding true love—a love that lasts forever, never tiring of the loved one's presence. And yes, Peggy was in Tuscany, and she had indeed found a true love to which she will remain faithful forever, throughout eternity, I do believe.

Now, standing inside this fairy-tale village, Peggy sees an escapade of enchantment. In every direction, she sees little shops surrounded with locally made ceramics. "Steph," she says. "Hurry and run. I found the perfect ceramic tiles for my kitchen." Peggy is jumping up and down as though she is holding for the toilet.

Walking toward her, I get a glimpse of something wonderful, and that's all it takes for my legs to shift into another gear.

"Oh look, I see a pair of hand-painted, ceramic Nubians," I say, racing toward them as though we were long lost lovers reuniting from a year's solo holiday pleasure. I pass Peggy in a puff of dust.

"Stephani, come back here. Come look at my tiles," Peggy shouts, lining up all the tiles in a row as she tries to decide which ones to purchase.

"Signora, do you want me to ship the tiles to America?" Alessandro asks as Peggy drifts toward his alluring, black-oil eyes. Walking into the shop not a minute too late, I see the love connection as a strong magnetic surge connects them beyond the sale of ceramic tiles.

"Peggy, let me see the tiles you found," I say, hoping to zap her serotonin level back up before it's too late—losing her forever to Alessandro. I know that when the serotonin level drops too low, it causes one to obsess, and from the looks of Peggy, I would say her serotonin level has plummeted.

Trying to break the love connection for just a moment, I watch Peggy and Alessandro chat and giggle like two heated lovers who are finally reconnecting. I don't know if it's the gorgeous ceramics surrounding her, or Alessandro's alluring, sexy smile; nonetheless, Peggy is in heaven, floating in pure ecstasy. She has found her kindred spirit, her soul mate, and perhaps her lover. I think about performing acrobatic flips right now, with hopes of snapping her out of this love trance. But the way it looks, that will not help.

Since Peggy's first Italy tour with us in May 2005, she has returned with us repeatedly. In fact, our Italy tour in May 2013 was Peggy's sixth tour with us. In addition, let me just say, she has purchased many more Italian tiles from her Romeo of a lover, Alessandro.

17

"Turn Around, We're Going to Napoli ... and Mamma Mia, Frank Flattens the Signora!"

The Italian music is floating throughout our coach as everyone sings the same chorus in broken Italian. The funny mixture of dialects, on board our coach, is comical, especially the strange but appropriate harmonizing sound bites of the clicking of cameras. Looking out my window, I see white-clothed tables flocked by ceramic vases with beautiful flowers. Towering over the long tables, I see flaming candles, illuminating a scene so spectacular that I shout, *"Basta.* Stop!"

"Mamma Mia, Stefania. What's the matter with you?" Tony demands, knowing good and well that the sharp, hairpin curves are no place to be stopping the bus.

The huge Mediterranean villa, clinging to the vineyard-covered cliffs, is stunning. It's beyond my English vocabulary to properly describe its architectural medieval beauty. The green vineyards to the right side of me are popping with purple grapes, and the silvery olive trees complete the picturesque masterpiece before me. All of this beauty appears to be a page out of an exotic magazine for the rich and famous. However, come to think of it, this is where the rich and famous come. They flock to Italy, especially Sorrento and the Amalfi Coast. The view before us in every direction is spectacularly gorgeous. The vineyards, olive groves, and the villas are all magically tumbling down the staggering, mountainous cliffs, plunging toward the turquoise-blue Mediterranean waters. Amongst the terra-cotta roof tiles, I try to memorize the vibrant colors of reds, pinks, and purples cascading down like a running waterfall.

As Nino makes another sharp, half-circle turn, I flash my camera toward the iron balconies that are exploding with vibrant colors of bougainvilleas on steroids. There's no other explanation for their bountiful growth and color other than the volcanic soil, which we already know produces the huge cantaloupe-sized lemons and the best-tasting tomatoes in the world.

We see the flaming illumination over the white-clothed tables clustered below us, suggesting an evening filled with family and friends. It's a scene I hope to capture with the click of my camera before Nino zooms around another hairpin turn just ahead.

"It's late September, the last harvest of the grapes," I say to the Americans as the picturesque villa slowly fades behind us while another one, just as magnificent, pops up. The Americans are hanging on tightly as Nino glides us around the zigzagging curves in this wonderland of magnificence.

We are in Southern Italy, and the panorama is breathtakingly magnificent. Everywhere we look, left to right, is a picture-perfect post card. The tiny U-shaped curves carved in the steep rock cliffs propagate more excitement and thrills within our coach. The mesmerizing views are surpassing the gorgeous Bay of Napoli, which was miles back. Nevertheless, every inch we go farther south is unbelievably spectacular in every way imaginable. Our eyes are magnetically drawn toward the staggering slopes and the picturesque vineyards racing straight down into the turquoise-blue waters. The brightly colored clothes flapping in the Mediterranean breeze present a flash of rainbow beauty amongst the colorful villas slapped hard against the mountainous, staggering rocks. It's a spectacular sight to behold.

"Outside of Napoli, life gets even more interesting for those willing to veer off the beaten paths," I say. "For people like me, who love traditional cultures mixed in with a lot of excitement from long ago, Southern Italy is definitely the place to be. I am wholeheartedly in love with Southern Italy. The Old World of Italy is where the old trades of life are still going strong from centuries ago. And Nino, our little bambino, lives in Napoli with his picture-perfect bride beauty, Susy." I reach over and pinch Nino's rosy red cheek.

"Cousin Bruno, who is identical to a computerized, picture-perfect Italian, lives in Napoli as well, along with his beautiful wife and his olive-kissed family. We are at home here. This is our welcoming station—that is, until we go a little farther south. Then it starts all again."

"Mamma Mia, Stefania, shall we go back to Napoli? Shall we take the Americana to see the artisans?" Tony asks while instructing Nino to turn around in the next available space, hoping to fit the turn of the coach.

"Si, si," I say. I want to jump up and down, but I'm confined to the front seat of the bus.

Trekking back to Napoli, laughing and singing to the Italian music, brings more excitement and adventure. On board with us now is a man whom I will call Frank, since I cannot disclose his real name. Frank is an American, working privately for the United States government, in a country that remains confidential. At Frank's request weeks ago, I arranged to pick him up at the Roma airport. I remember our telephone conversation well.

"Stephani, joining your Italy tour would be wonderful," Frank said in his deep southern accent. "My aunt Mary Ann told me all about your two annual tours to Italy, and from your website DecorateOrnate.com I know without a doubt this is the perfect holiday for me. It will be so nice to hear my American comrades' voices. Oh yes, it will. Can you make it happen for me? That is, if I fly in to Roma and met you?"

Turning the coach around and getting out in Napoli was a perfect idea. I love Napoli, and the excitement is starting to flow. As though playing Follow the Leader, we are wide eyed, strolling through the heart of Napoli. We stop more than we walk, making the rounds of every *pasticceria* while tasting from the extended hands of Tony, who is insisting we try every sugary conglomerate of dough we pass. Needless to say, we do so with pleasure.

Pulverizing the polished, glazed pastries in our mouths, chewing, crunching, and stuffing, we carry on, eagerly anticipating the "tucked-away" artisans nestled in the same neighborhoods as their ancestors before them. Looking upward, we see a colorful cabaret of flapping laundry and beautiful iron balconies, highlighted by more of the steroid-fed bougainvillea that cascades down like a picture-perfect postcard.

We are captivated, completely dazzled with the Neapolitan commotion. None of us wants to move our legs, but we do. We are semi-frozen, zoned in to the chaos before and all around us. We slowly trek behind Tony and Bruno while clicking our cameras and mimicking their

Italian hand gestures. From behind me, I hear the Americans saying, "Ooh la la" repeatedly, mixed in with the Italian words "Mamma Mia."

We are the marching band with no musical instruments, a welcoming homecoming for Tony and Bruno. Behind the two, we look like programmed, animated puppets, all of us marching as Sicilian marionettes through the narrow cobbled streets. With the pull of the iron hook, our arms magically go flying up, waving heroically while flashing our smiles. And with another pull of the iron rod, the words bounce out in broken Italian, saying, *"Ciao, Buongiorno.* Hello, good morning." We continue with great fascination as our words ricochet down the nooks and crannies of the winding, cobbled streets. We are tightly enveloped within medieval churches and tall towering living quarters. And every so often, after a few steps onward, we stop to click our cameras, all the while accepting with pleasure, from the hands extending toward us, tiny glasses filled with creamy yellow *limoncello.*

My face is already throbbing from the wide-stretched facial muscles that require this frozen, happy smile. Who wouldn't smile with all this blissful drama surrounding them? And, with a few more steps, we are right in the middle of Napoli, a city of pure, chaotic drama. The Neapolitans are loud, happy people. They are a boisterous rhythm of people who echo a distinct, loud dialect, which brings to my remembrance the reaction from the Americans on one particular day.

The next morning after Nino and Susy's fairy-tale wedding, the Americans on board our coach thought the two were fighting and arguing amongst themselves. Nino drove the coach and Susy sat in the passenger seat across from Nino. From the time we left Napoli, Susy never stopped talking to Nino. They were merely talking, expressing themselves. It was their Neapolitan dialect. The Neapolitan mother tongue that speedily flaps and wiggles to the beat of a loud, drumming voice. To the Americans, who had never been around such dialects, it seemed the two were in a heated confrontation, just hours after the wedding.

"Just a few more steps and we'll pass Rosalina's little shop, which is filled to overflowing with beautiful bottles of the famous limoncello," I say. "And, just a few more steps past Rosalina's is the tiny hole-in-the-wall shop. Only one person can fit inside, but it's filled with priceless antiquities such as the huge silver ex votos," I say to Louise Murphy from Houston, who is hoping to purchase one. Within a few more steps, the test of restraint will slap me hard in the face. I tell my legs, "No, you have plenty." Nonetheless, it doesn't work. Speedily, I dart off for a few minutes, grabbing Louise to go along.

We are gone long enough to purchase two *ex votos* while the others huddle around Tony and Bruno, enjoying the taste of the famous Napoli pizza. Within seconds, I've already purchased the handmade *ex voto* and speedily we arrive back, right in front of our group.

"I'm sure you all know that pizza was invented in Napoli, don't you?" I ask while standing in front of them, watching them devour the Margherita pizza that is now dripping from their stuffed mouths.

"The Margherita pizza was created exclusively for Queen Margherita. Look at the colors on top of your pizza. Do they resemble anything Italian?" I ask, watching them examine the few crumbs left in their hands.

"They represent the colors of the Italian flag. The three main ingredients of a Margherita pizza are red (tomato), white (mozzarella) and green (basil)."

Turning the corner, we witness more of the spectacle of the Neapolitans' daily life. Loud waves of hysterical laughter are bouncing down from the upper floors of the towering palazzo, one after another. We watch the signore living on the upper floors as they unfasten the colorful shutters, happily singing while displaying the family's wardrobe. Surely this is an illustration from an Italian Norman Rockwell moment. The tooting of scooter horns, the zooming around lounging dogs, and the squeeze of bicycle horns alert us to the arrival of fresh meat from the butcher's shop, wrapped in brown paper and tied with a string.

Simultaneously, with the parade of locals we watch the little Ape—a toylike truck—bump along over the cobblestones until it abruptly stops. It's the delivery of a big wheel of Parmigiano-Reggiano. The cheese is wrapped and tied with a string, ready to hoist up in the dangling metal bucket. Stories above, we watch the bucket, tied with a rope, dangle downward as the pulleys screech from lack of oil, I presume. We watch as the bucket descends straight down, and with one toss of the package, it goes back up. The signora, who's bending over her iron balcony eagerly awaiting her cheese, is immensely amusing to us. The Americans have never seen such as this before, not in real life. Surely, this is a scene from an Italian movie; like a funny, old movie wherein the signora smashes the grapes with her feet as her towering head of fruit perches on top.

Standing back, all of us in a wide-eyed huddle, we watch as the bucket dangles like a perfect acrobatic show. We are hypnotized, from the cartoonlike happenings before us, and then Jacque Gibbs, from Longview, Texas, burps out a hair-raising scream. Startled by the loud chorus of locals who are bellowing out cheers for the safe arrival of the huge wheel of cheese arriving at its towering destination, we join her with a jump. Afterward, we giggle like children and click our cameras, hoping to capture this Old World moment.

Strolling on, we stop and visit the artisans. They are delicately pressing and smoothing the clay as they form heads and bodies. Some are painting faces, and others sew their clothes. All around us, we see the *presepe*—the nativity; it's a world of artisans' shops, one after another. We are now on Via San Gregorio Armeno, the street and neighborhood of renowned artisans from generation to generation. This is one of my favorite streets in Napoli, the Old World of making the amazing presepe.

Browsing through the many presepe, some stand with amazement clicking their cameras, and we abruptly stop. Out in the narrow street lined with artisan shops, we hear hollering and screaming. We stare in disbelief as our Frank the American dashes out like a bolt of lightning and heroically restrains a screaming, hysterical signora. The lady is facedown with both hands molded to the cobbled street. She is stretched out like a dead victim ready to be outlined for the detective's case, with both legs kicking up and down and her red skirt twisted tightly up around her flattened body and neck.

Too shocked to move, we watch as Tony magically appears, waving both hands over his head and shouting, "Mamma Mia, Mamma Mia, what's the matter?" With eyes bulging out, Tony rolls out slang Italian, speaking speedily and hysterically, trying to find out what in the world Frank is doing as he straddles the pint-size signora with her dress twisted around her neck like a pretzel.

While the tiny signora slowly rumbles down to a low, helpless whimper, we watch with open mouths and ask ourselves, "Is this a movie scene? Surely it is, being filmed right here before us." With mouths opened wide, the shopkeepers hurriedly usher their customers out while Tony pulls Frank off the withering signora.

Flocking around the squealing array, the locals watch as Frank spills out in Texas slang, "I caught this woman stealing something from your shop, and she's hiding it in her brassiere!"

The locals, not understanding Frank's English words, rush to the deflated signora, who is now gasping for air. Without haste, Tony puts the much-needed brakes on Frank, who is attempting to reach for the signora's brassiere.

"Mamma Mia," shouts Tony as he grabs Frank's arm away from the hyperventilating, dazed signora. "Mamma Mia, Madonna, I don't believe my eyes." Standing up now and encircled with a mob of locals, Tony breathlessly explains some long, made-up story of how Frank the Americana has a medical condition that causes him to go crazy at various times, and for the first time, these horrible episodes must have sent him into a massive seizure, rewiring his brain waves to go haywire. Getting a second breath, Tony goes on to explain to the mob of locals how Frank's condition must have rewired his brain to think the local signora was stealing.

After the dust settles on the cobblestones, and the little signora is carted away on a white stretcher, Tony hollers, "Andiamo, let's go." We scurry around, grabbing our packages and wishing we were invisible, or at least I do. The Americans are laughing hysterically and believe this was an act, an audition for a movie, or perhaps a little entertainment for them, but no, it was real, all real.

I'm trying to think of myself as invisible, but walking through the narrow streets in Napoli, surrounded by one artisan after another on both sides of the narrow streets, is impossible. By the time we get around the corner, I see something right out of Alice in Wonderland. However, to be honest, everything here looks like Alice is strolling through Wonderland.

We eventually make our way to another street, zigzagging through the fairy-tale maze of Napoli, darting in and out, laughing and clicking our cameras, grabbing more pizza and going into medieval churches that are indescribable. The awkwardness of Frank and his strange behavior is not with us right now. No, Frank, along with Tony and a few others, went on ahead of us to the coach. Tony knows that leaving me with the Americans amongst this magnificent array of treasures is dangerous and not a good idea. He knows that I go crazy with excitement, taking the Americans to so many fabulous places and pushing the limits to overboard every now and then.

Finally, right before we step inside the coach, we turn to the locals and say, "Arrivederci Napoli. Goodbye." However, we don't go far, just a little way down the street.

We are now sitting at the table of Tony's friend, eating gigantic homemade rolls with hot creamy chocolate exploding inside our mouths. They are beyond delicious, and we stop for them every time we come to Napoli. There is no other word to describe what we're eating right now but *heavenly*.

Afterward, we toddle to the coach; some of us have chocolate evidence on our faces. We click our cameras to the beat of the chaotic rituals of the people's daily lives here in Napoli and thank God for his beautiful creations such as the Neapolitan people and the amazing landscape that takes our breath away, time and time again.

18

SOUTHERN ITALY, HERE WE COME! "WHAT IS SCHIACCIATA?"

Skya-CHA-ta: "crushed" or "squashed" in Italian.

We are miles from Napoli, and after several minutes of awkward silence on the coach, we're singing and laughing while Tony talks to Nino in Italian. Tony is trying to understand the episode with the flattened signora back in Napoli while Nino bounces back his opinions. The only opinion I have is that Frank was not kidding when he said, "I'm in great need of holiday pleasures with my American comrades." That was an understatement. From here on out, I hope that Frank will relax, chill out, and put his career on a holiday.

Surprisingly, Tony refrains from interrogating Frank about the hair-raising ordeal back in Napoli. However, it's probably because Frank went straight to the back of the coach where his large stash of candy is piled high. Turning around in my seat, I look back and see everyone laughing and oohing in the same way new mothers react to their firstborn in the delivery room. Even Frank is mellowed out. Sitting in his seat with giraffe legs protruding from a pair of black cowboy boots, he peels away one wrapper at a time as he plops bite-size chocolates into his wide-stretched mouth. It's comical to see his head tilt back and forth as though batteries were keeping him animated with the beating music. With a full mouth of milky chocolates, Frank passes an assortment of candy bars to the hand in front of him, insisting everyone take two or three. There is nothing mentally wrong with Frank, no. It's his career, being on active duty to protect and guarantee the safety of those around him. Frank did see the signora take something from the shop, but now we know that it was, in fact, her shop. And ... as far as slamming her to the cobblestones, well, he had a flashback perhaps, doing what he was trained to do.

Tony, who is swirling his arms over his head while singing and dancing in his seat and hollering out the funny sound of a braying donkey, makes me laugh. Our turnaround to Napoli was well worth it even though Frank thought he captured a local shoplifter.

"Look at the pastel villas dangling off the towering mountains. They are, somehow, magically clinging and hanging out over the sea. How in the world do the people harvest the grapes and olives without falling into the sea?" Pam Merritt, a blond, blue-eyed beauty from Overton, Texas, asks as she clicks her camera once again.

"I don't know, but I bet we will hear the celestial ding-dongs of the church bells echoing above the ceramic roof tiles in the morning," Laurell Mitchell, also from Overton, answers while pressing her adorable, silk-satin face to the coach window. We are relishing the magnificence of God's creation, and it only gets better as Nino twists around another perfect U-shape hook towering us high in midair. One of the Americans on Laurell's side of the coach says in awe, "Look, the ladders underneath the trees have baskets of lemons in them. Look at the men pulling the fruit. They're going to collapse into the sea."

"I'm pinching myself right now," says Cheryl, who's from Corsicana, Texas. "Is this not a dream? I can't believe what's before my eyes. Stephani, you told me there's no way to describe the beauty here, and now I understand." Cheryl leans over her daughter to get a better look at an old pink stucco villa.

"Look at the villas and the vineyards cascading straight down to the Mediterranean," Connie Robinson shouts, nearly knocking her adorable husband, Duane—Pooh-Daddy—slap-dab in the face as she grabs her Canon camera with the large Baylor University emblem on it.

Simultaneously, all of us grab our cameras, not wanting to miss a single photo; however, within a click, another American is saying, "Look at the flowers spilling off the iron terraces amongst the gigantic purple and green grapes. Ah, this is paradise."

We are like prisoners seeing daylight for the first time after years in solitary confinement. Oh, I love Southern Italy. No wonder kings and queens flocked to this area. There aren't enough words to describe the amazing beauty before us. With every twist and turn, my adrenaline shoots throughout my body, knowing we are nearing the Italian paradise of cantaloupe-size lemons and homemade limoncello.

I can already smell the enticing aromas of colorful vegetables exploding from the volcanic dirt and the mesmerizing pizza dough stretching its enticing mozzarella cheese across Napoli to Amalfi. The delicious, handmade dough expands and levitates through the Italian air, consuming my thoughts, my mind, and my vision. Looking out my window at the rainbow-colored garden, I feel my taste buds erupting with the taste of the perfectly blazed pizza crust. Ah, piping hot from the open-hearth oven, it creates a taste that comes only from the local timbers as they flame brightly. Crowned with a colorful array of golden eggplants, tomatoes, and mozzarella cheese, all are perfectly sautéed in its liquid gold olive oil. Surely it's dripping from my lips as Nino zooms away, leaving the colorful garden behind in a puff of petrol smoke.

"You do know that pizza was invented in Napoli, don't you?" I announce to Melba Burton, who responds to my question with raised eyebrows.

"Oh, yes, you told us in Napoli while we were eating the pizza Margherita," Forrest says, nodding.

"Just wait until you taste the pizza tonight. The bread dough is stretched into huge, flat rounds, creating the most delicious enticements you've ever put into your mouths. The Italians make so many different things with their dough, such as delicious pastries. In Sorrento, they use many lemons since they are so plentiful and large. And of course, an abundance of fruit abounds in the rich volcanic soil," I explain, tossing my hair behind my back.

"What about the grapes? The vineyards are everywhere. Surely they do something else with all of these grapes besides make wine." Melba is looking out the window at the vineyards stretching toward the Mediterranean.

"Ah, yes, in September the Italians celebrate the grape harvest with huge wine festivals," I say. "The Italians say *sagre* and we say *fairs*." There is always a festival celebration going on somewhere in Italy. They celebrate life, family, births, saints, food, wine, pasta, olives ... The list goes on and on with fun things to do. Just about anything you can think of is a reason or excuse for Italians to celebrate in a big way with family and friends.

"The three grand festivals that pop into my mind right now are the grape harvest, the olive harvest, and the sacred truffle-hunting season in Tuscany that's so popular because of the Americans' interest in fun. And let's not forget All Saints Day. The list goes on. But for now we'll just talk about the grape harvest." I reach for my sunglasses and take a second breath.

"Living in Italy is like living in a candy store for wine lovers. Every region of Italy produces wine, as you will experience on this tour. I'm glad you brought up the question of the grapes, Melba. There is one particular dish made for the celebration of the harvest. It's made with delicious bread and grapes."

"Oh, tell us," Melba pleads as she takes another photo through the window and licks her deep red lips as though she's just sipped the liquid red.

"The making of bread is a daily habit for the Italians. They make and eat their bread daily. God forbid they should save it for tomorrow. If so, ah ... well, then, they have created a hard rock. Yes, it's true isn't it, Tony?"

"*Che cosa?*" Nino asks, not understanding what I just told the Americans. "What, Stefania?" Turning to Tony, he says, "What does she say?"

"Mamma Mia, Nino. Did you know that the Americana buy their bread in a clear package and eat on it for a week or two? Mamma Mia, this is unbelievable," Tony says. "Yes, yes, it's true. And God only knows what the Americana put in the dough. It must be the injection of the dead. You know, the ... what do you say in English? Ah, you know the injection to keep the dead looking nice for months, Stefania?"

Rolling my eyes, I laugh at Tony and try to recall the word. But before I retrieve it, the blue-eyed beauty Gail Wilson, a scholarly legal nurse consultant from Mt. Pleasant, Texas, shouts out, "*Formaldehyde*. Is that what you're talking about, Tony?"

"Mamma Mia, what did you say, Gail?" Tony asks, not understanding the word in English.

"Che cosa? What do you say?" Nino asks Tony again. Tony spouts off the whole conversation in Italian to Nino in less than two seconds while Nino's eyes open wide with shock.

"No, I don't believe," Nino slurs in broken English.

"Yes! Oh yes, it is true. Mamma Mia, Nino, the Americana has many strange things they do. They eat things out of a can, a tin can! They drink the colas. They eat this bread for weeks in a clear package. Yes, that's why they have plenty of sick people. I'm telling you, the Americana eat very badly. They buy tomatoes in a tin can that taste awful. Unbelievable—they do these things every day. Look at Stefania. I'm telling you the truth, Nino. While in America, me, Pat, and Na'tura [Naiches] went to the market with Stefania and she filled the trolley with cans of vegetables. Mamma Mia, she cooked the Americana Thanksgiving *pranzo* [lunch] with these tin-can vegetables. And you know, Stefania eats too many dolce, sweets, and all of those diet colas. Mamma Mia, Stefania will not listen to me. I'm very worried she will die soon." Tony reiterates his universal knowledge to Nino, who is horrified by such terrible news, even though he hears it from Tony repeatedly.

Rolling my eyes again, I look at Tony with a slight grin. "Okay, let me answer Melba's question about the grapes. Didn't you ask what they do with so many grapes in Italy, Melba?"

"Yes, that's right, Stephani."

"Ah, let me back up to the beginning of the 'first harvest' of the grapes. From each family's vineyard, it's customary for them to take a basket full of grapes to their local priest to be blessed. After the blessings, the Italians begin baking for the celebrations. Of course, if we Americans were baking with grapes, we'd go to our local market and buy them in tin cans." I turn toward Nino and flash him a big smile while hearing Tony say, "Si, si. Yes, yes, I told you, Nino. Everything they eat comes in this bloody tin can."

"Speaking of grapes, let me tell you about the traditional bread made with the first harvested grapes in the Toscana region of Italy. It's called *Schiacciata*, pronounced skya-CHA-ta, meaning 'crushed' or 'squashed' in Italian," I explain, looking at Tony for his approval of my Italian pronunciation while my "tongue" lingers in its state of confusion.

"I remember every detail of Maria Rosa making the dolce bread in her little Toscana kitchen for my group of Americans years ago. Let me take you back to the day. Everyone breathe in for a second and follow me back in your minds.

"It was the day of the harvest feast. The long, wooden tables were staged like a Toscana movie set near the family-owned vineyard amongst the silvery branches of the olive grove. We were sprinkled amongst the immaculate groves; the olive trees follow one another in lines up and over the rolling hills. Amazingly, they are calculated at a perfect distance from each other. It rather reminds me of a marching band, each olive tree planted centuries ago, flowing together in perfect correlation. Never a tree out of step, and the grand finale is a beautiful rosebush standing proudly at the end of each row."

"Mamma Mia, Stefania, the rosebush stands in front of each row of grapes, not the olive trees," Tony hysterically corrects me with rolling eyes. "Stefania, you always tell the Americana about the bush, but you forget which tree it protects." He laughs, and then breaks the subject away like a train switching tracks, now shifting his focus to Nino, explaining why he must turn to the right.

Returning our thoughts to the Schiacciata grape bread, I clench the microphone below my chin, just underneath my red-painted lips, and continue to share the educational yet exciting evening with Maria Rosa.

"Stretching the bread dough into huge, flat rounds was the beginning of Maria Rosa's masterpiece. Afterward, she placed the grapes into a huge ceramic bowl, freely dousing extra-virgin olive oil until they floated. I watched as she reached for sprigs of fresh rosemary and fennel. Crushing them to small pieces, she sprinkled the aromatic herbs into the luscious extra-virgin olive oil. She bathed the grapes for an hour or so until they were infused with the wonders of the liquid gold and herbs, all the while enticing my hunger."

Larry from Shreveport, Louisiana, let out a loud exasperated sigh with catlike stretches displaying his iron-pumped muscles right in front of us as though he were stretching for the Olympic Games. "I'm confused," he said to Maria Rosa. "Didn't you say anyone can make this bread?"

"*Buon* pranzo, good lunch," Maria Rosa spilled out in Italian, waving her fist full of truths and swirling them through the air, assuming Larry understood her barrage of flying words. I will never forget Larry's inquisitiveness that evening, interrogating Maria Rosa with too many questions. However, in his defense he did request a session with an Italian cook when he signed up for the tour. I remember him saying to me, "I want to know the secret ingredients for the Italian oven-baked breads. I want to know every detail since I will be an international chef, living part-time in Italy."

"Nonetheless, the atmosphere was reminiscent of an operetta of bread dough and accompanying ingredients. White puffy cumulus clouds floated like explosions of cotton balls towering over us, and with the unexpected plop of brown sugar dumped forcefully upon the counter, the powdery parade of flour morphed into a cumulonimbus thundercloud. Puffs of flour hovered above us like a foggy tunnel. We marveled at the orchestrated dance of mamma and *figlia* [daughter] stretching and flattening the dough, swinging hands with fistfuls of *sale,* salt, as the dance continued," I explain.

"The grapes were laid to the side in a drained position. Maria Rosa continued to play with the dough, being very careful not to add too much flour. As she decanted more of the liquid gold, the dough began to swim. I was perplexed by the abundance of oil, but remained silently dazzled as her daughter refilled the communal ceramic pitcher from the gigantic green demijohn filled with the liquid red. Before I blinked my black-flocked lashes, Maria Rosa had gathered fistfuls of brown and white sugar, mixed them together, and then sprinkled it over the dough. In the golden-white puffy clouds of dough, the liquid gold and grapes swam sumptuously in the creases, sealing the lowest extremities with the yummy conglomerate of fruit. Within a matter of seconds, the schiacciata, the harvest grape bread, was shoved into her old hearth oven.

"I remember her dragging out the long farm table and benches and a crisp white tablecloth, along with plates and glassware. In mere minutes, we were feasting upon the most fabulous, impromptu *dolce Schiacciata con i'uva*—grape flatbread—I had ever eaten."

"Mamma Mia, Stefania, you gave them the whole formula for the schiacciata," Tony says. "It is unbelievable that you know these things. Do you know that the Etruscans made this bread during the harvest? It is a very ancient practice, before the Romans. Mamma Mia, Stefania, I do not understand why you tell the Americana these things but yes, it is all true, very true." Tony repeats everything in Italian to Nino, who is confused about why I'm talking about schiacciata, the wine harvest bread.

19

ARRIVING IN SORRENTO— LA TAVOLA DI LUCULLO

With every twist and turn, we gradually approach our Mediterranean paradise of enormous lemons and mouthwatering vegetables. We gaze upon an array of villas surrounded by orange, lemon, and olive groves with picturesque, narrow streets connected to the doll-size cars. Sorrento is magically beautiful, enticing, and delightfully located over white towering cliffs that plunge straight downward into the turquoise-blue Mediterranean with the Bay of Napoli waving proudly. If you hang your head out the window, you will certainly sniff the fragrance of oranges and lemon pies. And if you sniff a little longer, you will surely smell the aroma of limoncello, a liqueur made from the dolce—sweet—lemons.

Here in Sorrento, we're heading to our secret place where homemade pastas are made from scratch and the daily catch consists of something colorfully blue.

"Get ready to arouse your taste buds to the Mediterranean cuisine, the most spectacular flavors of all. Tonight, my friends, you are in for a culinary rendezvous that will leave you with lifelong memories," I announce while clicking my camera along with everyone else.

"Mamma Mia, Stefania, what are you talking about?" Tony asks, but before I can translate a few words, he returns with, "Ah, yes, I understand what you say now. There will be a love affair with the food tonight. Yes, yes, you are correct. They have no idea how wonderful the taste will be." He is beaming.

"We're having a Mediterranean feast at the family table of Tony's son this very evening. The many courses will consist of a huge array of fresh seafood caught straight from the spectacular Mediterranean prepared especially for us tonight, along with pizza and much more," I declare through the microphone.

"And if you know Tony Filaci at all, you know that being a full-fledged Sicilian entails a meticulous perfectionism for food. Therefore, it is only natural that his sexy son, Richard Filaci, would own and operate this incredible restaurant with the name La Tavola di Lucullo. It serves the most delicious homemade specialties in Sorrento—in Italy." My red lips all but kiss the microphone.

"Prepare yourself for fun tonight at La Tavola di Lucullo, the most spectacular meal of all in Italy. Didn't I just say that just a few minutes ago?" I ask, having fun with the Americans, who are glued to the window with their cameras, reminding me of little dogs sniffing the air.

"We're going to the old residential area of Sorrento. We'll be surrounded by beautiful Neapolitan villas of the most fabulous kind, along with more loaded lemon and orange groves everywhere. And we'll have dancing, the taste of the liquid red bursting throughout our mouths and hysterically funny entertainment by the famous Peppe, who will leave you tingling with excitement.

"La Tavola di Lucullo is famous for its simple cooking. The menu entails Mediterranean blue fish, an assortment of other fresh seafood, delicious antipasto, and, of course, homemade pasta and pizza. Their goal is to cook only 'poor food,' meaning the locals use their old recipes requiring the daily-harvested ingredients. The daily catch comes from the turquoise-blue waters of the Mediterranean surrounding Sorrento, and the explosion of flavor takes root in the rich volcanic soil. And oh, if Giada is around, we will have the taste of her famous tiramisu for sure." I shuffle my feet with excitement knowing we get to indulge, within hours, in the most delicious cuisine of all.

"And while in ecstasy with every mouthful of homemade delights, we'll be entertained with live, local music. The famous Tarantella, headed by their eccentric Pulcinella, is fantastically delightful. Richard's fun staff, which includes our dear Giada—Tony and Pat's daughter—along with the talented musician Peppe, will have us laughing so hard that our jaws will hurt. I guarantee your mouth will never forget the exploding extravaganza of each and every taste of the savory flavors as the fireworks of flavors erupt, bringing all of your taste buds to pure ecstasy. There's no food comparable to the local delights we'll consume at La Tavola di Lucullo in Sorrento, Italy."

The Americans on board right now are getting overly excited as we near, closer and closer, to our paradise home tonight.

"Oh, Stephani, tell everyone how much food we'll eat tonight. They don't need to snack before we get there," Melanie Bass from Pittsburg, Texas, reminds me.

Melanie is correct. After our savory feast tonight, we will wobble back to our coach with our love magnet at the wheel, Nino, our little bambino, singing and laughing with a very satisfied stomach and a lifetime of beautiful memories.

Right now, we are only minutes from arriving at our beloved sanctuary for the next three nights, the most serene place of all in Southern Italy. It is our home with our family: Villa Giovanna.

Arriving at Villa Giovanna means we're immediately surrounded by friends and family who will pamper us with sinful Italian delights, not to mention the heavenly tranquility of being immersed in the beautiful lemon trees and ancient olive groves. Villa Giovanna and its surrounding properties possess amazing powers. It's difficult to describe its supernatural enchantment that grabs ahold of one's soul. To understand this alluring love affair with tropical Villa Giovanna, one must experience it. You must sleep in the mesmerizing rooms that fill your soul with excitement. Then without a doubt, you will return. I can already smell the homemade cannoli with the rich ricotta filling erupting out of both ends of its crunchy shell. No one ever wants to leave this nestled lemony paradise, but with a nudge and a pull, I usually persuade him or her to hop aboard with me each day, promising to return in the late afternoon. Soon I will be looking out my balcony window, observing the beauty of the olive and lemon trees and, of course, Mt. Vesuvius.

Before I plunge knee-deep into my thoughts, Nino rounds our coach through the grand entrance to Villa Giovanna and everyone starts hollering with excitement. It's our home for a few nights and is owned by Tony and Pat's spicy son Richard Filaci, along with his beautiful, picture-perfect wife, Paola, and their beautiful children. Paola, along with her sister, is an *avvocato*—lawyer/attorney—in Sorrento.

Morning and night have already come, and after a dreamy night amongst the olive groves and the fully loaded lemon and orange trees, I bounce out of bed with my feet smacking the blue-and-white Mediterranean ceramic tiles.

What a gorgeous morning! I excitedly say to myself while opening the balcony doors. Being on the second floor, I stand outside overlooking the olive trees with their rolled-up nets attached to each of them. Behind them, I see the mesmerizing Mediterranean water and Mt. Vesusus. Right below me, I see a young woman pouring freshly squeezed Sicilian "blood-red" orange juice into clear glasses and another woman placing huge trays of freshly harvested fruits around the sizable ceramic table, whose top is popping with hand-painted lemons. Looking to the left where a beige hammock swings between two olive trees, I see lush green tropical plants enticing my eyes to take a photo. And before my eyelashes flutter up, the aroma of something delicious consumes the air, alerting my feet to hurry inside.

"Stefania, are you ready for breakfast?" asks Peggy Garmon, the lawyer, who is already bouncing with excitement for the day's adventure.

"Yes, yes, just one moment, Peggy Sue!" I excitedly shout back.

Within minutes of slipping my clothes on and painting my lips the perfect color of red, I say, *"Arrivederci"* to my little solace of paradise, nestled amongst the groves of olives and lemons. Dashing out of my room with a large shopping bag and my camera swung over my shoulder, an explosion of energy possesses my body, enticing my vocal cords to sing, "That's Amore."

Rounding the corner where Peggy Sue is already sipping the famous Sicilian "blood-red" orange juice from the ceramic table arrayed with fresh fruits and various juices, we take off, bypassing the huge demijohns sitting nicely on the ledge facing the Mediterranean. We walk past the beautiful waterfall and follow the aroma of freshly baked bread. Opening the door of the newly renovated breakfast villa, we see the luscious spread of Neapolitan delights piled high, resembling the Tower of Pisa.

"Buongiorno! Good morning, everyone!" I say with eyes opened wide toward the huge array of Neapolitan specialties. Looking over to the table, I see the Americans with plates piled with a mountain of heavenly delights. Amongst them sits Tony, tossing down a teeny-weeny cup of black espresso while waving his other hand in the air like a maestro

choreographing an Italian orchestra. Then, like a chorus choir obeying their maestro, they say, "Buongiorno, Stefania!"

"Stefania, you and Peggy have a seat." Tony insists as I accept large slices of freshly baked bread filled with the wide assortment of marmalades made from fruit grown on the grounds. Before taking my seat next to Tony, I hear Jack across the table asking, "Where are we heading today? Somewhere fabulous, I know."

"Oh, you just wait; it's beyond fabulous, just like every day is with us," I say, in anticipation of going to the famous Amalfi Coast and the Amalfi village, as well as a few other places that will blow them away with their beauty.

Wobbling to our coach, I greet Nino with a "Buongiorno." We take our seats behind him and anticipate the fun day awaiting us. We hold on tightly as Nino drives the coach around the enchanting coastline of staggering slopes. The exploding vineyards and fairy-tale villas pop out from the mountainous rock, magically hanging to the side of the towering mountains. Before we get half a mile from Villa Giovanna, we've started clicking our cameras and hollering to Nino, "Basta, basta. Stop!" The zigzagging road, high above the turquoise-blue sea, reminds me of a fishhook, spiraling around and then jabbing us hard with a hair-raising extravaganza so spectacular, so magnificent, and so way beyond our imagination, that it makes us realize the true meaning of a UNESCO World Heritage of beauty that words cannot come close to describing.

Tunneling around this corkscrew journey of magnificence is thrilling. Nino is winding up the cliffs, giving us mesmerizing photo shots of the lemon groves and amazing terraced gardens of huge plump vegetables mixed in with the beautiful umbrella and cypress trees. As we take one photo after another, we zoom around iron balconies dripping in vibrant pinks and purples with petunias and wisteria. We are on the edge of nothing, or one might say "in midair," with a sparkling wonderment of liquid paradise enticing us to look down. We are driving a dreamlike road that is a little narrower than two toy-sized Italian cars side by side. The Italians call the Amalfi Drive the Mamma Mia Road because those are the words you hear over and over as you make your way through this tunneling wonderment of pure visual delights.

We marvel at the steep terraces cut into rocky mountain slopes. The colorful villas dangle on the verge of disaster. *How do they hold on so tightly without plummeting into the Mediterranean?* I ask myself repeatedly. The challenges for caring and harvesting the grapes on these death-defying drops are nothing more than a trapeze act.

In all the many years of traveling this World-Wonder road, I've had only one American lady wet her pants in overwhelming, indescribable awe of such amazing beauty. Well, not exactly ... However, as my "forever-frozen" memory of that glorious day's events recalls, I must be honest and say that it wasn't exactly the amazing beauty that gave her a soaking. No, it was the hair-raising roller-coaster drive, along with the elderly bikini-strapped signora. The signora was flying at full speed toward us on her pink Vespa scooter, and it scared the cannoli out of her.

In a split second, a tiny Ape, a tiny, toylike, motorized truck towering tall with gigantic yellow lemons, zipped around our coach at full speed, meeting the nearly-naked signora head-on in the worst possible location: a sharp, hairpin curve soaring high over the gorgeous Mediterranean blue seas.

As I said, "The Amalfi drive is a Mamma Mia experience that will shoot your adrenaline through the roof in a matter of seconds and give you the most amazing photos you've ever taken." If you don't believe me, go to my website, www.DecorateOrnate.com, and see the photos for yourself, or better yet, hop aboard with us on our next Italian adventure every May and late September.

Before I explode with excitement, Nino makes another sharp curve and drives into a tiny spot barely large enough to fit the coach in for a quick stop. I jump up and holler, "Andiamo, let's go." We pile out in eager anticipation of today's adventure. Out in front of us is the Mediterranean, with boats bobbing up and down in the gorgeous blue waters, but directly in front of us is a scene that takes us back hundreds of years. We see the local men making their own fishing nets as though they are preserved from the biblical days. They are braiding the strings like a huge puzzle, and to the shock of the Americans, they are all wearing nothing but a narrow sliver of fabric—Speedos—that appear to be three sizes too small.

We zigzag around the little boats resting on the shore and stumble over the words on the verge of spilling from our mouths. I motion for the Americans to follow me, but peeling their eyes away from the Italian swimwear may take a while.

"Andiamo, let's go," I shout, and wave my arm toward the boat that is approaching us. "Come on—this is all ours and it's taking us out in the Mediterranean to see the famous Amalfi Coast and the gorgeous fairy-tale villas, plus much more. I'm not going to say another word about what you're in store for today, except ... get ready to experience a wonderment that will overwhelm you and leave you with fairy-tale memories to last a lifetime."

We cruise the Mediterranean coast with a chorus of clicking cameras and an operetta of "oohs" and "aahs" singing the praises of this world wonderment before us. I am a bundle of energy and enthusiasm, directing the Americans to look toward the left—the Amalfi Coast. To see the Amalfi Coast along with Positano from the water is indescribable. It's one of the world's most beautiful sites to behold, like a royal wedding cake saturated with sparkling diamonds, rare rubies, and sapphires sprinkled on top. It sparkles and glimmers, causing one to hyperventilate with exploding adrenaline rushes. In contrast, seeing and experiencing the Amalfi Coast from our motor coach is indisputably the world's most exciting bus ride. Zigzagging around the fishhook road with a 500-foot drop below to plunge straight toward the creamy swirl of turquoise waters is nothing comparable to the boat ride. The Amalfi Coast from the water is a total different experience, one that puts its name on the list of World Wonders.

"Welcome aboard to the Amalfi Coast," I say. "Are you ready for another adventure of a lifetime? Well, get your cameras ready and hold on to your eyeballs, because you are now among the rich and famous, and certainly the most beautiful place in the world." I wish I could backflip from one end of the boat to the other without landing in the water or breaking my neck. Simply observing this world wonder invokes a rock-star obsession within my soul. I wish to bring every American here, to share with them these hidden gems—not only the tourist destinations, but much more.

I am seated with the Americans on a yachtlike boat, along with our adorable local friend and guide, Cynthia Di Martino. We love Cynthia (Chin'see-ah) and always have fun with her. Although I have experienced the Mediterranean countless times right here in this very location, I bounce with excitement as if it were my first as our boat slowly embarks out into this marine treasure chest. It's not just the Amalfi Coast that shines so brightly. No. Countless villages parading in pastel colors overlook the mesmerizing Mediterranean. I'm in love with this place, head over heels in love with the Amalfi Coast.

We've traveled only a little way, and I'm already reacting as though I've won the Miss America Pageant. I frantically spring from my seat. *If only I had wings to fly.* The exciting thought zaps through my mind. I want to join in with the locals, diving off the soaring cliffs and plunging into the water, and then gracefully springing right back up into the cascading lemon terraces. I want to live in the amazing sand castle that stands so proudly on the edge of the sand.

"Stefania, what is the name of that village up there?" George never makes eye contact with me; he only clicks his camera repeatedly as though celebrities were modeling in front of him.

The questions from everyone bombard me like explosions inside a bag of popcorn. I start to explain Amalfi and the harvesting of the lemons between March and late July. I tell them of all the lemony delights in this region, such as the spongy baba cake and the limoncello, served chilled as a digestive drink. The Americans who travel with us are well versed in the citric paradise. Therefore, they start expounding. They overtake me with their words, flattening me out like a Frisbee and then tossing me into the sea.

They start with another village, the one dangling high above vineyards. "That is Ravello," a couple of them shout, and they skid into a halt and stare, waiting for me to take the reins and lead them on in explaining Ravello and its wonders to the new passengers.

"No, that's not Ravello up there," I say, chuckling. "That's the little church of Atrani. It's nestled on a rock cliff as if it were a white bird observing the magnificence of God's creation. You will see Ravello shortly. In fact, we are going there tomorrow."

Time passes too quickly, like the grains of an hourglass. Our bronzed Romeo of a captain glides past the villages of Amalfi, Positano, Ravello, Atrani, the Grotta dello Smeraldo in Conca dei Marini, Maiori, Minori, Furore Fjord, and the Li Galli Islands, and onward to Capri with the synchronization of a marching band. We journey like royalty through the heart of the Faraglioni rock formations and gasp as we travel through the pages of a storybook. The chorus of "oohs" and "aahs" resonates loudly, and on impulse, I blurt, "Would you like to get in the little rowboats and enter the famous Blue Grotto, the Grotta Azzurra?"

As I hear the words come out of my mouth, I robotically scan the Americans, analyzing their body sizes. *None of them are overweight, except for me,* I think.

It was years ago, probably my fourth tour of bringing the Americans to Southern Italy. I vividly remember the twelve Americans from all over the United States on board that particular tour. Laura from Oklahoma had especially requested to visit the Blue Grotto upon signing up for the tour. I relayed the same question then to the group of Americans: "Would you like to go inside the Blue Grotto, since Laura has asked to do so?"

Oh, I will never forget that tour: As soon as we approached the range of the rowboats, they began to paddle toward us. Laughing and chatting at rocket speed, I observed as each American stepped directly from our motorboat into the tiny rowboats. One by one, the Italian Romeos took the hand of each American, carefully helping them into the rowboats. The tradition was and still is to swing your leg over into the rowboat and hold the Italian's arm as he carefully helps you in.

One by one, the little rowboats gathered inside the grotto. "Remember to duck your heads as you go underneath the rock ledge," I shouted to them, watching them disappear inside the blue glowing cave. Finally, it was Laura and Amy's turn to load into the little boat. The memories of that ordeal bring a downpour of perspiration to my body.

With the motorboat beside the *tiny* rowboat, the Romeo worker instructed Laura to swing her leg into the rowboat and roll inside. Laura swung her hefty leg inside the toylike rowboat and the Romeo tried to pull her toward himself, but suddenly, as though she had been sliced down the middle, half of her flopped into the rowboat. The teeny-weeny boat tilted downward on its side, thrusting Laura's half body into the crystal-clear water. The Italian's desperately spewed cries of emergency, sending standby rowboats to her aid as quickly as possible. The pint-size Romeo squeezed her arm with all of his strength, pulling and tugging, stretching her arm as if it were bread dough, all the while praying to the Madonna for help.

Laura's camera and half of her body dipped into the Mediterranean's cool waters. Half of her face stared into the water. Amy had already loaded into the boat and clung to it for dear life, shrieking with nervous laughter and fear of splashing into the turquoise water with her new Italian hairdo that had been lacquered down with bottles of gel. The collective weight of the two women was well over 600 pounds.

Within seconds, a flock of Italian men pulled and tugged with all their strength while others tried to restore the tiny vessel. After what seemed an eternity of hair-raising comedy, they were able to push and tug her into the rocking boat. Once she finally flopped inside the tiny-tot wooden rowboat, it rocked and bucked back and forth like a bull on its first night at the rodeo. What a sight to see—a scar upon my memory, leaving me forever guarded about taking anyone weighing more than 200 pounds each into the tiny boats, unless they go solo.

At the sound of George's bellowing voice snapping me back to the present moment, I return my attention to the view before me. Ravello is another mouth-dropping village perched high upon the steep, rocky cliffs suspended just below the puffy cumulus clouds of Italy's Amalfi Coast.

Ravello possesses an intoxicating charm that magnetizes and attracts musicians from all over the world. It was a few years ago when Bon Jovi's guitarist Richie Sambora and Denise Richards were spotted in Ravello. I love the astounding stage in the villa gardens suspended over the shimmering Mediterranean Sea. Just the sight of orchestras performing on the free-hanging platform is enough to leave me breathless, a panorama inspiring a worldwide audience of poets, artists, and composers as well as lovers. The view is breathtakingly gorgeous and the gardens are divine. The Terrace of Infinity is one of Ravello's best sights. The terrace looks straight down onto a seductively curvy part of the coast. The effect astounds by the sharp drop of the mountain, giving the impression of looking down from an opening in the sky. The terraces of lemon trees decorate the mountain, and tiny cars trace the contour of the coast. Surreal.

20

Montalcino, Abby of Saint Antimo Monks

Rounding the Toscana curves like gentle waves stirs our emotions into hyper-drive. Many of the fifteen Americans on our coach have never been to Italy, and my heart's desire is to show them the fairy-tale hidden places that I love so much. Connie and Duane Robinson from Huntsville, Texas, are seated right behind me, singing and laughing as Tony sings along with the Italian music. Across the aisle, I see Peggy Garmon, the lady lawyer, sitting sideways in her coach seat with her leg crossed over her knee. She is bobbing her head up and down while using her foot as a drum on the side of Tony's seat. Our adorable Italian love magnet Nino is sitting at the wheel, driving our coach and keeping the beat to the music with his fingers as he accelerates the gas pedal, simultaneously leaving large puffs of Toscana smoke behind.

There is a world of enchanted creations before us and breathtaking shrines flickering with candles as we zoom past them. We are on the back roads in Tuscany, singing and dancing in our seats to our theme song "Tu Vuo' Fa L'Americano." Tony is singing at the top of his lungs while twirling his hands above his head. He's singing in perfect Italian harmony with all of us as I pretend the dashboard is my piano. What a beautiful morning it is here in Tuscany.

Our coach vibrates with celestial voices, and I stare through the windshield and marvel at the rolling vineyards. The view I see right now is exactly the view you see in famous paintings, art books, and dreams. Nino is driving us through a fairy tale indeed, and it's called the Val d'Orcia. Just the drive alone is a UNESCO World Heritage, and wow, it's so beautiful. The vineyards roll up and down in sweet harmony and behind me, I hear the Americans saying, "This is so gorgeous; it looks like a postcard." And shockingly, out of the same breath, I hear someone say, "I wonder why the Italians don't bring in some heavy equipment and level all these rolling hills. It sure would make the drive faster." I turn around, waiting for laughter or at least for someone to say, "I'm just joking." But no, the lady is serious.

I'm looking at the wealth of Montalcino as we slowly approach it; the grapes in this area produce the world's best reds, and one of the most expensive wines, the famous Brunello di Montalcino. In Italy, they have extremely strict laws when it comes to the vineyards that grow and produce the grapes for wine. By law, Brunello can be produced only within a very small region surrounding the town. And there is a four-year aging requirement, which controls the quality and price. Italians are serious when it comes to their wines. It's all in the taste of the grape, the aging process.

Brunello di Montalcino has a baby brother tagged with the name of its color and town, Rosso di Montalcino, another glorious liquid red made with the same grapes. What is the difference, then, if it's the same grapes from the same place? The little brother, Rosso di Montalcino, is not required to rest the four years of aging in the large barrels that are required for its big brother. If you really want to know wine and understand the big fuss, then you must hop aboard with us and experience it with Tony.

Tony, like most Italians, has been sipping the liquid red since birth, sucking it straight from the bambino bottle. And if you are in Tony's presence, he will insist you slowly sip the wine, allowing it to linger in your mouth for a little while before swallowing. Italians drink for the enjoyment of the flavor of the grape, not in excess so they can get drunk. In fact, Italians frown on drunkenness. They are unequivocally alarmed when they see an American guzzling down the liquid red like a starved animal.

The rolling Tuscan hills are sprinkled with many hilltop towns, and the architecture has changed very little in 400 years. Each village has its classic bell tower along with the castlelike fortress with the massive stone walls. We are curving up and down in our coach with hysterical laughter blending in with the Italian music. I pound the dashboard as my imaginary piano. Tony swirls both hands around and around in the air while tapping his shoes and shouting out a weird sound resembling a musical instrument unknown to the human race. The other fifteen Americans are singing and pretending to play their imaginary instruments. Nino is caught up in our Italian madness as well. He is driving the coach while singing in his beautiful Neapolitan accent, which sends us a little closer to pure ecstasy.

Rounding the curves, we see an explosion of silvery olive groves, lush green vineyards, and winding roads lined with the beautiful Italian cypress trees that I love so much. Just the drive alone supplies a countless array of picture-perfect postcards, one right after another. Like most hilltop villages, you can walk through the narrow and winding streets and smell the mouthwatering hot bread and biscotti baking, along with zesty tomatoes whose scents are steaming out through the window balconies. And if you stop talking long enough, you will hear the echo of the biscotti-cutting machine's chopping clatter. I know this for a fact from a few tours back.

Hearing the clatter, I stuck my head through an opened window to see the cause of the noise. To my surprise, I saw hands in flour, sizzling garlic, and squashed flowers bubbling along in hot olive oil. The magnetizing aromas were hard to turn away from, but I did without the disturbance of the owner of the hands knowing my eyes were upon her. Whew!

"Get ready to see something magnificent just ahead," I say as Tony blurts out, "Mamma Mia, Stefania, you are starting up again?"

Stretching my neck backward, I flash Tony a big grin and yes, I start up again. "Montalcino is a lovely medieval town sitting high upon this mountaintop."

"Mamma Mia, Stefania, it's not a mountaintop," Tony says, going into factual truths.

"We are about five hundred meters above sea level with the Orcia Valley flowing down, giving us this beautiful scenery in Tuscany. Now listen to me carefully. The Italian Riviera, where I live in Tuscany, is for me the most beautiful place. Yes, yes, it's true, and I must say, the southern area, Sorrento, where my son lives with his family, is very beautiful, too. But have you been to Sicily, my homeland?" Tony asks, turning around in his seat, looking at everyone.

Bringing the coach to a slow stop, we pile out, eagerly anticipating Montalcino and the taste of the liquid red that brought this charming hilltop village worldwide fame. Before we cross the narrow street, we watch a man swing an old straw witch's broom back and forth over the cobblestones.

"Wow! It's truly a fairy tale; look at the witch's broom. It's a real witch's broom. I mean, look at it. Can you believe they really use a broom like we see in the children's storybooks?" Sharon asks, clicking her camera for proof of such things and still not believing they use brooms like witches used.

Spending time in the hilltop village of Montalcino is fun and adventurous, and that is putting it mildly. Montalcino is indeed the frontrunner of Tuscany's holy trinity of hilltop towns, and if you ask the locals the names of the other two hilltop villages, they will say Montepulciano and Pienza.

We are slowly getting back on the coach when I notice Alice from Galveston, Texas, toting a large bag. "Buongiorno, *ragazzi*. Good morning, kids," Alice says to Nino and me. "Guess what I just purchased in the little shop over there?"

"Well, by looking at your face, I would say it must be something fabulous to eat. Is that peach or apricot marmalade smeared across your face?" I ask, feeling the urge to slide my finger across her colorful face for a nice taste.

"Ah, no, it's the locally made porridge. Oh, yes, I forgot. I did eat two of the large croissants, which I heaped with marmalade. Afterward, I asked for butter and received olive oil. I smeared a few drops of the liquid gold on top." Alice smiles widely, revealing more of the colorful marmalade over her teeth.

Everyone is now inside the coach, clicking their cameras. Looking downward to the flourishing vineyards, I hear the Americans saying things like, "This is what we see in the postcards, the calendars, and the paintings. Oh, this is beyond gorgeous. How can it get any better than this?"

"Oh, it does," I say, knowing they have no idea what's below us. In fact, Nino could point the coach in just about any direction right now, and it would be breathtaking. The Americans are going to scream with excitement when they see our next place, which is just about ten minutes from here.

On our tours, clinking about up and over the rolling hills, we experience something new every day. We stop along the way and taste the liquid reds. We holler with excitement when we see something as rare as the beauty before us. And like a bunch of crazy lunatics, we jump out of the coach at any given second to capture a photo or run toward a little shrine with glowing candles. It was only a few days ago when Nino was persuaded by the Americans to stop the coach in a skidding halt.

"What are those things hanging on the trees?" Mary shouts.

"Those are chestnuts," I say through the microphone.

"Stop the bus," some people shout in a panicky state of excitement.

"Mamma Mia! What's the matter with you?" Tony asks, startled by the sudden outburst of urgency. "Is it a number two?"

"No, they want to get some of the chestnuts up in the tree," I say.

"Mamma Mia, you must be joking. Who is going to get up there and get them?" Tony asks while tapping Nino on the shoulder, telling him to stop the bus.

We all wait patiently while Nino, along with my husband, Allen, crawl on top of the coach and then jump like two monkeys in hopes of grabbing a tree limb. We all hold our breath, watching them sway back and forth on the thin limbs. After a few minutes of skillful trapeze swings, they triumph in grabbing an abundance of chestnuts for everyone.

It's normal for Nino to stop in a skidding second, whether it's on a towering hilltop, a zigzagging curve, a sliver of ribbon stretching across a bottomless bridge, or in a heat of passion when an American sees an unexpected fairy tale or something as lovely as an Italian chestnut tree.

We round curves and see our next enchanting destination in the far valley, rising like a royal beauty among the rolling vineyards and silvery olive trees. It is so much more beautiful than the fairy-tale storybooks. I say nothing, though, not wanting to give away our surprise. But as Nino glides toward it, I hear the "oohs" and "aahs."

Nino backs the coach to a slow halt, facing us toward the Abbey of Sant'Antimo, and just like always, the Americans who have never been here before roar with excitement at seeing this fairy tale standing in all its glory.

"What's going on here today?" I ask Tony. "I've never seen this many cars parked here before. And come to think of it, I've never seen *any* cars parked here."

"Stefania, the locals are coming for Mass," declares Tony.

The moment my brain receives the message "coming to Mass," a metamorphosis immediately takes over my body and the transformation mode "out of control" takes over. I want everyone to experience the service, and if we hurry, we will make it.

Trotting up the short trail, we bypass the picturesque panorama of rolling vineyards with twisted olive trees, all fluttering in perfect harmony. To me, this is one of the most beautiful Toscana scenes. The panorama is spectacular. It looks just like a magazine photo, rising and falling; nevertheless, we don't stop to take in the beauty.

"Hopefully, we'll make it in time to hear the monks chanting the Gregorian praise," I say to the flock of Americans at my heels.

"Wow, this looks like something out of a dream," I hear from the ladies behind my heels.

We are at the back entrance of the Abbey of Sant'Antimo. Behind us, the men talk among themselves of the beauty before them. We all stand in awe. Before us are centuries of architectural travertine stone and onyx and huge, wood-carved doors separating us from within.

"This is a brotherhood of monks who have inhabited the Abbey of Sant'Antimo since the eighth century," I say in a low voice. "The monks live over there, just across the fence." I point to the monastery surrounded by lavender.

"Time stands still here. The monks renounced the world and live right here. They tend to the vineyards and olive trees, dwelling among the winegrowers of the most renowned wine of all, the Brunello di Montalcino. Wine lovers from all over the world covet the Brunello di Montalcino. And just think, we're within feet of the hilltop village Montalcino, which is the backdrop of the abbey." I turn away from the fence and walk toward the door of the abbey.

Standing outside of the abbey, we strain to hear the monks within. The bronze bells in the tower begin to chime, startling us. We giggle like children before stepping inside.

We are not prepared to witness such a divine moment. I have been inside this abbey many times, bringing groups of Americans twice a year, but this time is different.

Inside the abbey, we are spellbound, speechless, and overwhelmed with the ambience of thick fog engulfing the local people. We take a few steps forward and stand in reverence of the Holy Spirit that is filling this place. Straining my eyes to focus amongst the thick frankincense fog, I slowly make out images of white-hooded, robed monks chanting and swinging golden brass pots of smoking frankincense. The thick smoky plumes, floating throughout the medieval abbey, engulf us and leave us appearing as ghosts. Throughout the thick fog of frankincense, people begin to file out of their wooden seats, form a line one behind the other, and make their way toward the front where the monks stand.

We stand in a frozen cluster, all of us together, wide eyed and glued to the stone floor. Right in front of us, the last row of people files into the aisle. I grab Melba Burton from Kilgore, Texas, and pull her toward the aisle. Looking at me as though I am kidnapping her, Melba grabs the wooden pew and digs her heels into the worn stone.

"Come on. We must follow them," I say, motioning for the Americans to follow behind me.

Reluctantly, we all walk toward the thick cloud of frankincense fog. It's a silent and holy moment as we flow all in line, walking down the aisle on ancient stone flags worn smooth through the passing of faithful for hundreds of years.

Very slowly, we take baby steps between huge pillars of travertine and onyx, behind the local faithful. Our heads are bowed low, one behind the other, in the thick fog. With one foot in front of the other, I can barely see the monks. Everyone appears to be ghosts. I'm right behind a tiny Italian signora, who is slowly stepping behind another signora. Feeling as though Jesus could appear at any moment, my heart suddenly skips a beat with the burst of soft angelic chanting in a foreign language. It's a rare moment of holiness among the local people inside this old Romanesque church.

Within minutes of moving to the front, my eyes refocus, and I appear before a white-hooded, robed monk. He is chanting words unknown to me. He is serious, very serious, commanding me to do something, but I understand him not. His hand comes toward me with a white rounded wafer; I immediately open my mouth and stick out my tongue. The monk's eyes pop wider as he says, "No!" I try it again, but he shakes his head, repeating, "No, no."

Knowing I'm holding up the line, and feeling my face burn red, I turn to the left and proceed to walk away. I take three steps away and the somber harmony is broken by the slap of his leather sandals, flapping hard across the old stone floors. With a swish of his long, white robe, he hurries toward me as though I am a runaway bride. He grabs my arm, reeling me back to the position before him. Nervously shuffling his leather-bound feet beneath the robe, he holds up the same wafer once again and moves it toward me. Again, just like a rerun, I stick out my tongue, thinking that surely he will place the wafer on it.

In a moment of disbelief, another monk dressed the same as the first steps closer to him, trying to restrain his face from stretching into a huge grin. He clears his throat and then whispers something to the other monk holding the wafer before me. The local faithful come to a silent halt, watching and seeing the back of this strange but familiar American signora standing before Fra Domenico and Fra Giancarlo.

"Mamma Mia, what is the matter with her? Why must she require the assistance of Fra Domenico and Fra Giancarlo? Why did she try to escape?" the local faithful whisper among themselves, their eyebrows kissing their hairlines.

Still wondering what in the world these monks want me to do, I stand in front of them with my tongue out. I finally say, *"Non cepeto"* and slowly walk away to the left in hopes of escaping this time. But no such luck. The monk grabs my arm again, pulls me back, and this time takes my two hands, joins them with both palms up, and then places the wafer in them. His head quickly motions for me to taste the wafer, and without hesitation, I bring my palms up to my mouth. As if in a strong vacuum, the wafer disappears between my lips. A sudden breath of victory comes forth from the two monks' lips as their hands fly up in the heavy fog of frankincense.

Lingering no longer, I step to the left in hopes of making my escape this time. However, just as my eyes refocus through the heavy fog, I feel a sudden rush of heat overcoming my face. A flash flood of embarrassment consumes my body as I look eye-to-eye with the saintly congregation of Italians who cross themselves and pray for God's mercy over my sinful soul.

In American churches, we are not accustomed to monks, especially monks dressed in white-hooded robes with leather-strapped sandals, who swing golden brass pots with smoking frankincense that release smoky plumes in the church. In fact, if one should walk into an American church, as we do in Italy, they would no doubt call 911 for an emergency fire truck to be in hot pursuit of a burning building. Mamma Mia ...

21

ERICE, SICILY – SLEEPING AMONGST THE SPIRITS IN "L' EREMO MONASTERY"

"Look," I say as Nino takes a smooth left turn toward the most magical and unbelievable mountaintop village in Sicily.

"Mamma Mia, Stefania, they can't see a thing down here." Tony laughs as his hands circulate above his head in a swirling kind of way.

"Oh, I can't wait for you to see where we're going," I say excitedly through the microphone, and then I click my camera with my other hand, totally forgetting what Tony just said.

"Stefania, what are we looking for exactly? Anything in particular you see up there?" asks Dr. Isaac Osborne, who is seated directly behind me.

"Just wait until we start spiraling around the mountain and you walk inside the village of Erice. I will hear you saying, 'Mamma Mia' for sure," I say passionately, pointing to the mountaintop that is now dissipating within the fluffing clouds.

"We are going to Erice, one of the most sacred spots in the Mediterranean. It's a fairy-tale mountaintop that belongs in the storybooks of make-believe. It's a place so magical, so unbelievable, that you will not believe it is real and it is nestled way up there," I say excitedly, knowing we're nearly there and knowing they have no idea just how spectacular it truly is.

"Stefania, will we need our jackets since we'll be in the clouds?" asks Dee Tullis from Longview, Texas, who is slumping in her seat in hopes of seeing the mountain.

"Yes, I recommend taking it with you, because the climate is typically Mediterranean, but the altitude of Erice is nearly twenty-five hundred feet up, which makes it feel much cooler than down below. Oh, yes, one of the many things you'll ideally see in Erice is the mystical fog floating throughout the narrow streets and alleys. It's unbelievable, giving you—or at least it does me—a sudden surge of energy, accelerating your feet to follow it throughout the storybook dream you are surely in—or should I say, the dream you will be in very shortly."

Looking down for a brief moment to adjust the microphone cord, I start up again with more excitement than before. "I know it's the high altitude that gives Erice its mysterious and haunting effects of floating fog. Strangely out of nowhere with the sun shining brightly, Erice becomes shrouded with a fine mist of moving white fog."

Trying to demonstrate this strange maneuver, I swirl my hand over my head and around me, trying to show them the way the fog consumes the narrow alleyways, going straight through like a ghost before racing off through another alleyway.

"Oh, I nearly forgot to tell you, tomorrow when we're in Erice, don't forget to visit the castles. There are two castles that remain. The Pepoli Castle, which dates from Saracen times, and the Venus Castle, dating from the Norman period, built on top of the ancient Temple of Venus where Venus Ericina was worshipped, you know, as the goddess of fertility."

"In antiquity, Erice was famous for its stunning temple on the death-defying cliff where in succession, the Phoenicians worshipped Astarte, the Greeks Aphrodite, and the Romans Venus. This amazing temple stood for more than a thousand years where a sacred, flaming fire always burned from within its enclosure so brightly that sailors used it as a guiding beacon. It's absolutely indescribable, the very top of Erice with its fairy-tale setting of towering castles dangling over the dazzling waters, so aristocratically magnificent that you'll click your cameras over and over. Oh, I nearly forgot to tell you, it was here that the priestesses of Venus served the goddess with their bodies through the art of sacred prostitution. Yes, people traveled from everywhere to make this spindle-top climb to this sacred mountaintop to—well, you know, engage in orgies and prostitution, and only God knows what else."

"Ah, very nice. Mamma Mia, Stefania. What do you tell the people now? Do you think they need to prepare for this kind of activity?" Tony asks, pausing with raised eyebrows to show a little glimpse of meditation before laughing uncontrollably until he finds the breath to utter, "Fortuna's luck to you."

The coach bounces with laughter once again as necks stretch upward in hopes of catching a glimpse of this erotic time capsule we are destined to see.

"This pagan practice continued into Roman times, and the divinity Venus Erycina became so famous that a temple was dedicated to her in 217 BC in Rome while her cult spread throughout the Mediterranean."

"Mamma Mia, Stefania, you will not stop with this bloody story," Tony says, erupting like a laughing volcano, unable to continue with his words while others join in, laughing uncontrollably once again.

"Oh, Stefania, I want to hear the rest of the story since we're going to participate today or tomorrow," says Rose Jobe, who is now falling out of her seat from the laughter bouncing uncontrollably throughout her body.

"Ah, yes, yes, I know you will be participating as hard as you can tomorrow, participating in shopping for something spectacular for your fabulous home," I blurt out. My words mix with the contagious roaring laughter as well.

"Mamma Mia!" Tony spews out, laughing hard while Nino joins in as well even though he doesn't really understand what's so funny.

Trying to get my thoughts back on track, I "con-ta'-new"—continue—as Tony says in his beautiful dialect.

"Okay, remains of the original temple are still up here. They can be found in the Castello di Venere, a twelfth-century Norman castle incorporating some of the temple foundations. Inside the castle area, you can still see some of the temple walls, a Roman bath, and an ancient well. It's truly amazing. According to the scholars, this was Venus's private bathing spot. Still there, nestled and dangling high, it enchants with its naturally lush, fragrant herbs, grass, wildflowers, and perhaps, something else. Beneath the cliff, a dense, abandoned path leads to old stone steps that may have been used by the sailors to reach the temple. However, I would not recommend any of you trying these steps tomorrow. That is, unless you want to end up in the blue waters below."

"There is no way for me to describe this Sicilian village. You'll have to experience it and see it for yourselves. It will grab your eyes, making you think you're seeing something from Cinderella or Jack in the Beanstalk."

We are clicking our cameras like professional photographers as our coach coils around and around the Sicilian mountain, ascending into the fluffy clouds.

"Wow, this is amazing, absolutely amazing," Rose Jobe says to her daughter, Rose Ann Alexander from Austin, Texas, who is seated toward the back of the coach. "Look at the pastel oil painting down below. The bluest of blues. The Mediterranean is indescribable."

"Oh my, this is just beautiful," Rose Ann replies in her lovely southern accent as we unknowingly zoom by a little sign hidden amongst the greenery declaring "L'Eremo," which is a hidden gem.

"Stefania, let's go straight to the top of the village and let everyone experience the 'landing on the moon' encounter for a few hours while Nino and I take the luggage to the rooms," Tony says. "Va bene, okay?"

"Si, si. Va bene, yes, okay," I reply.

"After spending a few hours up here in Erice strolling through the mystifying village, we'll retire to our humble abode." I flash a large smile toward them and feel an explosion of happiness from the joy of knowing they're staying somewhere special and rare for the next few nights.

Describing a medieval village, one would talk of its cobbled streets, castles, the wall surrounding the village on a towering hilltop, the tiny shops of locals selling their beautiful wares, and the mesmerizing smells pouring out from their kitchens. However, to describe Erice is very difficult because it's nothing like the others I've seen. Erice belongs in the children's storybooks because it is so much more of a fantasy than a reality. And unexplainably, a hauntingly magical fog engulfs the village like a running train. This strange fog comes unexpectedly like a twirl of a magical wand. The mystical fog accentuates the supernatural atmosphere of this enchanted village, making you think, *I must be dreaming. This cannot be real.*

Erice's mazelike streets were not designed for cars, and it is overwhelming to think how the little donkeys must have struggled on their long, upward journey to get there. The 750-meter road rises straight from its foot at sea level and reminds me of Jack making his way up the beanstalk. It's enough upward twist to make our ears pop. There is a cable-car lift that will take us up to the top of Erice. However, with our beautiful Mercedes-Benz coach, our abundance of luggage, and, of course, our sun-kissed love magnet, Nino, who is at the wheel, why would we need such a thing?

Within minutes, we're racing toward the entrance of Erice, wide eyed and nearly stampeding the few locals in our paths who are slowly walking their dogs. No doubt, they were enjoying their afternoon beauty in their very own storybook setting until we piled out.

"Come on. Follow me," I shout to everyone, feeling like my legs don't want to obey the walking command. I give Rose Ann a slight whack on her back as she exuberantly zooms right past me.

"I want you to meet my friend Maria before she goes home." I feel a strong surge of excitement when entering Erice's fairy-tale entrance. Walking through the entrance is magical, enticing, and emotional for some. It grabs you and yanks you in with a glorious landing. The cobbled, polished, limestone streets are beautiful and old, dating back to 1200 BC. Walking inside, the cobbled streets greet you with adorable shops, one after another.

"This is unbelievable," I hear as the sound waves from Gail Wilson and Dee Tullis, who are mere feet behind me, zoom through the air. No sooner do I start to tell them to follow the aroma of Maria's shop than everyone darts off into the little shops and we all disappear into the wonderful world of enchantment for a few hours.

Knowing the tiny streets so well, I hurriedly jet off with my big bag and camera slung over my shoulder. I'm heading toward the mesmerizing aroma of Sicilian pastries, which magnetizes me straight to Maria Grammatico's pastry shop, the Pasticceria. All the Americans on this tour have already heard the incredible story of Maria in Erice. They've heard me tell her story many times, and of course, I show them the book *Bitter Almonds*.

Maria Grammatico was born in Erice, Sicily, in 1940, just in time to experience the tragedies of World War II. She was one of six children born into a poor family in Erice. The book *Bitter Almonds* is the story of her life, along with her little sister, who in the early 1950s, was taken by their widowed and poverty-stricken mother to the mountaintop village of Erice to temporarily live inside San Carlo. Little Maria and her younger sister were left to live and work inside the cloistered orphanage called San Carlo, which was run by an order of strict lay Franciscan nuns. Maria spent backbreaking hours, day after day, working and learning the craft of Sicilian confectionary.

Tony introduced me to Maria many years ago in her little pasticceria—bakery here in this mountaintop village. Thereafter, she showed me the book that spilled out her sad life. Thanks to an American lady, Mary Taylor Simeti and her Sicilian husband, Maria's story was told. At the consent of Maria, Mary Taylor Simeti took a recorder to Maria's pastry shop each day and recorded Maria telling her true story of life in San Carlo. It's an amazing, heartfelt story that Mary wrote as Maria told her story.

Every time Tony and I come to Erice, I find myself gravitating toward Maria Grammatio's pasticceria and San Carlo, time and time again. Sometimes you might find me at the very back of her shop, inside the little door, where I visit with her brother, who is usually sitting at the table rolling out dough and preparing the delicious pastries for the oven.

After visiting with Maria in her long, narrow pasticceria, and filling my bag with many of her delicious pastries, I stroll the few steps across the narrow street to another wonderful shop. This shop is stacked full of gorgeous, handmade tapestries and a nice assortment of Sicilian marionettes. After purchasing tapestries, I zigzag back across the little street to another shop with more marionettes, and this time I purchase one of them.

"Signora, *per favore*, please, will you ship this marionette to the USA?"

Within seconds, the mother and daughter jet across the street to find someone who knows how to ship to the United States. And before turning my head, five signoras appear, all talking at the same time. Within a flash, they zoom in closer and dart behind the petite counter. After forty-five minutes of talking and calling multiple numbers, a local signora comes to our rescue.

This shop is tiny and packed floor to ceiling with beautiful Sicilian ceramics, dangling marionettes, and locally made bags. Before surrendering my lovely marionette named Orlando to the signora behind the counter to ship, I carefully bring him close to my red painted lips and snap our photo together.

"Oh, this is not good at all. My lips are faded," I say to Orlando, who is painted to perfection with bright ruby-red lips and a black Sicilian mustache.

After applying a quick swipe of red lipstick, I hold my camera again and begin to click away. Lost in the moment of entertaining my newly found friend Orlando, I continue snapping the photos as though we have just walked the red carpet with thousands of screaming fans. When purchasing things to ship home, I always try to capture the moment with photos so I can remember what I purchased by the time I get home.

Walking toward San Carlo and stopping at a few more shops on the way, I suddenly feel as though I'm Dorothy in *The Wizard of Oz*. There's not a tornado coming my way, but within a second, I'm engulfed by the magical floating fog that's going straight past me and moving swiftly on ahead. It's not shifting around me. No, it comes from behind and goes through me. It's magical, simply magical. That's the only word I can think of to explain this unbelievable and fascinating mystical floating cloud. It reminds me of Casper the friendly ghost. It comes and goes instantly, and before your very eyes, it mysteriously runs in a fast hovering movement, taking sharp turns through the narrow alleys, bypassing the enchanting stone villas adorned with bright, cascading flowers bursting out with rainbow colors. Absolutely magical.

Mesmerized by this encounter, I catch my breath because of the beauty before me and take off walking behind its creamy white, floating force. I'm in awe. What a picturesque portrait. Appearing in slow motion from the floating mist are brightly colored sheets, lavender pants, and a few sizable brassieres flapping back and forth in the Sicilian air. Erice is simply breathtaking.

After a few stops here and there, I find myself standing outside the huge castle door of San Carlo, the orphanage. Looking up at the windows one after another, I find myself reliving every single moment Maria described in her book about being locked away inside, year after year. I am looking up at the opened window, wondering what's going on inside and wondering if that could have been Maria's room.

I don't have to wonder long, because a man pops out of the huge door, flashing a friendly "Buongiorno" and a quick smile.

"Buongiorno. Come stai? Good morning, how are you?" I say too eagerly, hoping to leap through the unlocked door before it slams shut. "Signor, can I please go inside? Please, I would love to see inside San Carlo," I plead desperately as he shakes his head.

"No, signora. I'm so sorry ... Signora, it's much too dangerous for you or anyone to go inside San Carlo. You see, they are repairing and painting the ceilings. Next time, signora."

"But it's me. You know me. I am Stefania, the Americana who brings so many Americans to this village. What must I do to go inside? Must I give to the church many euros? Must I give to the orphanage that is no longer operating as an orphanage?"

"Please, Stefania, it is for your safety. Please trust me, you will get hurt, and I am the one who will answer for your safety. You know that I tell you the truth."

I see his swelling tears and gripping compassion, and I know he's telling the truth. To console me, he takes my hand and leads me toward a door inside the connecting church of San Carlo.

"Per favore, please, Stefania, go inside here. You will like what you see. And you will return to Erice in a few months, and San Carlo will be okay for you then."

"*Grazie!* Thank you." I force my face to smile while still trying to reason in my head why I can't go inside San Carlo for just one second.

Heading back to the storybook square, I stop for a delicious afternoon snack, a sizzling vegetarian pizza. Taking my seat at the outside table across from the church, I can already hear Tony's words bouncing out, "Do not eat the bread. You will disturb the pleasure of eating the feast tonight."

Nevertheless, looking up and seeing the sizzling Sicilian pizza coming toward me, I forget Tony's voice inside my head and dive right in. I squeeze the yellow lemon slice inside my cola and open up my new book purchase of gorgeous photos of Erice. With my other hand, I reach for the sizzling pizza, cut it into slices, and devour it like a vacuum. Ah, this is delicious ... this is heaven ... this is a fairy tale.

Within seconds, I hear familiar voices, a chorus of chattering Americans hollering out to me. "Hello. Hello. Stefania, look what we've found in this amazing place."

Looking up with a full mouth, I watch six of the Americans quickly pull out chairs from my table and excitedly show off their purchases. In a matter of minutes, way too soon, my Sicilian pizza is completely devoured by all of us, and before I sip the last ounce of my cola, the Americans race off to another little shop.

Looking up with pizza crust still on my lips, I see Rose Jobe and her adorable daughter, Rose Ann Alexander, heading my way. I remember seeing them an hour or so ago, strolling near a shop where Rose and Rose Ann were drawn to an impressive tortoiseshell photo frame with a price tag of more than 700 euros.

"*Buon sera.* Good afternoon," I say to them, wiping pizza sauce from my mouth. "Are you having a fabulous time in Erice? Isn't it just amazing? Now, don't worry; we'll be here all day tomorrow." I rush my sentences together, not giving them a chance to answer.

"Oh, Stephie, look what I purchased. It's so beautiful!" Rose says, gently unwrapping the neatly bundled tortoiseshell photo frame she purchased a few minutes earlier.

"Wow, I love it." I say this with sincere honesty, reaching for my cola.

The expensive tortoiseshell frame is a perfect fit for the Marilyn Monroe lookalike Rose Jobe, who is, indeed, an explosion of sexy glamour intertwined with a perpetual appetite for the rarest of antiques and sizable diamonds of the most fabulous kind. This lady Rose, whom I love to call Roselina for fun, possesses, not in her home of course, a life-size walk-in vault loaded with hundreds of perfectly cut diamonds and precious stones that are much too rare for the ordinary to recognize. And this sizzling "hot mama" resides in a home that is wired with the rarest, high-tech security system and flashing camera mechanism that would guarantee absolute protection for the pope himself. Rose has exquisite taste and spent a rich man's fortune on a vast array of gorgeous antiques from all over the world. Many of her gorgeous antiques came from Decorate Ornate, such as the Carrara marble statues and the bronze statues, not to mention the most amazing castle doors. That's just for starters.

I wipe the red sauce from my faded lips, and Rose, Rose Ann, and I start our walk back to the entrance wall of Erice to meet Nino. Walking on the narrow cobblestones, we see the blond beauty Lana Niemann, a real estate tycoon from Gladewater, Texas, toting a large bag filled to the brim with something fabulous, I'm sure. And two steps down, we see the true meaning of erudite charm—Dr. Isaac, who is sipping on a nice glass of ruby-red vino in a lovely picturesque café. Just outside the café, right across the narrow cobblestone street, I see Leigh Clair from Omaha, Texas, holding a bag filled with Sicilian treasures.

"Buon sera, good afternoon, Leigh. Did you enjoy Erice? Are you ready to come back tomorrow for more?" I ask with a delicious pastry in hand.

"Oh, there's no way to describe this place. I'm coming back again and again," vows Leigh, bending over to grab another treasure before heading to the coach.

Erice has tantalizing views that are more than spectacular; they're breathtaking. The closest comparison to Erice would be a scenario of one closing their eyes, allowing their imagination to take them to a beautiful storybook setting such as *Alice in Wonderland* with Alice strolling the polished cobblestones, zipping in and out of the castles, and popping in to explore the San Carlo orphanage.

I've tried to find the words to express the beauty, the mystery, and the enchantment, but no words can express such uniqueness except for an imaginary storybook. High in the clouds, Erice looks over the city of Trapani and the salt flats, not to mention the gorgeous blue and turquoise waters. And on a cloudless day, you can see as far as Tunisia, in Africa.

We say goodbye to the village and hop into the coach. Before we click our cameras, Nino has made a few spinning curves, bringing us to heaven once again.

We are now inside the monastery, the amazing place we're so honored to stay. We have taken on the role of Alice in Wonderland again. We are giants walking down the long winding corridor with echoes singing out from our shoes. Before us are small doors, one after another, appearing to go on forever before veering off to the left or right. Taking a left turn, Tony and Nino shout out behind us, "Stefania, come look."

Unbelievable is the beauty we see at this moment. We are standing on an open terrace overlooking the most awesome sight to behold. We are speechless right now. Finding the words to describe such a magnificent holy place is difficult for all of us. Way down below lies a turquoise wonderment, the Mediterranean. Somewhere between this blue beauty and us float clouds of white fog with perfectly shaped trees peeking through. Before I can find words for this amazing beauty, I hear the other Americans shouting for joy. They've discovered their little cells—what we call rooms—with shuttered windows, now open, that overlook this mesmerizing paradise.

Walking into my little cell, I eagerly rush to the shuttered window, swing it open, and ... ah, I'm speechless. The view before me is indescribable, unbelievable, and so much more spectacular than anything else I know.

I'm two stories up, on one side of this amazing mountain, with my head hanging out the little window. The view is truly indescribable. Way below me underneath the floating fog, I see the color of deep turquoise blue. The Mediterranean waters faintly peep through the magical mist and are so beautiful, so fabled, that I wonder if this is nothing but a dream.

I turn my eyes to the left and look down. I see a huge vanilla-cream gate with a large cross on its front. Secured behind the gate, I note Gothic crosses standing proudly on tiny churches—mausoleums, one after another. A cemetery overflows with rainbow-colored flowers and marble tombs built like miniature Gothic houses. Some of the crosses and tombs remind me of a scary movie in a beautiful way. They are so Gothic, so *Dracula*-like. I want to run down the stairs, hollering loudly, "Hurry, we must see this amazing cemetery." But before I act on impulse, I hear Americans, jumping and laughing, thrilled that they're staying somewhere so magical, so beautiful, and so indescribably fairy tale.

I have returned to Erice repeatedly throughout these many years of bringing groups of Americans to Italy, seeing and experiencing this rare wonderment. And I must tell you my husband, Allen, spent four nights with me in a little cell of a room on our September 2012 Italy tour. However, we stayed in a different room, one I had never been in before. Of course, all of the rooms are similar because they are monks' rooms. There are rooms in this monastery that meander in many directions—more than 200 of them.

When above the monastery, Allen was overwhelmed. He saw the beauty and the mystery, and was amazed at the feat of building a fabled setting so far up in the clouds. The dangling castles on the very top of Erice and the history of it still standing as though frozen in time amazed him. And standing on the very top beside the huge castle, Allen looked down and gasped at the indescribable soaring beauty of the pagan temple ruins, another castle, that dangled like a magical illusion.

We were like children in the village of Erice, running and exploring in a mythological storybook that is still going strong with the locals living and residing as they did from the beginning of time. Allen met my dear friend Maria Grammatio and her sweet brother inside her adorable pastry shop, the Pasticceria. And, like a page turning the next chapter of the book, Allen stood with me around the corner, looking up to the window where Maria spent most of her life with her little sister locked away from society with a strict flock of nuns in San Carlo Orphanage.

Allen introduced himself to the local men who sat talking on their wooden bench each morning. He laughed and talked the best he could in broken Italian to convey his world to their world, which is a completely different planet compared with America. He smiled and laughed as Pat and I tried on hats and furs in the local shop that had the most gorgeous Italian designs. We enjoyed the freshly tossed pizza outside on the small piazza, laughing and eating with the Americans while watching a Cinderella-like wedding within feet of us at the local church. We exchanged stories about the wondrous things we saw just minutes before consuming our pizzas. And at their request, I called Tony, who was having his afternoon siesta at the monastery and told him the Americans wanted to stay longer and not to send Nino with the coach for at least three more hours. The Americans are like children, excited and mesmerized by a world so different and so dreamlike. We click our cameras toward the castle that appears to be a royal ornament atop a breathtaking wedding cake.

Finally returning to the monastery, we are greeted by waving arms extended from our dear friend Calogero. Behind him, we see Tony flashing a happy smile and hear his Italian greetings as if we had just arrived from America. Calogero is a beautiful man and dear friend who graciously opens his arms to us, making us feel special and loved. He oversees this hidden treasure chest as if it were his newborn bambino. He possesses a genuine love that reflects a sweet and godly spirit as if he were a monk himself. However, Calogero is not a monk. No, he is married to a beautiful woman and has sons who are as handsome as the statue of David himself. In fact, one of them oversees the nearby orphanage here in Sicily that we love to visit so much. The whole family has a special heart, a godly heart that serves and provides goodness to others.

"Stefania and friends, come stai—how are you, my dear ones? Please enjoy yourselves and prepare for the feast tonight," Calogero says to us, bending over in a slight bow, giving us a gentleman's smile, and then slowly disappearing down the long corridor while singing a celestial song in Italian.

We gather for a delicious seven-course meal. And with the sun going down and the amazing glow of the castle way above us, we laughed and talked among ourselves. After laughing and talking until midnight, we finally say our goodnights and meander out in different directions throughout the spellbinding monastery.

With the old key gripped in Allen's left hand and his other holding mine, we make our way up the meandering stairs, giggling like children and feeling as though Casper the friendly ghost will pop out from the many doors any second. The old floors creak and thunder strange sounds as we softly walk the long corridor. The midnight glow is somehow flickering beams of dim light in front of us, making me wonder where the source is coming from. I feel the urge to knock loudly on some of the little doors as we pass them by. However, since Allen is with me, I restrain myself and think, *You are an adult, so try to act like one.*

Standing in front of our dwarf door, Allen takes the old key and turns it twice, one left click and one right click. The turn of the key resonates hauntingly like a bellowing siren throughout the long corridor, and for some reason, I feel as though the head monk will surely pop out, reprimanding us to be quiet. "Respect the tranquility of others," he would say. However, the only others on this floor are my group, the Americans. Tony and Nino are way down below. And I'm sure Tony has found another bed, something more sizable, if he's lucky. With the turn of the key that unlocks the wood door, we hurriedly push it open to see our toylike bed neatly made with the sparkly moonlight shining through our balcony window.

Allen sleeps with me on the toy-size bed in the old monastery, feeling the spirit of God's amazing beauty inside the indescribable setting. We sleep with our window swung open so we can look at the dangling castle on top of the towering mountaintop. We see glowing lights flickering way above the clouds and hovering on top of the castle, and when we look at the castle, intermittently we see the misty fog streaming around its very top as it chases something around and around. Then in a speedy moment, the misty fog takes off running through the star-studded sky. It is magical, nothing comparable to anything else I've ever seen, except in Erice. The misty fog is coming toward us, toward our little balcony window here in the monastery. It is a view that can't be real, but it is … an experience that can't be anything but a dream, but it's not.

Inside our tiny cell with the window flung open every night, we slept and cuddled as though it were our first night together. We watched as an unexplainable vapor filled our room, perhaps the same mystical fog that floats and tarries inside the walled village of Erice as though ghosts are running through the village. The walled village is just above us, only a few twists and turns around the mountaintop side of the monastery. This unexplainable vapor consumed us each night, taking our minds and bodies to new heights. And when the morning rose, we awoke refreshed, renewed, energized, and connected as one in thought. It was amazingly wonderful, so surreal it left Allen reminiscing to this very day the moments we shared. And yes, Allen will tell you, there is indeed, something strange and magically alluring that entices your soul, inflames your senses, rebirths your desires, and simulates your libido, all in one big package, on the mountainside of Erice in the old monastery of 'L'Eremo.'

22

BISACQUINO & CORELONE, SICILY

After a delicious Sicilian breakfast, all ten of the Americans make their way to the coach. I can already hear their laughter and chatter as I step inside and take my seat across from Nino, who is already at the wheel and looking eager to go. And like always, Tony is in the mix of laughter seated behind Nino.

"Buongiorno, everyone, how are you this morning?" I ask through my microphone as Nino steps on the gas pedal and we shoot off in a magical sort of way.

The credit for this day's adventure goes to my dear friend Dee Tullis from Longview, Texas. Dee asked me before signing up for this tour if we could go to a remote place in Sicily called Bisacquino and without giving it a second thought, I replied spontaneously.

"Absolutely, I see no problem at all going to Bisacquino. We have our own coach, so why not."

I remember Dee's response as she stretched her perfectly red-lined lips across her geisha-silk face.

"Mamma Mia, sign me up. I can't wait to tell my friends that I'm actually going to Bisacquino. Oh, by the way, you do know that Bisacquino is the breeding grounds for the mafioso, don't you?"

"Hmm, well not really, but don't worry. Sicily is beautiful," I responded back, watching Dee flashing her dark eyes with a certain look of caution in her voice as though the mafioso were hearing her every word in Gladewater, Texas.

Now, leaning over to talk with Tony, I remind him of our promised adventure for the day. Or should I say "my" promised adventure.

"Mamma Mia, Stefania, what do you mean we must go to Bisacquino and Corleone? What's the matter with this Americana? There is nothing to see in either of these places," Tony fires back with comical hysteria,

155

reminding me of Rodney Dangerfield with his wide Italian eyes going back and forth in a cartoonish kind of way.

I point to the guilty one, Dee Tullis, who is laughing hysterically with another southern-bred beauty, Gail Wilson, both of whom are seated toward the back of the coach, oblivious to what we're saying. To get a better look, I stretch my neck around and the two of them are still carrying on like two wind-up Chatty Cathy dolls.

Turning around to see Dee, Tony starts.

"Dee, Dee, Deeeeeee!"

"Oh yes, angel?" Dee replies in her adorable southern accent of sweet endearment, her black flashing eyes enhancing the southern animation.

"Mamma Mia, Dee. What's the matter with you? Why must we go to Bisacquino today? What do you plan to see, Dee?" Rodney—I mean, Tony—says to Dee.

"Oh Tony, I plan to see the mafioso, and Stefania said we can go to Corleone as well," Dee says jokingly, giving Tony a wide smile as she turns back around to continue her laughter with the blue-eyed beauty, Gail Wilson from Mt. Pleasant, Texas, whose personality is identical to the beloved Lucille Ball.

Throwing his hands up in the morning air, Tony twirls back around in his seat, saying to Nino, "Andiamo, let's go. Mamma Mia, Stefania, where do you find these Americana?"

Without hesitation, I laughingly say, "In America."

Tony lovingly laughs and gives in to Dee because for one, Tony loves her stretched-out southern drawl, reminding him of the old American spaghetti westerns. Every time he gets within arm's reach of Dee's smiling face, a sudden urge sparks him to say, "*Ciao, puppetta*. Hello, dear one." Then without thought, Tony reaches for her flawless face, the puppetta face, a baby doll face that triggers him to squeeze her cheeks with a slight twist at the end.

Being here in Palermo creates an exploding rush of adrenaline through my body as Nino drives through the crowded streets this morning. The buildings, the churches, the people, and the open markets transfer us back at least 200 years. With every twist and turn, we see flapping laundry among the towering neighborhood flats along with the many concrete houses built by the mafioso. To our left, we

156

see a young Sicilian boy rolling a colorful wooden cart loaded down with freshly baked breads, and behind him is another multicolored cart bumping along over the cobblestones with fresh fruit towering. I wonder how the towering pyramid of fruit stays so perfectly balanced on the cobblestones.

Palermo is enticing to the eyes. It makes a perfect movie scene with the real life actors going about their daily lives in a world so foreign, so rare, and so tantalizing. Everywhere we look, we see a conglomeration of pandemonium fun bouncing through life as an old Sicilian movie, and we are still on the coach.

Reaching over and picking up the microphone, I announce to all of the Americans, "This morning we have a special adventure for those of you who are brave enough to go along with us. And any of you who want to stay in Palermo while we're off to … Bisacquino and Corleone, let me know, and you can stay in this mysterious wonderment of Palermo today."

"Mamma Mia, Stefania, no one wants to go to Bisacquino and Corleone except Dee. Everyone else wants to stay here in Palermo and see this beautiful city," Tony barks, twirling his hands in the air with a distraught face.

Before Tony finishes his sentence, everyone, it seems, hollers out, "Yes, yes, we're going with you to Bisacquino and Corleone."

In a flash, Lana Niemann, the beautiful real estate tycoon and vivacious owner of Rocket Realty in Gladewater, Texas, along with Leigh Clair, a blond-hair beauty from Omaha, Texas, declare they are staying in Palermo to shop the exotic street markets with the local Sicilians and absorb the exciting chaos that comes only from Palermo.

"Mamma Mia, yes, I knew you wanted to stay in Palermo." Tony smiles at Lana and Leigh, who are already standing in the middle of the aisle, bouncing on their toes, ready to hop out into the chaotic Old World of Palermo.

"Yes, we're staying in Palermo," Lana says, rushing her words excitedly, knowing there's a wonderful array of designer purses and sunglasses awaiting her large shopping bag.

"Lana and Leigh are the only two staying in Palermo while we're in Bisacquino and Corleone," I reiterate to Tony, who is already fretting about not having Lana and Leigh amongst our flock.

Dragging the palm of his right hand down his pant leg and then nervously rubbing his stomach as though ping-pong balls are ricocheting within, he painfully blurts out his familiar mantra. "Mamma Mia, why must you escape from us today?" Before Lana or Leigh respond, Tony delivers his verdict in a low whispering voice, causing everyone to lean in toward him. "Okay, now listen to me," he says to Lana and Leigh as though they're little children going out to play with other children from a different planet. "We let you off here and the street markets are right there, va bene, okay?" Tony instructs, pointing to the right.

"Okay, Tony. We're going to have loads of fun today and we'll see you guys this afternoon," Lana says as she hops off the coach with Leigh at her heels. She waves goodbye and shows Tony her cell phone, which should give him the reassurance of calling if needed, but it does not.

"Mamma Mia, Stefania. Everyone wants to go to Bisacquino and Corleone? Unbelievable. I can't believe all of you want to go with us in lieu of staying in beautiful Palermo." Tony swirls back around in his seat with a comical, confused look on his Sicilian face while making a phone call, asking for a few extra eyes on Lana and Leigh, who have already disappeared among the array of dangling market wares.

"Tony, do you really think we'd let you, Stefania, and Nino zoom off without us? I mean, come on. We all know how 'adventure' follows you guys, especially Stefania," Dr. Isaac says, flaring his beautiful whitewall teeth beneath wooly black eyebrows that merge toward his hairline of lacquered curls. Dr. Isaac, by the way, keeps us laughing with his delightful personality of scholarly intellect.

We maneuver through the crowded streets of Palermo oohing and aahing at the animated surroundings of honking horns and galloping horses adorned in flamboyant tassels. We see the handmade marionettes dangling from the vendors' horse-drawn buggies, and a split second later in front of us, we see a vendor waving his wares below a set of black eyes resting lazily on huge cheekbones painted with ruby-red blush. We watch as a Sicilian signora grabs all that she can from the vendor while flipping her purse upside down. In a mad rush, the euros roll out and hit the cobblestones, jingling and jangling.

"Mamma Mia, I hope she has enough coins for her impromptu purchase," Dr. Isaac says, laughing and wrinkling his brow as he tries to get a better examination of her purchases.

"For heaven's sake, don't let Stefania out the door. She'll take what that lady can't carry, for sure," Gail Wilson says, fluttering her liquid-blue eyes toward Chuck, her studious, *farmacista* lover who is also her devoted and handsome husband.

Still laughing and clicking our cameras, we see more trotting horses pulling fringe-laced buggies with olive-tone lovers caressing each other as though they are chiropractors, massaging the muscles and kneading the skin. The variety of cultural influence is wide in Palermo. We see Moorish architectural and Arabic writing on the enormous basilica standing before us. And right in front of the massive building is a huge wooden wagon of some sort. It looks as though Cleopatra will pop out any second with her servants, waving huge palm leaves. It's nothing like an American wagon. No, it resembles a topless ship painted in muted colors. It's used for the many celebrations such as Easter and the parading of the Madonna and patron saint through the narrow alleys.

With all of the foreign beauty surrounding us, the alluring aromas of baking breads levitates among the chaotic rhythm. We inhale the fragrance of yeast rising in the hot ovens and envision the exploding red tomatoes bubbling with garlicky herbs. I glance over to Billy Craig from the alligator swamps of Louisiana, who signed up for this tour while shopping for castle doors in Decorate Ornate. I observe his pointed face, which resembles a smiling dachshund theatrically sniffing the exotic aromas of Arabian Knights, the exotic spices of cooking that bring a torrential downpour inside his mouth. Surely it does ... I see him swallowing hard, repeatedly, as though trying to swallow a large vitamin. Afterward, he swirls his tongue, elongated like that of a leathery lizard, and wraps it acrobatically around his mouth with thin lips. My taste buds are blasting in ecstasy too, but I restrain my tongue, locking it within my mouth, and refusing to display such a theatrical show.

Farther up the street, just a few tiptoes ahead, we see Arab-like alleys and street markets zigzagging in every direction. I feel as though I am watching a showbiz circus parading around. Everything is so enticing, even the dogs are smiling. The passengers are competing with the same drug-induced hysteria as the Hollywood paparazzi as they snap photo after photo of this extravagance of a world so foreign to their American way of life.

The medieval madness stirs us to more excitement, if that's possible, when I look straight ahead and see the Porta Nuova framed by huge, turbaned Arab statutes standing cross-armed and glaring toward us. It prompts me to shout with hyperventilating excitement. "Nino, *lento, lento*—slowly, slowly," I say and have everyone's attention and scrambling for their cameras as a mental numbness yanks my thoughts for a brief second. The traffic is pushing us forward, demanding we go through the framed passageway with the gigantic Arabs guarding our entrance. I want to jump out of the coach and demand the zooming scooters and tiny cars to stop. I want to freeze this moment for thirty minutes and allow us to stand in front of this amazing history and hear of its secrets. Ha, I must be joking. The local people see no history before them. They are desensitized to this entire conglomerate of national madness. They embrace their heritage and dance amongst the ruins of beauty. Even the local fishermen are frozen in time. They still weave their nets and dangle their toes in the cool sea, preparing for the day's catch.

For a brief second, I allow my thoughts to expand, but as we get closer to the entrance, I explain. "These are the Arab statues I told you about earlier. They symbolize the reign of Arab power of Palermo's seven hundred years of domination. Look at them on each side of the entrance, highlighting the exotic influence from the Arabian Knights who once occupied Sicily for so many years," I reiterate as they whoop and holler with glass-shattering vibrations.

"Oh, I can't believe my eyes. They ruled Sicily as kings and queens. I've studied this history for years," Billy Craig shouts out, now resembling a pointed-nose possum since his tongue is nowhere to be seen.

With our mouths still open and our fingers clicking the cameras, Nino squeals a right turn onto a very familiar street. It's a long side street with old shabby buildings, one after another, on each side of us. It's the street we stop at when we're in Palermo. The street pours out beautiful, medieval treasures, enticing us like an open treasure chest with magnetizing, magical powers. We are animated "smiley faces" with our mouths stretched wide.

"Mamma Mia, Stefania, do not look to the left or to the right. We must not stop," Tony bellows. In a split second, our faces release and slam together like a musical accordion.

"Oh yes, we must stop," I shout, along with the others, who are now whooping and hollering with climatic excitement.

We've barely rounded the corner into this nestled treasure chest and amazingly within a split second, everyone is hollering out like a roaring tornado, "Basta, basta. Stop!"

"Mamma Mia, Stefania," Tony shouts as he brings his hands to his ears with his eyes bugging out. "Mamma Mia, I thought we must go to Bisacquino and Corleone. What do you mean, 'Basta, basta?' We will never get to Bisacquino and Corleone if we stop here," Tony cautions, breaking out into a huge smile and saying, "Okay, you get out right now, yes, yes, you get out right now. Nino and I will stay here with the coach."

"Um, this doesn't mean we're getting out of going to Bisacquino and Corleone. We'll only stay for a while, just long enough to see what's here," I say to Tony, knowing he thinks we will stay for hours in this mountainous pile of fabulous antiques all of which is tucked away on this hidden, narrow street in Palermo.

With Tony giving us the okay, a sudden burst of hand clapping starts and Nino presses the button for the door to swing open. In a flash, we all fly out and run to the little shops, hollering like wild children. Flocking to the various shops, one after another with huge assortments of antiques spilling out to the tiny street, I'm instantly drawn toward the huge marionette dangling from a ceiling rope. Speedily breezing through the piles of treasures, I dive into a vast array of marvelous furniture that surely came from a haunted castle. What a joyous reunion of things so rare and unusual. Glancing up, I see another brilliant piece: a colorful Madonna painted on glass.

Looking around for help, I see no one, so I step up on a pile of wooden debris and grab hold of the large painting. It's unusual, and I'm already in love with it. Walking a little sideways with my neck stretched around the Madonna, I haphazardly carry it to the front. Trying to find some help, I see the striking beauty Gail Wilson toting a large box with an antique chandelier protruding out of the top.

"Oh Stephie, look at this beautiful light fixture. Oh, I love it," Gail says, rushing back to the shop to hunt for more treasures.

"*Quanto costa?* How much?" I ask the Sicilian man with a cigarette dangling from his mouth. Raising his hands in the morning air, he speedily talks in his local dialect with a strange Sicilian twist.

I fumble through my purse for an ink pen and paper. Finally, I place a crinkled piece of paper on the nearby wooden crate and hand the pen to the Sicilian shopkeeper.

"Quanto costa? How much for the Madonna?" I ask again, shoving the pen toward his hand.

"*Non parlo Italano.* I do not understand the Italian you speak," I say to him, pointing to the ink pen and paper.

"Va bene, okay," he says, scribbling 25 on the paper.

"Ah! Va bene, okay. Grazie, thank you. And yes, I do want this Madonna," I assure him with a huge smile while caressing the Madonna like a newborn bambino.

"Oh, I love it so much, but let me see if it will fit into my luggage," I say, forgetting he cannot understand a word I'm saying. I have an extra luggage in the coach so I walk toward it, waving the Madonna in front of Tony and Nino who are still resting inside the coach.

Piling out, I hear Tony already saying, "Mamma Mia, Madonna. What have you found, Stefania?"

"I found something wonderful. Do you think it will fit in the extra luggage? I need to see if it will fit before I pay the man."

"Va bene. Okay," Tony answers as Nino heads to the back of the coach to get the empty luggage. Excitedly, the shop-owner along with his son takes the Madonna painting from me and places it toward the opened luggage.

"Oh no, it's too long and wide for the luggage," I say to the man, not knowing what to do now.

Instantly, the shop owner's son, Valentino, springs up from the ground with the luggage and explains to Tony that he will get larger luggage just down the street.

"*Perfecto*, I will go help you with the luggage," I shout excitedly, not realizing there's no need to shout.

"Oh Stephie, will you please bring me a large luggage, too? I need another one for my chandelier I'm purchasing, and I think Dee wants one, too," declares Gail as I follow behind Valentino, who is swinging his leg over his motorcycle.

As though I'm playing Follow the Leader, I swing my leg over the seat right behind him and away we go, peeling off like a speeding rocket. I brace myself for a sudden stop at the end of the little street, but surprisingly, Valentino revs the motor louder and away we go again, shooting out into the oncoming spaghetti mixture of traffic. Zipping in and out, barely escaping the crashing of little cars, I feel the rush of panic slapping me hard in the face. I soon realize I have no helmet on, and Valentino doesn't stop at the end of the street where I thought we were going to buy the luggage.

"I'm going to die," I scream as he zooms and accelerates the engine, darting right between two oncoming cars and brushing my elbow against a little truck stacked high with swaying melons. Zigzagging in and out of the cluster mix of cars, I fervently pray. Forcing my eyes open, I scream louder as I see a truck loaded down—or should I say loaded up—with crates of yellow vegetables of some sort that sway back and forth like the Tower of Pisa. Wrapping my arms around his waist, I scream and holler like a raging lunatic, seeing my life flash before me and thinking, "I've finally gone too far."

Squeezing my eyes shut while my fingers grab tightly to his black leather belt, I inhale a strange odor and soon realize this Romeo has forgotten his deodorant. The overpowering stench in my nostrils is overwhelming, but my nose soon forgets the smell as my body dips hard to the left, coming within inches of the cobblestone street. Before I grab my heart left on the cobblestones, Valentino yanks the motorcycle back up, skidding it sideways around the corner like a professional circus performer.

I am dazzled, discombobulated, and now face-to-face with the locals on the open street market. I see hundreds of Sicilians shopping among the colorful array of wares. Nonetheless, without waiting for people to move, Valentino sounds off his ear-popping horn, warning everyone to jump aside as we dart in and out as if we are in a high-speed chase.

Zooming down another side street, we fly through the crowds, zipping in and out, and causing the locals to jump back before Valentino abruptly kills the engine right in front of a luggage shop.

"Andiamo, let's go," Valentino hollers as he leaps off his motorcycle while leaving me more discombobulated than before. My hair is standing straight up in a whiplash sort of way. I force my leg over the seat while balancing my other leg on the cobblestones.

Taking two steps forward, I hear a loud gunshot. I scream while holding my heart. Immediately I look for red blood that's surely pouring from my blouse. Somehow, faster than the speed of light, I sprint to the nearby shop where Valentino is leisurely conferring with the shopkeeper.

"Do you see any blood on me?" I ask hysterically.

Ignoring my alarming injury, he pretends nothing out of the ordinary happened, and asks for the large luggage dangling from the ceiling. Then he looks at me and says, "You okay, me okay, va bene?"

"Mamma Mia, don't you understand? Someone shot a gun," I declare, keeping my eyes focused on the door while holding my hand over my physiological wound.

The shopkeeper flashes me a quick wink while happily whipping out a long measuring stick. At once, he measures the bright yellow luggage, and then slowly nods, saying, "Too short for the Madonna."

"Andiamo, let's go," Valentino verbalizes in his Sicilian accent, darting out the door with me at his heels.

Simultaneously, we leap onto the motorcycle with me wrapping my arms tightly around Valentino's shirt. Within seconds we peel off, zigzagging in and out of cars once again. When we have been on the road less than five minutes, Valentino's metal buttons rip from his fabric shirt, clattering to the cobblestones, and in no time at all, his shirt parts like the Red Sea down the middle and flies toward me, engulfing my head and leaving his upper torso stripped. Needless to say, I must have yanked a little too hard on his shirt.

We stop many more times, asking luggage merchants if the Madonna will fit into any of their luggage. Finally, we zoom out from the narrow alleyways, flying full throttle with Valentino shouting loudly too many words to understand with the wind punching me in the face. I've seen the hidden jewels of Palermo this morning. I've seen the hidden flats tucked away in the narrow alleyways where the children play in the streets, and I've come face-to-face with death, just barely missed by a speeding bullet heading straight to my heart.

We are now weaving in and out of the heavy bumper-to-bumper traffic, and before I can blink my eyes, we come to an abrupt skidding halt. Thanks to a tiny fruit truck loaded down with red strawberries appearing from nowhere, the back wheel of the cycle is sent skidding up in the air like a bucking bronco performing at the rodeo in Gladewater, Texas. My heart flies into my throat once again and then *bam*, crashes down hard, forcing me to scream like a hysterical bambino. Everything within me freezes. I'm completely addled, probably close to a nervous breakdown, or at least that's what I think one would be likened to: a person shocked beyond repair after a near-death situation and seemingly no end to it in this Sicilian morning horizon. My face has never felt such a blast of air like the one that's whipping it like a professional boxer.

After less than twenty minutes or so, the harsh beating to my face subsides and waves of excitement slap me as I see street vendors loaded down with wonderful Sicilian wares, all lined up underneath white tents. Sadly, though, my excitement diminishes as Valentino skids to the left alleyway, slamming us toward the cobblestones once again. Then in a lightning flash, he yanks us back up in a wild, whiplashing performance.

In the midst of our bucking-bull ride, I swallow an insect. Minutes later, Valentino abruptly stops. This again sends the back tire of the motorcycle upward and then crashing back down hard with a bouncing spring at the end. For some unexplained reason, we are both consumed with smoke, reeling from the burning rubber tires. From the loud squealing and popping of little pebbles flying underneath the sweltering wheels, one would surely assume an army of machine guns was sounding off.

Stopping and jumping on and off in front of more luggage shops, we hear the same story: "No large luggage for the Madonna," so we finally start to zigzag our way back.

We zip in and out of the cars and trucks all the way back to the narrow street, and somehow, I realize we are nearly back to where we started. Before I can bat my whiplashed eyes, our rocket of a motorcycle stops in an abrupt skidding maneuver that would probably win Valentino some kind of trophy for being the most acrobatic driver in the world. The minute I look up, I see Tony and Nino staring at us.

My next maneuver would probably win me a trophy because I heroically fly off Valentino's motorcycle as if burning flames are torching my seat and run toward Tony and Nino.

"You will not believe what I've been through," I say breathlessly to them, grabbing Tony's arm and feeling my adrenaline tingle throughout my limp body. "I nearly died! Oh yes, trying to find that stupid luggage, someone shot at me. And on top of that, Valentino caused a fruit truck to flip over, bringing all of the oranges in Sicily to be flattened by an oncoming cement truck."

"Mamma Mia, Madonna! You are unbelievable. I'm telling you, Stefania, you are truly unbelievable. I cannot get out of your sight for just one minute without you getting into an alarming situation," Tony observes, laughing with dilating eyeballs and twirling hands.

In between laughs, Tony blurts out, "What happened to your hair?"

Immediately, I bring my hand to my hair and realize it is sticking straight up.

"I was nearly killed while with this lunatic man. Somebody shot at me. Ask him. He'll tell you," I frantically explain to Tony as Gail Wilson pops out with the same chandelier in her arms as before.

"Stephie, what happened to you? Oh my, look at your hair. Did you find the luggage?" Gail blurts out and then explodes into out-of-control laughter while trying to be sympathetic as she flattens her own hair down as though it were mine.

"Never mind the luggage. You don't need it now. The papa sent his other son to get lots of bubble wrap and strong tape. Mamma Mia, he's been working very hard wrapping the Madonna up over and over with bubble wrap. You can carry the Madonna on the plane like a large carry-on. He made you a nice handle with the tape, too." Tony and I walk toward Valentino, who is now standing beside his papa, holding the large bundle of bubble wrap.

"Is the Madonna inside?" I ask, unable to see anything but a big bundle of bubble wrap tied around and around with clear tape.

"Si, si. Yes, yes, it's ready for you to go," Tony declares before asking, "Why do you like this so much, Stefania? I do not understand why you pay so much for this piece."

"I love it. It's perfect, and the price is amazingly low," I reply, running my hands through my wiry, tangled hair.

"Mamma Mia, Nino, did you see this Madonna she likes? Unbelievable. She pays too much for this painted Madonna. Oh well, if you like, it's okay. Va bene," Tony comments as he raises his eyebrows and shakes his head in disbelief.

"*Grazie*, thank you," I say to Valentino and the papa, who are staring with grins, expressing their happiness in finding a solution to my luggage dilemma. It is comical to look at Valentino, standing with a huge ball of bubble wrap in hand.

"Ah, va bene, okay, very nice, very nice," Tony says to the papa as Nino reaches with both arms for the bubble-wrapped Madonna, receiving it as though it's a newborn bambino. Simultaneously, the papa holds his frail, olive hand out for his euros.

"Oh yes, let me pay you. Just one *momenta*." I reach into my purse, taking out a twenty and a ten, placing them in Papa's hand. I stand with my arm extended, my palm facing upward, patiently waiting for him to return five euros to me.

The Madonna was twenty-five euros, so yes, I need five euros back, I think to myself while standing with my hand out. Strangely, Papa continues to hold his hand out as well, clenching the thirty euros.

"Why is he not giving me my five euros back? Signore sir, you owe me five euros," I say as Tony repeats in Italian, but he looks confused as though he misunderstands.

"Mamma Mia, signora, what do you mean? You must be joking. You owe me many more euros. You must pay me two thousand and five hundred euros, minus the thirty euros you give me for the Madonna," he demands, handing me back the thirty euros and extending his other hand for the twenty-five hundred euros.

Tony and Nino look at me with raised eyebrows.

"Stefania, stop trying to be funny. Give the man his two thousand, five hundred euros. You gave him only thirty euros. And we must hurry if we are driving to this bloody Bisacquino and Corleone. Ah, but if you want to stand here and play with this man, we don't go."

"What? Are you kidding me? His son told me—no, he wrote down— twenty-five—on paper. Twenty-five euros. You must be joking. I'm not paying two thousand, five hundred euros for a Madonna like this," I say feverishly. Nino immediately hands the bubble-wrapped Madonna back to Valentino as though it were piping hot right out of the oven.

Leaning over to my ear, Tony says in English, "Get to the bus *now*! Get everyone to the bus."

"Che cosa, what?" Papa asks, looking toward me with black, dilating eyes as his son Valentino shuffles his leather shoes in the grass while holding the large bundle of bubble wrap.

"Mamma Mia, Madonna," Tony says again with his eyes bulging out like a cartoon character caught with his hand in the cookie jar.

"Unbelievable, the things you do, Stefania. Do you know the papa spent hours getting enough bubble wrap, plus taping and packaging the Madonna up for you? Did you really think the old Madonna was just twenty-five euros? Mamma Mia, Stefania. You know the things we have in Sicily are not as those in America. We have genuine antiques here. You are paying for the antiquity, do you understand?" We hurriedly walk to the bus with empty arms, except for Nino, who is carrying the empty luggage that was too small.

"Si, si, yes, I understand, but that Madonna is not a twenty-five-hundred-euro piece," I say, defending myself.

"Stefanie. I can't believe what just happened back there," Gail Wilson says, laughing uncontrollably while holding her chandelier as though it's a newborn bambino on the bus.

"This is just too much. My jaws are hurting from laughing so much," Dee Tullis spills out, not knowing why she's laughing.

"What the heck just happened back there?" Dee asks Gail, who is laughing too hard to respond.

"What in the world did you do for us to make such a sudden haste to the bus?" Dee asks again, hoping Gail will stop laughing long enough to answer her question.

Dr. Isaac, shaking his head with a big grin on his handsome face, looks at Tony and releases a mantra of Mamma Mias before sounding off a roar of laughter as well. Rose Jobe and Rose Ann are still trying to regain their composure and heart rates from the sudden alarm of me shouting, "Andiamo, let's go, *hurry… Run* to the bus—it's an emergency."

"Mamma Mia, Stefania, this is unbelievable. The things you do; the way you dance through this life is not normal for us here in Italy," Tony blurts out as Nino peels out like a speeding bullet, leaving the papa and son holding the huge bundle of a ball securely bubble-wrapped with the beautiful Madonna painting still hidden inside.

"Ah, yes, Stefania, answer me this one question. What do you mean someone shot at you? Valentino said the shot came from a car backfiring in the alleyway," Tony inquires with a huge grin stretching the span of his Sicilian face.

"Mamma Mia," shouts Rose Ann from the back of the bus, laughing hysterically while mumbling to everyone, "Mamma Mia, this is just too much."

"Stefania, we never go back there again. Absolutely not! No, we cannot ever go back. You cannot do such as this to Sicilians. We are in Sicily. Mamma Mia, the things you get me into are unbelievable," Tony says. He switches back and forth from English to Italian, trying to make Nino understand why I wouldn't give the euros for the Madonna.

Hours later, after the laughing slows down, I tell Tony, "Oh, on our next trip when in Sicily, I want to get one of those huge marionettes. I want the one that was hanging in their old building. I should have gotten it, but I forgot about it after the ordeal on the motorcycle. Anyway, I hope it will be there when we come back."

Tony says nothing, but throws his arms up in the air and takes a deep breath. Nino looks at me with a huge smile and says, "Mamma Mia, Stefania."

I ease back in my seat while contemplating my next trip there.

23

"Couvent Royal Saint Maximin La Sainte-Baume"

Italy to Provence—France

Spending more than a week in the regions of Tuscany and Umbria, zooming up and down the hilltop villages and going to fairy-tale places, has been beyond magical. We bask in the lifetime memories of what we've seen and experienced; thankfully this amazing adventure is nowhere close to being over.

After a magical week in Italy visiting nestled, fairy-tale storybooks they call villages, eating and dancing with a genuine count at La Certosa *ristorante* with our dear friend and owner, Count Salvatore—the famous owner of I' Falciani, and adventuring through an old monastery that's been restricted from outsiders since the beginning of monks, tasting the harvest of the grapes that have been crushed and fermented in old wooden barrels, riding in our very own boat out in the gorgeous Mediterranean, seeing things that can't be explained in mere words, and looking upon mouth-dropping creations that existed before Christ are just a few of the magnificent things we've done. And oh how we laughed as we rode the curves in Tuscany, stopped on impulse at the family vineyards, and ate the swollen lumps of dough that were pressed and stretched to sizable perfection and then doused with an abundance of the extra-virgin, liquid gold before sliding into the old Tuscan ovens.

"Excuse me, Stephani, can I say a few words to everyone?" Betty asks, walking toward the front of the coach as her fingers twist a long strand of blond hair that sprouted miraculously overnight. Just yesterday she sported a short, velvety red neckline hairdo. Now she has more blond hair than the whole group put together, thanks to her colorful wig collection.

As Betty turns to face the people, she reaches for the elastic band of her yellow pants and gives them a hard yank to hike them up, way too far above her swollen ankles. "I'd like to say a few words and share my memories from this past week," Betty nervously says, clicking her white tennis shoes together as though she is trying to get back to Kansas—off the yellow brick road.

"This past week of memory-making has been much, too much. There is no way to choose which memories are my favorites. Every hilltop village is spectacularly wonderful, all having their own personalities. And the people who live within the hilltop walls are likened to the storybooks from my childhood. We know how the Italians cook and prepare the pasta now. We know the perfection and care they take to roll the pasta by hand, thanks to the signora's rattling instructions to us at the same time with the wave of orchestrated arms. I loved the magic show before us when they switched to another bowl, mixing and plowing the dough, all the while saying how easily the dough submits when smashed back down, flipping it back before tossing a cotton cloth over it ... and then leaving it to rise and swell as the magic show continues on to another heap of pure delight, a towering bowl of squash blossoms waiting for their performance."

"Thank you, Betty. Yes, you have a lifetime of memories that will replay throughout your mind forever. And remember, we have another week to go," I say as Jerry from California reaches for the microphone and insists Betty, along with her abundance of hair, scoot out of his way.

"Well, now, I am a master gardener and Louise, my wife of twenty-three years, retired from the local florist shop. We love flowers and the floral beauty here in Italy. Well, it's definitely beyond words to describe. I retired from my lifelong career as an architect, designing bridges and things for the great state of California. I've always wanted to visit Italy. I heard about Stephani's tours from a client designing a garden wedding in Beverly Hills. In fact, she flies to East Texas to buy from Decorate Ornate. She says Stephani finds the best architectural pieces and the most beautiful castle doors for her celebrity clients," Jerry rambles, nervously yanking the fabric of his jeans as if his reproductive organs were shouting loudly, "SOS"—the international Morse code distress signal.

"Well, let me say, the churches we've seen this week are spellbinding. The beautiful, fresh flowers that fill the nostrils with divine smells of a glorious spring day—the bountiful bundles of roses, lilacs, jasmine, all

171

mixed with a smidgen of something wonderful was intoxicating. The wooden benches, worn over thousands of years from bended knees, the robed priests and saints gazing down from their lofty perches high above, the hand-painted icons with red rubies and other precious stones highlighted by the glowing candles, the amazing sound from the heavenly organs piped from the gigantic walls, and the old wooden crosses with Jesus nailed to them, all gives us a tingle of reality of the pain he suffered for all of us. This is what I've seen in the old Toscana country churches pure magnificence. A region of Italy that is a zillion times beyond my comprehension. I will never forget this tour, and yes, if God's willing, Louise and I will be back with you again, Stephani, Tony, and Nino. Thank you so much for opening your hearts to us and making us part of your family," Jerry says, brushing his thick dark curls away from his blue designer glasses while flashing his teeth as though waiting for the cameras to click his photo.

The girls from Texarkana, Texas, are laughing hysterically toward the middle of the coach. I have no idea what they're laughing about, but laughter seems to follow us wherever we go.

We're on our way to France this very moment. We'll be spending a week in the Provence region of France and then on to the French Riviera, home to the rich and famous. The Italian music is playing softly in the coach this morning and the memories of this past week are continuing to replay through my mind as Nino drives us through this amazing country.

"Stefania, do you mind if I say a few words to everyone while we drive?" Barbara asks while reaching for the microphone.

"Please, yes." I turn myself around to face everyone seated on the coach.

"Well, I would like to say how amazing this trip has been and how blessed I am to be here with all of you. I can't believe we're already heading to France, the French Riviera. Oh, I'm so excited! I feel like this is a dream, a fairy-tale dream that I hope to never wake from."

"Mamma Mia, Stefania, this is very nice," Tony says. "Barbara is very nice, and I like her very much. She must come again with us. Yes, yes, she must come again." Tony reaches up to grab Barbara's face and give it a big squeeze.

Laughing at Tony's words and rubbing her squeezed face, Barbara continues. "I will never forget Tuscany, and I will return again with you, Stefania and Tony. I don't know where to start; the whole tour has been beyond my wildest dreams. Just a few days ago in the Tuscan hills of Italy, we tasted the harvest of the grapes, which still makes the saliva run wildly throughout my mouth. We ate like starved Americans, consuming the most delicious vegetables bursting with flavors. Ah, the freshly baked breads doused in the liquid-gold olive oil and the towering heaps of pasta sprinkled heavily with the mozzarella cheese were simply divine. It's a taste that perpetrates pure ecstasy within our mouths, causing one to immediately eat more and more until the next course is placed before you, which causes you again to plunge deep into the plate, licking the very essence of a mere drip or speckle of spaghetti sauce. We dived in deep, didn't we? And I'm already anticipating my next meal, which will be something wonderful, I'm sure. Probably French cuisine," Barbara finishes and hands the microphone back to me as she returns to her seat, leaving us in a state of hunger for another towering pile of pasta.

Passing a double-decker bus packed full, I think to myself how blessed we are to take smaller groups of Americans to Italy. We're nothing like the big "touristy" tour groups packed in like sardines, having to line up for miles down the road to use the toilets or eat lunch. Thankfully, we're nothing like the big commercial groups, prodding the Americans around from one point to another like a herd of goats. Anyone can hop aboard on such as those—you know, the big tour companies promising so much for so little when in reality, it's just the opposite. You pay for so much, but get so little.

"Excuse me, Stefania. Can I please say a word to everyone through your microphone?" Dr. Williams asks, standing right behind my seat in the narrow aisle.

"Oh, yes, of course you can," I say with great surprise by his gentle nudge on my shoulder, that causes me to reach for the microphone that's resting in its holder between Nino and me.

Handing the microphone to Dr. Williams brings a whirlwind of questions beaming from Tony's wide eyes, which are looking at me right now. Not being able to stay silent, Tony asks, "Mamma Mia, what is this, *Dottore?* Perhaps you can sing?"

173

With a slight nod and the microphone in hand, Dr. Williams stands in the aisle, facing the Americans with his mouth gapped open like a donkey flaring his teeth for a posed smile. He shuffles his blue tennis shoes around as though warming up for ballet and starts in a slow, stuttering voice.

"Stefania, if Nino were to take us to the airport right now, I could truly say I've been blessed beyond words and will relive this adventure over and over within my mind. I can't believe the places we've seen on this tour. I will relive this dream forever," he says, tears streaming from his eyes. He appears to be in pain, but he is just recalling his memories, I presume. We are left in suspension for a brief moment of silence. He starts back again with a series of deep breaths and a happy smile exposing the wide gap between his teeth. Scratching his polished egg of a head, sparsely rooted with Irish red strands, he takes one last skipping breath and starts with a nervous cough.

"Thank you for taking us to your friend's castle. The meal was superb, and the castle was more than a fairy tale. Thank you for taking us to the floating village and meeting Mamma, and eating in her wine cellar with the professor with the broken heart. And oh, partaking in the harvested grapes. Then afterward, sitting at the family table with so many courses piled high while hearing their stories of everyday life. Oh yes, joining the medieval festivals as though we're family and awaking to the chiming church bells with singing voices of monks and the saintly sisters was truly heavenly.

"Going to the medieval village of Arezzo on market day and finding so many treasures. Well, I don't know whether or not I should include that as a thank-you, but my dear sweetie pie sure had a heck of a time, and, well, the best part of that for me, was seeing the places where they filmed my favorite movie ... I can't seem to think of its name. Was it *Life Is Beautiful* or *It's a Beautiful Life?* Heck, I can't remember, but it's my favorite for sure. I will never forget the Cappuccin Crypt in Rome, Stefania. That was overwhelming for me to see as a doctor. I hope you all understand my curiosity of wanting to get a better look. Seeing more than four thousand bones of monks with the soil brought back from Jerusalem was worth all the trouble I caused. Well, I mean the trouble I caused you, Tony." Dr. Williams turns aside and flashes Tony a helpless puppy-dog smile as if he were truly an Irish setter, yearning for a massage atop his head.

"I didn't mean to cause such a commotion inside. I only wanted to get a better look at the bone structure of such people from the era of 1528 to ... what did it say, 1870? I never thought it was such a big deal, jumping over the rope, but then, I had no idea that Rome, the ancient eternal city, would have such modern equipment as red laser beams alerting the officials of going past the restraint.

"Oh well, I hope someday I can repay you for the many euros you passed under the little table to that burly nun. I assume her name is Maria, like all the rest of them. And I can't begin to explain my joy and excitement of being with all of you, Tony, Nino, Stefania, and my new Americana friends. Thank you from the bottom of my heart for such a magical adventure. And please, put my name at the top of the list for your next Italy tour. I would not miss out on this much fun for anything." Dr. Williams is emotional as he expands his chest with a deep breath of fresh air while wiping the wetness from his eyes before starting up again with more emotion building like a volcano.

"I would like to dedicate this tour to the love of my life, the one who gave me three children, Marty, Bobby, and dear Lori, all of whom have master's degrees from Baylor University. Oh Helen, I love you so much, darling. You are the wind that pushes me each day out the door. You are the voice that brings my ears to full attention. You are the one who cheers me on to keep going, working for the sake of the sick, laboring late hours, and giving my time on weekends. Helen, you are the one who keeps my covers pulled back as I slip underneath your favorite D. Porthault sheets, guaranteeing my comfort for a tireless morning. And ah, you are my tireless accountant, shifting accounts to here and there for the sake of someday retiring, perhaps here in Italy. Oh yes, I want to live here in Italy, close to Tony and his family, yes, I would like ..."

"Mamma Mia, Madonna, what's the matter with you, Dottore? You must be joking. Absolutely, you are joking," Tony spews in a fast adrenaline rush that jolts his body like a streak of lightning. "Mamma Mia, where did you find this one, Stefania?" Tony asks, rolling his bulging eyes up and down while his hands fly in the air. He's looking at Dr.

Williams, who hands me the microphone and beams with pride and joy as he skips back to his seat.

"Mamma Mia, Stefania, why does the dottore say such things? Does he think just because he wants to live in Italy he will find a piece of land and villa so easily? Absolutely not. He knows not where I live, does he, Stefania? Mamma Mia! I do not understand where you find these people."

Sitting a few seats behind me are my two dear cousins, sisters Judy Prestridge Smith and Jane Diane Prestridge Mullett. Judy lives in Texarkana, Texas, and Jane Diane lives in Austin, Texas. I'm contemplating on calling Judy to the front of the coach. I want her to tell everyone about her famous inventions. Being the spontaneous person that I am, I grab the microphone from my lap and ask with over-the-top Texas enthusiasm, "How many of you have heard of Wine-a-Rita or Wine Glace the delicious concoction in a box that can be mixed with wine or juice in a blender?"

Motioning for her to come forward, I stretch the microphone to Judy, the famous mixologist who now faces everyone while holding a box of Wine-a-Rita. On the seat's edge, spine straight up as a wood ruler, she is posed like a news reporter ready to give an update on her latest breaking news, which happens to be her fabulous Wine-a-Rita. Before she speaks, everyone starts speaking.

"You are the one that invented the Wine-a-Rita? Wow, I can't believe it. I love every flavor of Wine-a-Rita. Oh my, it's absolutely delicious. This is unbelievable, Judy. What a great product you invented. I've got to call my sister and tell her the creator of Wine-a-Rita is on board with us. I buy all of my girlfriends Wine-a-Rita every year for their birthdays and Christmas, and we love it for our friends' gatherings," say the various American accents, ricocheting throughout the coach, while Judy sits with the microphone in hand, ready to give her news update.

We have laughed, talked, listened, sung Italian songs, and made stops throughout our adventurous drive, and now we're arriving in a place that is special and unique, a place that belongs in the storybooks from long ago. A place where white-robed monks stroll the corridors and sleep in tiny cells, praying to God while singing praises of worship. We're now in Provence, the beautiful region of France.

Nino turns the corner, driving the coach through the narrow entrance of the Basilica of Saint Maximin La Sainte-Baume, and all at once we "ooh" and "aah" at the magnificence of what's standing before us. It looks like something out of a dream, an old fairy-tale dream of stupendous castles and Gothic gargoyles flapping their wings to ward off the evil spirits. We get out and stand in awe, speechless and overwhelmed by the majesty of something so old.

Breaking the silence, I hear Mary Louise say, "I can't believe we're here, standing in front of this piece of history. Right here in Provence, the region of lavender. I never thought I'd be in France, but here I am."

We click our cameras, and before we take the next step toward the entrance, we are greeted by a 'look-alike' of Julia Childs, along with the same Julia Childs voice.

"Mamma Mia, it's Julia Childs, right here in the flesh," I say, feeling the urge to greet her in French, which I do. "*Bonjour*, Julia."

"Mamma Mia, Stefania. Shall we all speak in French now?" Tony asks with a surprised look on his face, and then says, "Why do you call her Julia, Stefania? Her name is not Julia."

"I know, but she looks and talks just like Julia. You know, Julia Childs?"

"I do not know who this Julia or Childs is," Tony says, wondering what I will come up with next while looking at his highly paid professor with condolences of me calling her a name he has never heard of until now.

Calling her Julia was a big mistake because she immediately switches to her French tongue, rattling on and on, leaving me discombobulated because of my limited French. I feel stupid, but feel thankful to Tony, who springs to my rescue and replies in fluent French dialect.

"This must be Julia Childs. She looks like her, she talks like her, and she dresses like her," Mary Rogers says with her New York accent, while clenching her designer leather purse tighter.

"Yes, I agree. She must be Julia, or perhaps her twin. You know what they say about everyone; we all have a twin. However, this Julia is a scholarly professor chosen by Tony from the Louve in Paris. Isn't that right, Tony?"

Clapping her hands together as though we are schoolchildren, Julia says to us in difficult to understand English, "Welcome to France. You've arrived at a place so special and so spectacularly unbelievable. Just around the corner adjacent to this monastery and down in the grotto, rests a saint."

"Ah, let me explain," Julia says as we lean closer to her, trying to understand her Julia Childs's accent. "In the antiquity manuscripts, there is a list of passengers who set out for Marseilles, France, to escape the horrible danger that existed after Jesus was crucified. By boat, Joseph, with many disciples on board, traveled from the Holy Land and landed at Marseilles, France, a Phoenician trading post in the year 35 AD. The manuscripts say that Joseph went on to England to establish seminaries and send out missionaries preaching and teaching the gospel of Jesus Christ. It goes on to say that at sea in a vessel without sails or oars, the boat drifted and arrived in Marseilles, and they were saved from the terrifying waters. From Marseilles, France, it is known in the scripts that Joseph and others passed into Britain. Afterward, while preaching the gospel there, he died." Julia takes a quick breath and then continues.

"Ah, but do you know that Cardinal Baroniu, Curator of the Vatican library, gives this account? But let me explain for you to understand. You are Americans and I know you know very little of this history. I must start from the beginning with you. Shall we start from the beginning, as in with Mary and Joseph?"

"Pardon me Julia, but no, we are all very intelligent people and as Americans, we know the Bible. We most certainly know about Mary and Joseph and the birth of Jesus Christ," I say, spreading my fingers out in a fan across my breastbone, shocked and embarrassed for my wonderful group of Americans.

"Ah! Do you really know about Mary and Joseph in the Bible?" Julia asks us, slapping her hands against her pale face, disregarding what I just said. "Well, then, I will proceed very slowly for you," Julia says with a slight roll of her eyes, tightening her fingers around a beautiful leather-bound book as though she will explode.

"As I said, they were exposed to the rough sea in an old wooden vessel without sails or oars. Miraculously, the wind-beaten vessel drifted to Marseilles, and they were saved from the raging sea. Now the question you must have: How many of the disciples were with Joseph of Arimathea during his short stay before going on to Britain? That is hard to say. Now listen to me carefully, because various existing records agree in part with the Cardinal Baronius' record, naming among the occupants of the castaway boat:

Mary Magdalene, Martha the handmaiden, Marcella, Lazarus whom Jesus raised from the dead, and Maximin, the man whose sight Jesus restored. And other records state that Philip and James accompanied Joseph. Others do report that Mary the wife of Cleopas, and Mary the mother of Jesus, were also in the boat. Shall I tell you Cardinal Baronius' complete list of passengers? Yes, of course." Julia answers her own question while we stare with raised eyebrows and growling stomachs.

"*Scusi,* madame, that will not be necessary. Not today. *Merci beaucoup,* thank you very much," Tony says in perfect French.

"The Americans are very hungry for they have not eaten in the last hour or so. And Madame, thank you very much, but this is too much to hear," declares Tony, hoping to escape her explanations until tomorrow.

"Ah, yes, but they must hear them now," protests Julia, as she continues rolling out their names in broken English before Tony could object: "St. Mary, wife of Cleopas; St. Maximin, the blind man; St. Sidonius—Restitutus; St. Joseph of Arimathea; St. Mary Magdalene—yes, Mary Magdalene from the Bible; St. Martha; and St. Lazarus."

"Madame. Basta, enough—stop," objects Tony in a raised voice, but Julia Childs hears nothing.

"The records state that James and Mary the mother of Jesus, were also in the boat. Many ships came with refugees from Egypt. On record, it says that Mary Magdalene, along with Mother Mary and her two daughters, landed there along with Joseph of Arimathea and Jesus' brother James," Julia spills out in a speedy rush as Tony throws his hands up with a roll of his eyes.

"Mamma Mia, this is too much, Madame. We cannot hear all of this right now. No, absolutely not," Tony says with great exasperation dancing on his face.

Julia stomps her feet in a dancing shuffle. Within seconds, she proceeds on as though Tony were invisible.

"Yes, right here, where you are right now, just around the corner, are some of the 'saints' I just mentioned. They are in the sarcophagus near the reliquary of Mary Magdalene in the basilica. For safety reasons, we do know from the scripts there were many who left the Holy Lands via Egypt after Jesus was crucified. Yes, it is known that the women in particular traveled and stayed in the South of France then known as Gaul. They were still in danger and had to go about their mission of spreading the teachings quietly and almost secretly. Ah yes, do you know that Joseph of Arimathea traveled with others to his familiar territory in the Britannic Isles and began his teaching there? He went on to establish the first Christian Church at Glastonbury. It was not so dangerous there even though it was still part of the ancient Roman Empire."

"Mamma Mia, Madame. Enough, basta, stop," shouts Tony, and then looking at me says, "Stefania, andiamo. Let's go! We must go to our rooms, settle in, and relax before the big dinner tonight. Mamma Mia, this French Madame is talking in excess. You just met her and she gives you a whole day of teachings. Baugh, baugh," spouts Tony with a slight grin stretching his Rodney Dangerfield face. He walks over to Julia, pats her on the back and speaks in perfect French.

Thanks to Tony we're staying here, right here in this towering old monastery straight from the Bible days. Tomorrow we'll visit the convent just around the corner.

"Mary Magdalene's tomb is just around the corner, side by side, right here," I say to everyone. "And Julia said the convent was founded in 1295 by Charles II of Anjou, the king of Sicily and Count of Provence to house the relics of Mary Magdalene, whose tomb had been discovered here in 1279," I say while everyone joins in with his or her own thoughts.

"Mary Magdalene is down in the grotto just next door, and from what I've heard, many have experienced a divine presence here. The very presence of Mary Magdalene," Dr. Williams informs his wife while clicking his camera at every angle.

Stopping in awe again, we stand in front of this Gothic convent. It's absolutely incredible and so old. It was entrusted to the order of the Dominicans until 1959. The basilica and the royal convent are indeed the most beautiful Gothic edifice in the southeast of France. It says so right here in front of us, and I must totally agree.

"Wow, can you believe we'll be here for the next four nights? Right here in St. Maximin, among sixty-seven rooms spread out and up over several stories tall. This was the home of the Dominican fathers," Dr.

Williams says to his wife, who looks as though she's seen a ghost and clings tightly to his brown polyester brown shirt.

Words cannot describe the monastery we're in right now. The Couvent Royal Saint-Maximin La Sainte-Baume is hauntingly fabulous. The niches and entrances dart off in so many directions as we follow the French porter up the winding stairs. My eyes widen and my heart explodes with awe. I feel as though the monks will appear any minute, strolling down the long corridors.

Opening my door, I'm awestruck by the old stone walls and the little shuttered windows. I drop my backpack loaded with my laptop on the blue plaid bedspread and rush to unlatch the shutters. Pushing the shutters outward, I stretch over the balcony window and stare in awe again. I see old ceramic roof tiles and a parade of singing pigeons just a few feet below. Surrounding me are shuttered windows in a horseshoe curve. The presence all around me is a brush of angel wings. I feel a loving presence hovering all around and think, *If only angelic music were playing, this could be heaven.*

Right after that thought zaps through my mind, I jump, startled with the thought coming true. I lean over the balcony and stretch my neck out as far as possible without plunging down below. I look up and down at the balconies above and below me, and then I look to the left and right. I see nothing, but angelic music is playing. I'm hoping to see some of the shutters swing open to verify that I'm not dead and already in heaven. How could this be? Where is the music coming from? I turn around to look around in my little room to make sure I'm not dreaming, and then turn back toward the balcony and shout out, "Hello, Hello!" No one responds, and the music keeps playing softly. I stand in utter amazement at the view before me. I watch the closed shutters, hoping someone will swing them open, but they don't. I only see flapping pigeons on the ceramic tiles that appear angelic as well. I hear violins, harps, and chimes, beautifully sounding all around me.

Turning around from the window again, I see nothing but my little storybook bed and backpack. *This is the perfect place to write*, I think, pulling out my laptop and setting it on the ledge of the balcony. Looking around, I see a little chair that must have belonged to the monk of this room. Immediately I start typing, looking out over this musical paradise, expecting to see angels all around.

When I look out my balcony window, I sense God's holy presence. I want to stay here longer. I want to stay inside this room, this cell, and write more chapters in my book. I want to meditate on God and thank him for his loving mercy. I want to stay perched right here, looking out my window with my laptop resting on the windowsill. I want to watch the pigeons resting on the old ceramic roof tiles and toss them some French bread, and I want to listen to the angelic music playing softly down below.

I know from the beginning this place was entrusted to the order of the Dominican monks. Looking up, I see worn gargoyles to the left of my balcony window. There are four stories of white and gray blocks of large stones, similar to columns, but no, they're not columns. They remind me of tall houses, each one adorned with a rooftop, and the front guarded with worn gargoyles. This place is amazing, so celestial, and the music plays on until the bells ring out "ding-dong, ding-dong," interrupting the saintly music for a few moments, to alert everyone that it's time for dinner. The feeling here is surreal, a dream, a fairy tale from long ago, and walking down the stairs to dinner is enchanting. I see and understand why this place is tagged "The finest gothic building in the South East of France, built to house the relics of Mary Magdalene." No wonder her spirit smiles upon this place. It's a wonderment of serenity and heavenly beauty.

Walking out into the "groin vaulted" veranda, I turn to the left, stepping inside the cloister under the cross vaults. Before reaching the dining area, I pass a sign with an arrow saying "Grotto" pointing down a stairway leading into darkness. Knowing I have time to detour for a second, I step back, dart to the right, and take the stone stairs to a world below. To a grotto that no doubt will bring shivers to my body and a sudden brush of angel wings across my heart.

The next morning, the Americans say that staying here brings out strong emotions and a certain feeling of being in the presence of God. "We feel the holiness of awe lingering down the hallways," they say in a whispering voice as though they are in church. "We can visualize the monks chanting and singing praises to God. We feel as though we're in the biblical days and some of the patriarchs such as Father Abraham, Isaac, and Jacob are just around the corner."

The following week here in Provence is magnificent. We hop aboard our coach and experience the magnificence of Provence, along with 'Julia Child' in tow. We purchase the lavender soaps and explore amazing places. We go to the countryside vineyards and partake of the many local wines. We dine with pleasure the exquisite, abundance of French foods. Every single day in Provence is magically fabulous. The memories we make will last a lifetime.

One in particular will be the day we drove to an enchanting village perched high over the blue waters overlooking the French Riviera. Oh, how we loved the dollhouse village of Eze. The medieval village is entirely pedestrian; there are no cars at all. Walking into this storybook setting immediately brings fairy tales to reality. The narrow cobbled streets are accentuated by several enticing small town squares. The stone paths and arched passages are beautiful. And around every corner we saw the stone-built houses, resembling caves dug in the rock. Our eyes bounced from surprise to disbelief. Every step we made was overwhelmingly magnificent. The whole village of Eze is like a magical stage, a set for the make-believe actors to fall into motion. We were enchanted by the wood-carved doors and the fabled houses teasing us to come inside. We clicked our cameras until the batteries ran out and lingered inside the little doll-sized shops, wishing we could load everything in the coach and bring it back to the states.

Afterward, Nino drove the coach higher, climbing to the castle ruins and arriving at the Fragonard perfumery laboratory. The small village of Eze has two perfumeries: Fragonard and Galimard. Fragonard and Galimard are the manufactures of ingredients for the world-famous perfume house names. We went to the factory on the Moyenne Corniche between Monaco and Nice. Upon arrival, we flew into the Fragonard perfumery laboratory and watched the amazing production process. We saw baskets full of harvested lavender, sunflowers, and the list goes on and on. Fragonard is where I purchase my favorite perfume every time I return to France. It takes only one tiny drop and it will last for days.

We held on tightly as Nino rounded the curves, bringing us up into the luxury of royalty. We stepped out into another storybook setting,

Monaco, which happens to be 0.8 square miles. The first time I went to Provence, I was amazed at the size of Monaco, which is pretty much the same size as Central Park in New York City and is the smallest state in the world after Vatican City. Monaco is truly amazing, nestled high on the gorgeous blue Mediterranean Sea and surrounded by France on three sides as though a royal wedding cake. Monaco lures people from all over the world, entrancing them to taste the seducing flavors of its royal pedigree.

Monaco has a perpetual calling for the rich and famous and is a playground welcoming beautiful people. Even Hollywood legend Alfred Hitchcock chose Monaco as the location for his 1955 movie *To Catch a Thief* starring Cary Grant and Grace Kelly. Since Monaco loves beautiful people, a year later on April 18, 1956, Monaco's Prince Rainier III married Grace Kelly in a blissful fairy-tale wedding that brought the world's attention to the royal setting. The fairy-tale couple ceremoniously danced atop the wedding cake for more than twenty-five years until the death of Princess Grace in 1982.

After saying our farewells to the royal elite in Monaco as well as Monte Carlo and Nice, we jetted off to the playgrounds of Aix en Provence, shopping the lavender-filled shops and buying too many aristocratic, feathered-netted hats. Afterward, we drove through the vineyards and found ourselves devouring the French cuisine along with sipping and slurping the liquid reds at Chateau Grand Boise. While everyone was floating inside with the liquid reds, I slipped away and walked toward the huge iron gate. Once inside the lavender fields, I stood still, allowing my nose to fill with the aromas. Seconds later, looking toward the towering villa, my legs magnetized to the unknown thrills within. Suddenly, without thought, I drifted toward the old villa and waved to several men who were sitting underneath tall trees, sipping the liquid red from glass goblets.

"Shall I go inside?" I shouted to them, but they understood no English. "Va bene. Okay," I said to them, forgetting I was in France, not Italy. Within seconds, I was inside the old villa, completely blown away. I remember seeing the country French entrance: a creamy white with yellowish undertones and many beautiful things. I visualized parties spilling out into the gardens adjoining the picturesque property. I could see elegant parties with dancing for 100 and a cadre of elegantly dressed French men and women dining around the long wooden table. Somewhere among the guests, I imagined ornately dressed servers stepping out of history in their beautiful suits and bow ties.

Afterward, in the afternoon, we rode the whimsical, toylike train to another breathtaking Mediterranean town nestled with rainbow-colored shops and bobbing boats. We were at the seaside town of Cassie in southern France. Greeted by the miniature train awaiting our arrival, we jumped off the coach. "Wow, another fairy-tale storybook comes alive," someone said. And yes, it was very much alive.

24

THE FLOATING VILLAGE—
CIVITA DI BAGNOREGIO

On a foggy morning, it's a village magically suspended in air above the mountains. It appears floating—risen from the grave, soaring high into the heavens. You could say it has overcome, for now, death and the grave. Life is very much alive upon its rocks even though it's been close to death many times. "The Dying City" is how Italians refer to it now, although it's very much alive. There is only one entrance, unless you drop from the sky. We walk the mysterious bridge that takes us over the majestic mountains, clicking our cameras while oohing and aahing.

This particular village is truly enchanting; a hidden treasure from way before Christ's time. Of all the villages in Tuscany and Umbria, this is the most mouth-dropping village that exists as it has from the beginning of time, except for a few shifts and turns of the earth below.

My granddaddy spoke of this place long ago. He said, "Someday you will see this place, I'm sure. You will fall into the story, at least a chapter or two, and the pages will turn swiftly, evaporating right before your eyes. You are my shadow, the adventurer. You will metamorphose when the time comes, I'm sure of it." Strangely, I remember those words spoken to me kind of like a hazy dream. There is power in the words you speak in someone's life. There is power in your mouth—for good or for bad— according to God's Word.

In late September 2000, I went to Civita di Bagnoregio, Italy, taking twelve Americans who had signed up for the "Decorate Ornate's Italy Adventures." Fourteen years later, I'm still taking the Americans to visit this mouth-dropping village once a year and sometimes twice a year. There are no words to describe this place. It transfers you back thousands of years just like a movie set, and the locals still live the same as they did generations back. The magnificence of looking upon this village perched on top of a mountainous hilltop with an altitude of 1440 feet above sea level is truly the most spectacular wonderment these American eyes can ever see here in Tuscany.

Civita di Bagnoregio is truly a world wonder. The only way to reach it is by the narrow sliver of concrete that's suspended over the wide crater. It seems to go forever, endlessly leading you to a fairy-tale world. When walking the bridge, the wind always seems to blow, giving us the feeling of riding a ship over high seas even though sharp dips and peaks of golden-brown meringue whip below rather than waves.

As soon as our feet touch the bridge, something magically happens within our bodies. It's sort of like a power surge zaps inside, intoxicating us to act like wild children. The force pulls us up the bridge like a magnet, causing our legs to go forward as though a wild tiger is at our heels.

Reaching the top, we enter like a proud army ready to celebrate our great victory with a greater exploration. We run and scatter into this new world where sarcophaguses sleep in the tunneled necropolis, deeply rooted in the tufa stone. The ancient corridor is down below, running north to south and crossing the entire village. Maria, a local resident, shared one day that it is used as an access road for farmers and donkeys. And speaking of donkeys, those precious little guys are indispensable to the locals. They are in the donkey races in front of the church square twice a year, but the farmers use them for many things, such as riding to the fields loaded down with equipment, among the cliffs, and across the sand hills.

Civita and Bagnoregio used to be two neighboring villages connected by the mountainous landscape with the Convent of San Francesco and other buildings between them, but that's history now.

When I talked to the granddaughter of one of the locals a few years back, she shared her love and passion for this amazing village and asked me to bring the Americans. I will never forget her thoughts as she poured them out to me while sitting in her nonna's cool cellar surrounded by huge barrels of the liquid red that rested peacefully, slowly aging along with the big round reels of cheese that were deep in the earth.

Leaning against a dusty barrel while motioning for me to sit in the chair next to her, she began her story.

"As the Roman Empire slowly crumbled, the repercussions flowed out to us here in Bagnoregio, Civita's neighboring sister. As the empire collapsed, neglect of the drainage tanks started the destruction as the clay became a soaked sponge. On top of the neglect, the trees surrounding the area were cut down for marketing, removing the deep-rooted support of the mountainous terrain, and the erosion started a catastrophic nightmare of landslides. Little by little the soil disappeared, and then entire neighborhoods dropped into the earth, which totally swallowed them up until nothing was left. As a result, Bagnoregio and Civita are now separated by this huge crater, connected only by the narrow concrete bridge. I visualize the bridge as a *cordone ombelicale*—umbilical cord—a bridge of life to a medieval village suspended in the air. And without this lifeline, Civita will surely die."

"Oh, Stefania, visualize how they were once a single city joined only by neighborhoods but with the neglect, the mudslides, and the earthquakes, there is now this huge crater separating the two. This is where the concrete bridge of life to Civita starts. Do you understand?" she asks, her deep topaz eyes willing me to comprehend.

"Yes, I understand so much more now. I understand how the church and most of Bagnoregio, sitting in the middle of the two, collapsed and fell down," I say, visualizing how it once looked.

"Yes, Stefania, and before all of this, there was no need for a bridge, but that goes back hundreds of years. And of course when Hitler invaded Italy, the Nazis blew the masonry bridge to pieces with explosives in 1944—which was the last remaining connection between Civita and the rest of the town. More landslides occurred in the year of 1964, causing a newly rebuilt bridge to collapse," she said with a lot of passion.

Arriving in our new Mercedes-Benz coach with Nino at the wheel, I tell the Americans, "Yes, here we are. This is Bagnoregio, so have a fabulous time on your own. Shall we get out and explore?"

"What? This is Bagnoregio?" the Americans shout at me.

"Where is the beautiful mountaintop village you described to us?" they ask, stretching their necks in every direction.

"Ah, let your imagination run wild. Can't you see the mountaintop village?" I joke as a broken-down, old bus wobbles around the corner, coming to a sudden stop right in front of us.

"Andiamo, let's go," I shout while jumping on the bus, waving them on. "Bagnoregio is just around the corner, completely hidden from our view. And don't forget your cameras; you will need them for sure."

Civita is the village we're going to visit, but I usually say Bagnoregio or Bangladesh with a huge smile.

Bumping along in the rickety, old bus while holding tightly to the rope dangling from the ceiling, we zoom around a few narrow streets and finally incline just a tad before coming to a complete stop. Bouncing off the raggedy bus, the Americans look up, not believing their eyes. The view before them is totally a fairy tale. More than a fairy tale, if that's possible. It's surreal and beyond comprehension.

"This has to be a figment of my imagination. Where is the transportation to take us up there? Is there a ski lift somewhere?" Mattie Murphy from New York City asks.

"No, you will not find a ski lift here, my dear. And it really is suspended in the air," I respond.

A young boy riding a blue Vespa zooms near us at a blazing speed and slowly fades away. "Now that's how I want to ride," Mattie jokes and then declares, "Ah, a donkey will do, but where are they?"

"Mattie, the Vespa has nearly replaced the little donkey. The *Vespa* can do a lot of the same work as the donkey … such as transporting the residents' groceries and necessities up the long sliver of ribbon. But sadly they still use the little donkeys. I saw a donkey loaded with large concrete blocks in Amalfi. And yes, I see them in Greece too. I think it's terrible to treat them so cruelly," I ramble on with my eyes on the prize—Civita.

"I can't believe my eyes. A city suspended in the air … but how can a human being build something like this? I've traveled all over the world, but this really takes the cake." Mattie clicks her camera while asking many questions before I have time to answer even one.

Running toward the long bridge like little children is always the first reaction, but right before they start the walk I shout, "Let's get a photo of our group." But being too excited to stop, most of them keep going except for a few. Sandra Crow, who resembles a whimsical animated doll, excitedly explains to Tony why she is trying to decide whether to stay with him for a nice towering scoop of gelato or ascend the bridge with everyone else.

"Ah, come on, Sandra, we'll walk slowly with you," promises Shawn Young, from Rockwall, Texas. He and his wife, Holly, grab Sandra by each arm, leading her toward the bridge.

Walking up the deceptively steep bridge is not as difficult as it looks, though it looks like something right out of a misty dream. The rocky concrete bridge starts out on ground level and within a few steps the earth underneath totally disappears.

Trekking up the pathway suspended over the wide crater is absolutely an "out-of-body" experience. Everyone starts out walking and then stops every few minutes to take photos before reaching the top. At times, we see little donkeys loaded down with baskets of grapes and vegetables, making the upward journey along with scooters zooming past. However, the transportation is mostly legwork. There are no cars or trucks allowed on the narrow sliver of ribbon bridge.

Sandra is already stopping to lean over the bridge, telling Shaun and Holly to go ahead, that she will be fine. Steps behind her, Connie and Duane Robinson from Huntsville, Texas ask, "Isn't this amazing, Sandra? Just wait until you reach the village."

Walking through the arched-stone entrance is almost supernatural. The feeling is overwhelmingly magical, not believing what's appearing before your eyes. I'm sure this is a similar feeling to walking on the moon for the first time.

Entering the village, we pass through an Etruscan arch created more than 2,500 years ago. To the left are ancient Etruscan chamber tombs being reused as tool sheds. To my surprise, before making it through the entire arched entrance, I am greeted by a young lady standing at the doorway of a newly opened gift shop. This very cave was previously used for the little donkeys. I remember walking toward the back wall and seeing the water trough where the donkeys quenched their thirst. Today, I'm excited to see this rare treasure chest emerging from its deep sleep. *It was built 500 years before Christ*, I think to myself and wish I could bring every American to see this wonderment.

The whole village is surrounded by open air. In other words, if you walk straight to the back, passing the church and many cavelike houses, Mamma's stone house will be on the left with her wine cellar toward the back. Straight ahead, you will pass an iron balcony overhead that usually explodes with gorgeous flowers. Unknowing to the visitor, they have bypassed Etruscan caves used as stables, a fascinating chapel that was carved into the stone with a little ceramic tile depicting the Madonna and child, and so much more. The main stone path coils to the left and then winds downhill with a surprising view that will take your breath away—a view that overlooks a planet Mars-like movie. Absolutely incredible! After one surely takes a hundred photos, the pathway that has now turned to dirt leads to another world—an Etruscan world of amazing tunnels.

The artifacts found in the territory of Bagnoregio date back to the Stone Age and the first recorded traces of human existence belong to the Etruscan people, who were here before the Romans. Studying the Etruscans, seeing their tombs throughout Italy, I know their customs consisted of digging caves around their villages so the burial of the dead could be close to them. And not only close; they wanted their deceased loved ones to be very visible as a perpetual reminder. That's not uncommon at all in Italy. The dead are everywhere. They are in tombs, glass caskets, standing up, hanging around, and so forth. The Etruscan Acropolis is within feet of the tunnels, the caves, and the burial tombs.

I discovered the cave tunnels years ago while showing the Americans where they keep the demijohns and cheese in the cellar. And now, stepping into the tufa stone cellar, I see huge barrels of wine and garden tools hanging all around, along with a little table and chairs in the far corner. To the right, I see carved out steps descending into another room with wicker demijohns full of the liquid red, more barrels aging gracefully, and big reels of cheese. To the left, I see a carved crucifix on the tufa stone over the arched, carved-out entrance leading down to another dark tunnel. I want to go down and see this cemetery for myself but just as I place my hands on each side of the tufa black stone, I hear the Americans hollering for me to come eat. The moisture from the deep tunnels makes the carved-out steps slippery and leaves a hint of black on my hands. Nonetheless, I brush my hands off, ridding them of the black moisture, and head out from the cellar.

Like always, we gather around the Tuscan tables with local friends, eating and drinking until we can't anymore. Afterward, we excitedly scatter again, running to the stone houses with beautiful geraniums smiling in bright red blooms that sit perfectly on each step. We all look like characters in a storybook, strolling around from one adventure to another.

Hanging my head over a fence to look at the mountains down below, I suddenly hear Diedra Camp from Gilmer, Texas, hollering, "Hurry to the square. There is a marching band dressed in medieval costume."

Needless to say, we flock to the square where the old church, St. Donato, stands. And yes, we are amazed again. The colorful band plays their musical instruments as though they were back in time, centuries ago. They are festooned in beautiful period costumes, appearing to be animated cartoon characters. Immediately I feel the storybook page has turned and is continued on to the next page of wonderment. We are standing here watching them play, awe struck at the scene before us.

Here in the square, it is said that the Church of St. Donato was built sometime in the seventh century on the site of a pre-existing pagan temple. Looking up at the church, I remember several years ago when this church had very little inside. The walls were dark and the Madonna stood lonely. It was sad to see the church in such despair.

I still remember Tony's haunting words as we were approaching Civita di Bagnoregio several years ago. "Stefania, I heard on Vatican radio this morning that they're sending people to Civita di Bagnoregio today to investigate the whereabouts of the old religious relics that were hidden in the underground tunnels as Hitler invaded Italy. They question whether or not the relics were returned to the area churches after the war."

Excitement rocked our coach that day as I repeated Tony's words through the microphone. And yes, just a few years ago on the day we arrived, the Vatican officials were inside, bringing out unbelievable relics. Somehow, perhaps looking back through the old archives, they discovered the order given in 1943 for all local churches to hurriedly take the relics to Civita di Bagnoregio and hide them down in the tunnels, protecting them from Hitler's invading army. Could all of the relics still be hidden in Civitad di Bagnoregio after all these years? That was the big question the Vatican officials were asking that very day we arrived.

On that day as we walked into the church, we saw men bringing out candelabras and a glass tomb with a beautiful young woman resting inside. Her dress and shoes reminded me of Juliet, as in *Romeo and Juliet*.

I remember many of us leaning over the glass reliquary/casket to see her better and how we gasped at the hole cut from her chest. Her heart had been taken out with the same sword that pierced through her body. She was a Christian martyr.

To repay the village for keeping the relics safely hidden for all of these years, the Vatican restored their church. Every year, sometimes twice a year, I witnessed the ongoing restoration of the church. I was there when they brought in many things. I watched them install, hang, and place many beautiful things in the church. My heart explodes with happiness for the locals to have their church so beautifully restored. There are now two saints resting peacefully in glass caskets toward the front of the church, one on the left and one on the right. It's amazing to see how magnificently decorated the church is compared to earlier.

After the band marches on, I lead some of the Americans to another friend's wine cellar. They drink from the large green demijohns filled with the liquid reds as though we've had nothing at all to drink. We peek at the large wheel of cheese silently aging in the cool cellar down below, and we talk with Maria, who is sitting in her garden beside her stone house.

I recently read that Maria is no longer around, perhaps deceased. It's not true, though. She is fine, doing as well as expected for her old age. Maria's family tells the few who visit Civita that she is not there, not around anymore, which is true in the months of late fall and winter. But now in late May, Maria sits in her garden right past her little stone house with her hand held open for a few coins.

A few years ago, I suggested to Maria that she offer her garden for a tour to the visitors in exchange for a few coins and she does. I've visited with Maria throughout the many years, threading her needles, bringing her little tree trunk chairs outside her stone house, uncorking a bottle or two for her pleasure, and the list goes on and on with so many wonderful memories.

Strolling around in this fairy tale, I see another surprise: a sign hanging on the entrance to the underground shop Antica Civitas leading to more Etruscan caves. This little white sign makes me giggle. It reads *Entrata*—Entrance—1,00 euro—Bambini Gratis—Free Children."

"Ah, you get free children here," I say with a smile. And to my surprise, I never knew this adorable cave of a shop was used as Geppetto's workshop in the 2008 film *Pinocchio*.

Jetting off to the right, I walk the cobbled street to get one last photo of the amazing cliff-hanging backyard that's tucked behind the main street of this enchanted storybook. Leaning over the ledge with my camera pressed to my eye, I hear the echoing voice of a woman with a perfect British accent. Looking to the left, I see an iron-fenced yard that's dangling over the soaring cliff with a female stretched over a man with curly, black curls who's holding a glass of the liquid red. They are oblivious of me. Her long, slinky body presses his back against the red damask pillow entwined to the iron lounger. His body covered in silky black fabric is Romeo-like. He appears, from what I can see through the camera lens as an Italian movie star with a blond beauty strapped romantically on top of him. I zoom the lens closer and see right down to her black roots of her bleached-blond hair. He kisses her softly and romantically. And with a deep exhale, this love scene skyrockets to the moon and back. They are completely out of control. Trying not to drop my camera or disturb their heated passion, I adjust my zoom lens. Within seconds of pressing the button, I hear Sandra Crow shouting. "Where is Stephani? She's got to see this marching band performing in medieval costume."

Sandra doesn't know that many of us have already seen the marching band, but hastening to her call, I go. Leading toward the piazza, the center of the village where the church stands proudly, we see the marching locals tooting horns and trombones honking out Italian tunes. It appears to be a dream—a page from Cinderella or Jack in the Beanstalk. *Oh how I wish to bring more of the Americans here*, I think again, knowing that too many Americans will never come to Italy because of fear and the unknown of being in a foreign country. And of course the obsession of saving the money.

"Yes, you save the money and give to Saint Peter when you arrive at paradise," Tony says to Ollie after hearing his wife beg for three euros to purchase a little book describing the church in Civita. Embarrassed, I presume, Ollie peeps skyward and sniffs the bubbly tomatoes that are surely steaming from the pots nearby while shoving both hands in his denim jeans. With a blinking red face and pretending not to hear Tony, Ollie jiggles inside his pockets and produces a handful of euros.

Next door, I notice Jim and Louise. They stop to buy fresh jams. Inside, the owner proudly shows off his huge olive press that is about 1,500 years old. He confides that not so long ago, in 1969 or so, blindfolded donkeys plodded in a circle to operate the press, crushing the olives. "This was an ancient factory where olive oil was produced," he says, pointing toward the stoned wall. "Those harnesses are donkey harnesses and the large round stone had blindfolded donkeys harnessed to it. After the donkeys labored, pulling the large stone, the crushed olives went to the next press—a finer olive oil press to produce the finest oil. Afterward, the treasured oil was stored in the underground caves."

"Maria still has her olive press in her cellar, just a few feet behind us," I say to him. We've eaten many meals in Maria's cellar, sipping the liquid red along with eating an abundance of bruschetta, the bread toasted on an open fire, drizzled with extra-virgin olive oil, rubbed with spicy garlic, and topped with chopped tomatoes. Ah, so delicious.

With the band gone and out of sight, we laugh and talk amongst ourselves and observe a lady carting a load of glossy aubergines, or some say *melanzana* (eggplants), as though they were bambinos. No sooner does she vanish around the corner we notice one of ours, than Frank from Burbank, California, is pulling a chair out for a beautiful Italian woman who appeared out of nowhere. Just a few minutes ago Frank was sitting with Tony, laughing and eating pasta. Now he's serenading this beautiful Italian with liquid-black eyes and seducing lips.

We watch from across the table as Frank bravely slides his arm around her slender bronzed shoulder. Impulsively, we lean toward them as though it would help to hear more clearly the words coming out of Frank's smooth-talking mouth.

"I love you. Do you understand?" Frank whispers in a boisterous tone.

"Mamma Mia," spews from Tony's mouth that's full of spicy pasta. "Mamma Mia," we hear again as he simultaneously coughs and starts choking on a heaping swirl of pasta that's now lodged somewhere in his throat. Immediately tossing down glasses of the liquid red, he regains his disposition and leans in toward Frank, hoping to hear more of his impromptu love affair that is taking place right before our very eyes.

Seconds later, Frank inches closer to her ears, whispering once again. We giggle like teenagers and lean forward, struggling to hear the words. Tony places both of his elbows on the little table and shuffles his weight forward in hopes of hearing more clearly. As the movie reels toward a romantic love affair, our little table suddenly collapses sending us all toward them. While trying to protect my expensive camera, I land sprawled on top of Frank with a hard hit. And like a trapeze act gone terribly wrong, Tony's stomach punches lady love right in the face as his arm soars through her shiny black wig, sending it flying through the air. We are one big conglomerate of tangled bodies. All of us discombobulated and speechless as we discover ladylove is in fact, a man. Mamma Mia ... I wish to bring more of the Americans to this place.

25

PARMA CHEESE IS IN NEAR SIGHT!

Driving through the Appennine Mountains to Parma, Italy, with Nino at the wheel has me talking on the microphone again. I'm preparing our group of twelve Americans for the big event of actually seeing the huge wheels of cheese resting silently and aging to perfection. Sadly though, Parma is not visited by very many tourists but to the Italians, Parma is magnifico. If you are going to Italy as a tourist or sadly squeezed into one of those huge, double-decker tour buses advertised everywhere, you will certainly not see Parma. The tour buses completely bypass this amazing place and head to Milan.

Parma is full of wonderful foods, such as the famous Parma ham called Prosciutto de Parma and the Parmigiano Reggiano cheese. Its scent is already drifting through the mountaintops, permeating our coach as Nino glides us up and down the Appennine Mountains. We know we're nearly there as the aroma gets stronger and also, we pass a colorful sign alerting us to the fact that their renowned celebrity, Prosciutto (Parma hams), is just ahead. I know Tony and Nino are thinking about the taste, while I'm thinking about something very different.

"Stefania, how long have they been making the cheese?" John hollers out from a few rows back on the coach.

"Oh, John, they've been making cheese here for many generations. If you ask one of the locals how long, they can't seem to say exactly but they will give an estimation of somewhere around eight hundred years or so."

"Mamma Mia, you know more than I do. Very nice," Tony laughingly says as Nino spins the coach around to a sudden stop.

Walking into the tall, wide building, we're overwhelmed by the smell of cheese and the towering rows of shelves, one after another. On the left and right of each row, I see large, round wheels of cheese. This is unbelievable. So many wheels of cheese as large as tires ... hundreds of them. Down the wide aisle, we see a worker with something resembling a hammer in his hand, soaring high beside the shelves of cheese while standing on the outer part of a forklift. The forklift is in the process of lifting him way up.

Looking down a little, we see the driver on the lift busily maneuvering the controls. Over on the other side of the building, we see bright sparks of fire flying in the air. It looks like a Fourth of July sparkler. The man is too far away for us to recognize exactly what's going on, but before we take another step, one of the Americans asks what the man is doing with the hammer. In great detail, a worker explains that the man takes each wheel of cheese and taps it lightly to hear the sound. We are talking to experts—generations of experts—who live each day working to produce the most famous Parmigiano Reggiano. They are serious about every minute detail.

Looking up and around, we see a spotless array of large round wheels of cheese resting and waiting, aging to perfection. We watch with amazement as the forklift takes out one wheel of cheese from way above on the top shelf. Within seconds, the inspector takes his hammer, for lack of a better word, and lightly taps around the circumference of the rind. Listening very closely to the oversized wheel, he keeps his ear drawn near, hearing its reply. This is unbelievable to the Americans. Watching and observing such unusual behavior reminds them of being in an examination room, awaiting their physical examinations. The doctor of cheese, listening to the heartbeat through his cold stethoscope to determine the aging process, is truly hard to believe.

Way up on the tall shelf, a huge wheel of cheese has been chosen from amongst the other hibernating wheels. The Italian worker stumbles with his broken English and reverts to Italian while explaining that this particular wheel of cheese sounds unacceptable. Like a newborn bambino being examined by the doctor, the large wheel of cheese is emotionally vulnerable to the expert's opinion. We stand and watch as the deficient wheel is taken by forklift, heading to the area of inspection where the torching process begins.

When we walk to the other side of the building, we again see the man holding a sparkler. As we get closer, we realize he's holding a torch. He appears to be intensely occupied with the torch, holding it to the wheel of cheese while sparks shoot in every direction.

"This particular wheel of cheese has not achieved the process of being tagged Parmigiano Reggiano cheese," the worker tells us sadly, as though he were relaying bad news to the parents of a new bambino. "This wheel of cheese has some kind of imperfection, such as the coloring being a tiny bit off or perhaps something even worse," he says with sad eyes.

The wheel of cheese has been disgraced, and its acclaimed Parmigiano Reggiano status has been demoted to a lower grade of cheese. Regretfully, this wheel of cheese will not receive the proud stamp in pin-dot writing around the circumference of the rind. It will receive the dreaded horizontal lines running through the words, meaning the wheel of cheese was rejected by the consortium because it failed to meet the quality control, which is very strict.

If you are looking at the entire rind, you'll find the fire-branded logo of the consortium, a number indicating the identity of the producer, and the year of production. To receive such a reward, it must be aged for a minimum of twelve months, but it is recommended to age it eighteen to twenty-five months. The longer the cheese gets to age, the darker the color, the richer the flavor, the stronger the aroma, and the higher the cost. Very similar to fine wine, you might say.

Luckily, you don't have to drive to Parma, Italy, to purchase the cheese. You can buy the fabulously divine Parmigiano Reggiano cheese all over Italy. However, its production is protected by the government. In fact, the sacred cheese is ranked in the minds of all Italians as a rare heavenly piece of real estate that will forever be prized as royalty.

After our royal treatment and an overabundance of liquid red floating happily inside our stomachs, we laughingly get back on the coach. As we laugh and talk together, Nino spins the coach around the corner, sputtering up and down the rolling hills until all of a sudden, we smell the cheese.

"Mamma Mia, Stefania, I can still smell the cheese. It's very strong. Much stronger than inside the building. Do you smell the cheese, Stefania?" Tony asks me with a disturbed look on his face.

"Si, yes, I do. It's very strong," I say, sniffing in the air like a dog.

Turning around in his seat, Tony looks at the Americans and asks them, "Do you smell the cheese?"

201

Immediately, someone says, "Yes, it's stronger than ever inside the coach."

"Why is that so, Tony?" Susan asks, pulling her red collar up to her nose.

"Mamma Mia, I do not know. This is very strange to me," Tony says, mystified by the growing smell.

The smell of cheese is getting stronger, it seems, while Nino drives us through the most breathtaking roads. In the midst of our laughter, Tony gets a call from one of his local friends, insisting we stop at his nearby vineyard for a taste.

Without alerting the Americans of our impromptu decision, Nino zigzags around the flowing hills, takes a right turn, and swirls gently around the many chestnut trees. Within seconds, we're rolling up to hundreds of silvery olive trees with a picturesque farm table resting peacefully underneath its silvery canopy.

The old farm table appears to be miles long with pink, red, and purple flowers exploding down the middle. To the right, we see the old villa and a hundred hands bringing out platters of food through the aged double doors. And out of nowhere we see more hands bringing out green demijohns full of the liquid red. The setting is typical Italian.

Before I take a sip of the liquid red, I hear Sally Parker from Houston hollering for Nino to unlock the coach. I assume she forgot her camera or perhaps her purse, but seeing her rolling out the huge, tire-size wheel of cheese from underneath the luggage department nearly makes my eyes pop out.

"Oh my, I can't believe it. Sally took one of the rounds of cheese. How in the world did she take it?" I ask out loud, not even sure if anyone is paying attention to me.

Nino's eyes grow large, displaying the shock of such a huge parcel underneath the coach. However, before anyone else notices the large cargo rolling toward us, I get up and walk toward Sally.

"Sally, how in the world did you load this huge wheel of cheese?" I ask.

"Oh, Stephie, it's a gift for everyone. While all of you were absorbed, I slipped away with Marcello and purchased one of the big rounds," Sally explains, smiling a wide Pinocchio smile.

26

CORTONA, ITALY ...

Here we are, all thirteen Americans plus Tony the Sicilian, standing in awe in front of Frances Mayes's villa. We are staring upward at the villa, comparing the memories from the movie *Under the Tuscan Sun*. After a few moments of clicking our cameras at the villa and taking turns posing in front of the shrine where the old man placed flowers in the vase each day, I hear Tony.

"Buongiorno Signora, come stai? Hello, lady, how are you? Stefania is here with the Americana. Stefania and the Americana would like to come in for a visit, have a look around, enjoy a nice glass of vino, and talk with you for a few moments," Tony explains in Italian to a woman thought to be Frances Mayes who is leaning out the window, looking down at us as though we are space aliens.

Alarmed at Tony's request, I say to the woman, "No. I mean, excuse me, signora, we cannot come in. Tony was just joking with you."

"What do you mean, Stefania? Of course, I ask to go in with the Americana. Absolutely ... yes, these Americanos are crazy for this *Tuscan Sun*," Tony says as both of his hands whirl through the air, forgetting about the woman leaning farther out the window.

"Oh, sir, I'm not Frances Mayes. No, I am her sister from America. I'm sorry, but I do not understand," she says with an alarming tone, as though we have just arrived to invade the villa and drink all of their vino.

"Oh, signora—I mean, madam—I'm so sorry to have intruded. I bring Americans to Italy twice a year and this is one of the places we love. We're not asking to come in, but of course we'd love to say hello to Frances if she's in," I hurriedly say before Tony starts up again.

"Oh, I'm so sorry, but Frances and Ed are away at the other villa they purchased," she replies, still leaning out the window.

The Americans continue taking photos of the famous house while hesitantly walking toward the coach. I watch the Americans throw their arms up in the air, waving as if they are leaving their dearly beloved lover while Nino smiles, shaking his head with a roll of his eyes.

"Mamma Mia, I do not understand the reason for this visit," Nino says to Tony who is also shaking his head, mumbling Italian words that translate the same sentiment.

Loaded back on the coach, we pass the entrance gate to the medieval walls of Cortona, and out of nowhere I hear someone hollering behind me, "Stop the bus, stop the bus! We must get out."

"Mamma Mia, Madonna," shouts Tony, who thinks someone must do a number two again.

"What's the matter with you? Must we stop for the number two?" Tony asks in alarm, turning around in his seat and now looking at Mary from New Jersey, who is in love with Cortona from watching *Under the Tuscan Sun.*

"No, but we must go inside Cortona," Mary says with excitement.

"Basta, basta. Stop, stop," Tony tells Nino, who is now backing up the coach and opening the door for us to flock inside the medieval walls of Cortona.

Trekking up the narrow, cobbled streets in Cortona is so whimsical. We laugh and we dance in the middle of the ancient streets. We zigzag from one shop to another, and see the gorgeous flowers spilling out from the old ceramic pots. It's a parade of "buongiornos" and "hellos" spilling out from the aproned women who are sweeping the front of their shops with the twiggy witches' brooms. Some of them are carrying buckets of soapy water from their doorway, swishing back and forth on their shop windows, while others are pouring water into their colorful array of flowers, laughing and calling to one another as they sweep the steady stream of suds toward the steep cobbled incline. Most of us have already stopped and purchased wonderful things along the way, and in front of me I see Diane and Gary Huddleston stepping over the trickling suds that are now racing down toward me. The way of life here in Cortona is magical. Time has frozen.

Hank is happily showing us the leather shoes he just purchased from the little shop a few feet back.

"My shoes were made right here by her own hands. If I lived here, oh my, I would have a new pair made every day," Hank says, bringing the shoes up to his nose, sniffing the Italian leather as though it is an expensive perfume.

"Look at my shoes. I got the pink leather sandals she made," Kathy from Houston says, waving one shoe in the air.

"*Scusi, scusi, scusi,* signora," says the local shopkeeper, waving a beautiful box in the air. "Signora, these are for you," she says, smiling and forcing a box of *pignole* cookies on Karen, and then shuffling back to her shoe store.

"Grazie, thank you." Kathy smiles, holding the box of pignoli cookies as though a magic genie granted her wish for the day. *How peculiar. Free cookies for purchasing shoes.*

We reach the top of the narrow street, and right in front of us, we see the animated piazza, the main square. A beautiful bride and groom walk down the long steps from the same church that was in the movie. I remember Diane Lane standing by the church at Christmastime, talking with the real estate friend while holding his child.

"Oh my, we're in a dream," shouts Nellie from Savannah, Georgia, in her southern accent.

"Stephani, come here. You've got to see this amazing shop," shouts Connie Jo, who is dangling something fabulous in her hands. "You must come see this," Connie shouts again. Standing at the bottom on the left side of the church stairs, I see Connie holding a ruffled bundle of something.

"What is it?" I ask.

"Look at the beautiful creation. This is so you, Stephani," Connie says, leading me through the tiny opening by the church stairs.

Taking a few steps inside, we are in a cavelike shop with two beautiful women chattering in Italian.

"This is the mother and daughter, the owners of this amazing place," Connie Jo declares, holding up the ruffled, handmade wraps and gorgeous ruffled tops in various shades.

Immediately wrapping my neck and body in reds, purples, whites, and other various colors of the rainbow, I look at myself in the tiny, handheld mirror and announce to them, "Oh my goodness, I must have them all."

I would have never known a shop was here, underneath the church steps, if it had not been for Connie Jo. I have no idea how she discovered the shop, but the beautiful pieces I just purchased from the mamma and daughter are going to be my favorite things to wear. The name of this shop is Arcobaleno, and it is hidden below the stairs in the medieval piazza of Cortona, Italy.

Life in Cortona is truly beautiful. It reminds me of a snow-globe, shaken hard. Afterward, everyone happily ice-skates around, doing his or her own task in a secluded world. Its huge, medieval walls protect it, and once you walk inside, everything becomes animated as though Santa Claus and his little elves will appear any second with Rudolph, happily skipping across the cobbled pavement. Of course, I know every town has its problems, but as guests for a few delightful hours, we would surely tag Cortona as one of our favorite chapters in this old storybook life here in Italy.

27

VENICE AND MORE

We have already spent three magical nights in Venice, and for many of our perpetual American travelers, saying goodbye to this magnificently designed floating island is too hard to do. Regardless of the number of times I've been to Venice—which is more than I can remember—I am always surprised and astonished by its beauty.

Nino is driving our coach, and I am sitting on the passenger side with the microphone dangling in my hand. We are already miles away from the floating city but my mind seems to linger there a while longer. Seated here, I reminisce about Venice and its powerful, magnetic grasp on me. It's not just the famous sights of Venice that takes my breath away, though they are beyond impressive. No, it's the way you can meander through the seemingly endless maze of backstreets, popping in and out of gorgeous shops, grabbing a delicious piece of pizza, and then find yourself in the most enchanted square completely alone, so you think, when all of a sudden out pops something totally wonderful in the busiest time of the day. There is no other place in the world like Venice. It's the way you get lost in the magical transformation of being in *Alice in Wonderland*. And at the end of the day, don't think it's over. It's only beginning. We usually drop in to visit our friends at the *ristorante* on the right side of the prestigious, famous opera house La Fenice Theatre and enjoy a delicious surprise of their latest creation. We laugh and sing together, acting like little children who are reuniting with their playmates after a long, hot summer vacation.

Like always, zigzagging in this human maze, we are only a few twists and turns from the most famous square in the world: Saint Mark's Square. And on the opposite end, behind Saint Mark's Square with a few zigzags and turns, we end up at the best place of all to eat pizza. Tony and I always take the Americans here, and oh, what fun we have indulging our faces with Italian delights and the liquid reds until we cannot shove another thing into our mouths.

It's been only a few nights since we were all seated at the long table, laughing and talking with electrified emotions from being on this magical island. We gave little notice to the long board running down the middle of the table right in front of us. The Americans sipped the steady delivery of liquid reds, and I sipped the Coca-Colas with floating lemons on top as Tony continuously complained of me drinking such toxic liquids that would surely send me to an early grave. We laughed until our mouths hurt while anticipating the famous pizza that would soon makes its grand appearance.

Eventually, I tried to explain the long board in the middle of the table, but before I finished, out walked two Venetians carrying another long board loaded with mouthwatering slices of pizza. Venice is the only place I know where pizza is stretched out so long on a flat board and placed before you.

In all of its floating glory, the city of Venice is one of the most magical places on earth. There is nothing like a city floating on petrified wood. Venice was built entirely upon water, and its streets are nothing more than wide canals that meander throughout the entire city. Time seems to stand still here, and when going into Harry's Bar, one would expect to see Ernest Hemingway seated over in the far corner, sipping the famous Bellini, which was invented sometime between 1934 and 1948 by Giuseppe Cipriani, the founder of Harry's Bar in Venice. And if you ask the locals inside Harry's Bar, they will say that nothing has changed since Hemingway except for the fact that they're all getting a little older. That seems to be the story with all of Venice.

There is an irresistibly enticing power in Venice. Even the locals seem to be under the city's enchanting spell. I always suggest to the Americans that they hop aboard the handcrafted gondolas that glide them through the romantic canals, one after another.

I will never forget James from Miami, who is seated three or four rows behind me right now. He asked many questions about Venice's sinking situation, which gave me the opportunity to encourage him to focus more on its beauty than on its burial. If you ask any of the Venetians, "Is Venice sinking?" They will tell you, "Absolutely not."

While Nino drives us along this morning, the Americans are talking and laughing among themselves, and I continue to daydream. For some reason, my thoughts revert to yesterday.

"Stephani, it's been my lifelong dream to come to Venice. You do know that, right?" James asks me, forgetting he has already repeated his sentiments to me and the rest of the group numerous times.

Not surprising at all, James drooled at the elegant windows of famous Italian designer-couture boutiques while strolling along the picturesque alleys, taking the time to immerse himself in the daily lives of the locals. He was amazed at the talented local artisans crafting elaborate masks, beautiful writing paper, precious jewels, and whimsical toys such as Pinocchio. He stood in awe and practically exploded with happiness inside the famous La Fenice Opera House. He told us about the hidden churches, palaces, and family courtyards so amazingly designed. He even made it to the famous Rialto Bridge and ate with some of the others in our group, reciting all of his discoveries for the day.

Then out of nowhere, James fell head over heels in love with an Italian beauty while on his first thirty-minute gondola ride. James said it was "meant to be" when he stepped into the gondola at the same time as the stranger. I can still hear his words echoing in my ears.

"Oh, Stephani, I held Maria's hand as we floated down the picturesque canals, enjoying the most romantic views of the city. We floated under small bridges while being serenaded by a red-striped gondolier. Oh, it was a dream that I will never forget. I know this woman feels the same way I do. She held my hand and leaned toward my chest. My whole body broke out into a sudden sensation of sweaty drops of water that made me feel dizzy. I have never felt this way before, and I know for sure that I am in love. Yes, I am in love."

For the first time, I did not know what to say. I don't know how to reply to James. Therefore, I do what Tony usually does inherently. I repeated over and over, "Mamma Mia," and before I sounded out the last vowel, James started again like a broken record, refusing to stop.

"Stephani, you must help me find her. Please, I beg of you to help me. You are the only one who knows how to find her. Don't you see, it's meant to be, me marrying and living right here in Venice. This is my dream and prayer coming true. And just think how beautiful our children will be, all

Italian and American mixed perfectly. Ah, it's a perfect recipe blended by God's own hands," James said passionately. "Can you arrange everything for me? Will you please?" James begged like a little child in desperation for a lollipop.

Then out of nowhere, Tony appeared. He had heard only a few sentences of James's desperation, but that's enough to get him started. And like always, Tony's hands shot up in the air, swirling around as he said, "Mamma Mia, you must be joking. Here we go again with another Americana." He explained to Nino in Italian the story James had just told us plus a few additional sentences.

"Mamma Mia, Stefania, where did you find this one?" Tony asked me with raised eyebrows, shaking his head.

But what can I say? Venice has alluring enchantment over its guests. It truly grabs your heart and mind, Velcroing your very soul to its history and beauty. It brings one to the state of mind that they will do whatever it takes to emerge and live as they do. Visitors want to reach up and grab ahold of the romantic air that possesses their hearts and emotions. Venice is truly marvelous.

Even getting to Venice is special. It has the most spectacular public transport system in the world, the *vaporetto* or water-taxi bus. Arriving by sea in a vaporetto is the normal, but we have more than a vaporetto. We float spectacularly in our own personal boat, a Rolls-Royce of a boat that takes us down the Grand Canal alongside the gondolas and the large, crowded vaporettos. And on arrival, we are greeted with the happy face of our dear friend Adriano. He is family to us—a loyal friend who reminds me of a magic genie, always popping up in Venice just in time with a helping hand. And just like Adriano, a refined Venetian, everywhere we look is a picture-perfect postcard.

The Doge's Palace, a Gothic masterpiece, rises out of the water like a star-studded stallion, towering brilliantly. Standing nearby is the Basilica of San Marco—Saint Mark's Basilica. We greatly admired the marvelous masterpiece of such amazing creativity. Every time I look upon Saint Mark's Basilica, I'm amazed by its beauty. Inside and outside is a mixture of Byzantine, Roman, Venetian, and Gothic styles. Stepping inside, we behold gorgeous columns, arches, gigantic inlaid domes, and the most incredibly precious Golden Pala, an altarpiece with sapphires, emeralds, pearls, amethysts, rubies, agate, topaz, and garnets that total more than 1,927 stones inlaid into gold leaf. And inside this mouth-dropping basilica are the precious remains of the apostle Mark. Yes, did you get that? The apostle Mark, as in Saint Mark in the Bible.

Inside, we took a deep breath and experience Saint Mark's Basilica as almost nobody else does except for the Doge himself, alone except for our guide and the keeper of the basilica. We were celebrities going inside at dusk after the crowds were locked away. Who else gets special privileges as we do? Being inside the most gorgeous basilica in the world with the apostle Mark's remains down below was truly amazing, and it was thanks to Tony, as always making unbelievable things happen.

We saw things like the crypt, which the keeper unlocked for us, where the bones of Saint Mark are kept. There is no way to describe the magnificent gold mosaics at night. All 43,000 square feet of them lighted up, glimmering, and sparkling in the dark is truly amazing.

Inside the basilica, we heard the adventurous story of how the apostle Mark arrived in Venice. It is a story of kidnapping and a dangerous sea voyage. We learn where the precious stones decorating Saint Mark's came from, which had something to do with the conquest of Constantinople in the Crusades.

History has it frozen in time that Venetian merchants stole the relics of Saint Mark the Evangelist from Alexandria, Egypt, which is home to my friend Sayed. That is another story that I will not go in to right now. If you ask the historians, they will tell you the story of how Saint Mark's body/relics were hidden in a pork barrel to get them past the guards. The wild adventure is depicted in the thirteenth-century mosaic above the door, farthest left of the front entrance of Saint Mark's Basilica. You can see how the beautiful twelfth- and thirteenth-century interior mosaics, all with messages of Christian salvation, depict scenes and events from both the Old and New Testaments.

And, of course, we went behind the scenes of the Doge's Palace to explore the secret collections of original art; the senate; the courts, torture chambers, and palace floors; and the prison cells, including that of the famed Casanova himself.

The Rialto Bridge (Ponte di Rialto) is another truly unforgettable place we flock to, including James. It's an arched bridge, having been there for more than 400 years. It reminds me of a white umbrella cockatoo, spanning its wings of little shops.

On our second day in Venice, the Rialto Bridge is the very place we find Sandra Crow buying beautiful gifts for her American friends in Bogata, Texas, and Lafayette, Louisiana. I will never forget her surveying the finished products dangling from both arms: six colorful bags filled with gorgeous Venetian glass. She takes a deep, gratifying sigh, twinkling her black eyes balanced blissfully on cherub cheekbones. Satisfied with her purchases ... but anticipating the next shop.

The other island Murano is where we go to visit old friends at their glass factory. We watch them blow the gorgeous Venetian glass. Afterward, we relax in the family office sipping liquid red from a bottle tagged more than three hundred euros. Afterward, Connie Jo quivers with the effort of controlling herself as she skips away with a gifted bottle— as in a free bottle of wine— and a wide grin that can't be contained no matter how hard she tries.

Begging for lace, we float on over to another small island, Burano, where the most beautiful and exquisite Venetian lace is still being handmade. Tony insists we taste the local seafood, and we do so with pleasure at the table of family friends. Filling the boat with too much lace, we head back to the island of Venice. Still electrified with excitement, most of the Americans hop aboard a gondola to be serenaded by a handsome Venetian in a striped shirt. And we all know that James walks away from the gondola a very happy man.

Afterward, we jet off to Verona, home of Romeo and Juliet, that is truly a storybook town. Every morning after breakfast, we are off to experience amazing places. On this particular tour, I decide we're going back to Lake Como, but before getting there, we stop and purchase some of the luxurious silk fabrics they produce in the area. Afterward, we make a detour to join Tony's friend, who is knee-deep in harvesting the grapes.

Arriving at Lake Como brings many happy faces, especially to the women who see George Clooney hop on his motorcycle, which I fail to see since I am on my knees, crawling like a bambino down the aisle to find my eyeglasses. Lake Como is home to many celebrity holiday villas; the two that I am familiar with are George Clooney's and Donatella Versace's, which are situated directly on the water.

Blame it on strong grappa or a moment of weakness—whichever it was, Janet from Dallas had a heck of a time rendezvousing underneath the Italian moonlight with the cool Lake Como waters splashing against her midlife-crisis body. Oh, how she rumbled below my balcony window. It was earth shaking. The commotion caused the Murano crystals in my chandelier to vibrate. I wasn't the only one to hear a strange ruckus knocking against the stucco wall. The next-door occupants did as well.

When I heard the loud noise, I was already nestled in my memory-foam bed. Well, it wasn't exactly memory foam, but with the high piles of fluffy pillows elevating my body so high on the little mattress, it was the closest thing to memory foam I had ever had in Italy. And like any other normal person would do, I tossed my pillows away and forced my body out of the perfect cocoon.

Looking out my balcony window, I saw below in a perfect moonlight glow two twisted human pretzels amongst a bed of flowers, and a flock of colorful men. There they stood, the local police in their colorful uniforms, encircling Janet and her Romeo. This was better than any late-night movie, because in a matter of minutes, the local police step closer to them, step by step, silently signaling each other to proceed to the alleged "wild boars" rooting and wallowing in the tall beds of flowers. To their surprise, it was only you-know-who.

After sailing around Lake Como and dreaming of living there, we stood frozen at the festival of white-robed monks singing behind a celestial flock of ornately, white-robed priests holding the Madonna and baby Jesus on a tall, wooden stand. Like curious little children, we followed them through the village, bypassing the beautiful old church, zigzagging around until we came face-to-face with the gathered crowd of locals who were singing and crossing themselves as the white-robed, saintly flock slowly walked right in front of them with us dragging up the rear.

Like animated robots, we dropped our heads, crossed ourselves, and walked into a beautiful old church where we were greeted by another conclave of saintly bishops, all wearing gorgeous ruby studded mitres (headdresses).

We were in a strange predicament. Clearly, we were not supposed to be inside. Therefore, not knowing what to do or say, I turned to the

Americans and motioned for them to follow me back to the church door—the one we came through to begin with. Not thinking about the gathered flock of locals waiting outside, we opened the castle door, and music blasted out and waves of excitement ignited the air. The Italian tongue slapped us hard as we came face-to-face with hundreds of them. The loud drums pounded along with various musical instruments vibrating our bodies. We stood frozen in shock, staring wide eyed at the local flock. There always seems to be some kind of an Italian predicament that follows me as I make my way through this life.

After making so many lifetime memories at Lake Como, we surprised the Americans by zooming off to Switzerland, which was less than an hour's drive. We spent the day eating Swiss chocolates, coveting Rolex watches, and tasting just about every edible thing dangling in front of us. Two of the American ladies darted into a pharmacy that had a large sign advertising this "miracle" antidote for wrinkles. Inquisitiveness finally got the best of us, and we all toddled out with towering boxes of this invention guaranteed to wipe away any blemish, wrinkle, sag, flawed pigmentation, or repugnance of any of our inherited facial features.

Needless to say, it was indeed a miracle. The creamy white concoction worked magically for Betty and Arlene, who to this day beg me to go back and purchase more of this miracle antidote when in Switzerland.

28

Santa Margherita, Italy—Love!

Arriving at Santa Margherita on the Italian Riviera has put everyone in a joyful state of musical jubilation, as though they've consumed too much of the liquid red. We barely get our feet on the ground before we hear the church bells dinging and donging along with a violinist playing beautiful music. Santa Margherita is breathtaking. We see its picturesque setting of candy-colored buildings, luscious palm trees, and romantic seafront promenade calling our names.

On board this mid-May Italy tour are twelve Americans—five men and seven women. One in particular is Annette from Frisco, Texas, a vivacious bombshell in her midforties. Her blond hair is layered in long wavy curls, and her flawless face portrays a perpetual surprise as if spying Santa Claus coming down the chimney with his sack of toys. She says her cosmetic surgeon was her narcissistic ex-husband, a real jerk and philanderer who worshipped himself more than her.

I vividly remember our meeting in my store, Decorate Ornate. She bounced through the front door accompanied by an entourage of girlfriends. Upon separating herself from her friends near the back of the store, Annette zipped to the front counter and introduced herself to me once again.

"Stephani, I've read about you in various magazines and heard you speak at the Dallas Country Club's social event. I doubt you remember me, but I returned your shoe to you when you enthusiastically kicked your leg up while giving a demonstration on the platform. Oh my. You do get excited when talking about Italy. Thank goodness that I caught it, or it could have hit someone in the head!

"Oh well, I want to sign up for your Italy tour. However, I do have one request. I want a Casanova, a sexy Romeo who will snatch me off to a lovers' paradise for the whole thirteen days. I'm not picky about his hair. No, it can be straight, curly, or no hair at all. I just want to fall in love in Italy—the country where women are worshipped for nothing more than being a woman. I know how the movies portray Italian men—worshipping their mamma and all."

Watching Annette right now, I see her flirt with Antonio, a local olive beauty who is married with three small children. Sipping his glass of vino, the liquid red, Annette flashes her long lashes of a poodle, intentionally enticing him. I linger at my table and watch. Annette giggles at nothing in particular while forcing her chest upon the stage of performance. Within seconds, she shoots up from her chair and walks past him, intentionally dropping her purse within feet of his view. She is squeezed into a fashionable pair of low-rise American jeans with crystal-studded pockets now sparkling in Antonio's face. I watch as she brazenly displays her size 6 rear end in a slow orchestrated movement as though she will grab a pole and start whirling any second.

My eyes flash to Antonio, who is clenching his napkin in one hand while awkwardly turning his eyes to a small pink rose peeking over the top of a Murano vase. He plays with the delicate rose petals, rubbing and massaging them. It's obvious to see he is desperately trying to avoid another American entrapment, another American woman begging for love and romance while forcefully flaunting her assets.

I look to the other side and watch three Italian men return her flirtatious advances, obligingly flashing their smiles with an alluring wink. Annette melts, knowing she is the center of attention and now has her pick of the litter, or at least from the table of three.

The next afternoon, laughing and sipping a diet cola, I bask in the Italian Riviera sunlight, watching the locals dip into the turquoise-blue waters. *Ah, this is truly heaven, surely it is*, I think to myself as Annette flops down beside me.

"Oh, Stephani, can I please stay here forever? I've never seen such beauty as here." Annette tosses her blond curls over her bare shoulder and scans the men as they walk by.

"Oh, I know, Annette. The gorgeous pastel buildings and medieval churches are beyond fabulous. I could live here forever in this storybook setting," I reply, sipping my diet cola and dreaming of bringing the same color to Main Street in Gladewater, Texas—the hometown of Decorate Ornate.

"Oh, Stephie, you are too funny. You make me laugh. No. I'm not talking about the buildings and churches here. Ha, I'm talking about the Italian Romeos. They are so fine. Well, not all of them, but the one I was with last night. Oh girl, everything I've heard about the Italian stallions is true. Yes, so true. They are romantic, caring, and have the slow hand with the long soft kisses. I'm already in love. Thank you so much for making my dreams come true. You have fulfilled my wish, but of course, this is just the beginning of our tour. I can't imagine what the rest of this tour will bring me." Annette reclines in a lounge chair that she hurriedly scooted beside me.

"Stephie, how did you catch your husband? How did you fall in love with him? Tell me how it felt to know he was the one and only for you amongst this treasure chest of beauties." Annette swipes her thin lips with a soft raspberry lip gloss and then turns to me with the expectation of hearing the juicy details.

"Well, Annette, I used to ask my sister Victoria, 'How can a person know if he or she is in love? How does it feel? I want to be in love and feel the invisible, magnetic force that binds a woman and man into one that will last a lifetime. I want to be held tightly while dancing the tango with heated passion racing throughout my body. I want to read sincere love notes written by his own hand, and I want to be held and kissed as though it were our last night together before the *Titanic* goes under. And of course, I want a man, a godly man with Christian morals who has eyes only for me.'

"Laughingly, my sister said, 'True love is rare and if you find it, trust me, you will know it. The thing about falling in love is this: once it happens to you, there is little that you can do to stop it. Therefore, do not put yourself in a place where you could fall for the wrong one.'

"I went through life for so long never knowing, understanding, or experiencing true love or any of those feelings. Until a miracle happened.

"I fell in love with a tall, dark man. It was an electrifying experience, similar to being plugged into a 220-volt electrical outlet. My appetite ceased; my heart rate exploded; my adrenaline and dopamine levels reached an all-time high that immediately sent out joyous, floating feelings of pure ecstasy racing throughout my brain. My emotions were transformed to an all-time high, and my brain circuits redirected to respond in a ridiculous, adolescent, hysteria-like way. At the most unpredictable times, his sun-kissed face would pop into my mind like a roaring tornado, causing my other thoughts to speedily melt away. My mind was kidnapped, thrown away, and replaced with angelic visions of him that appeared unexpectedly twenty-four hours a day. My whole being felt an earthquaking shake within, ferociously awaking every vital emotion, causing me to feel as though I were soaring high into the clouds, flying like a bird with no worries or troubles, only pure happiness.

"It's true, it feels just like a heated thermometer rising, but it doesn't stop. It explodes over the top. That's the feeling of falling in love and, Mamma Mia, what an emotional ride. The ride takes you so high before it slowly starts to glide back down to reality, seeing him for who he really is all along.

"That's how the hormonal fluids work in the brain. Once the fatal chemicals drop back down to their normal levels, get ready for the shock of reality, because that's when you see the 'real' man that couldn't do any wrong for the first six months or longer.

"Amazingly, when we subject ourselves to lust—you know, the emotion below the waist—something happens within the brain. The brain has significant levels of hormonal fluids such as, just for starters, testosterone and estrogen, and they react to the happenings that are influencing our minds and views when it comes to lust.

"If you get past lust, the next stage guarantees the powerful flow of adrenaline, dopamine, and the most potent chemical of all when it comes to love: serotonin. Oh yes, the good old magical fluid that sent me spinning into a world that I'd never known or experienced before in my entire life.

"Once the serotonin in the brain starts to drop, there are no medical antidotes to reverse the fatal bite, the love bite, as I refer to its destined diagnosis. Perhaps that's why God warns men not to lust after another woman; the fatal liquid starts pumping like a magic potion. And when this emotional ride starts, get ready to see a whole lot of changes in a person's behavior, such as a total transformation, the silliness of acting so strangely, doing things beyond the normal. It's easy to recognize a victim, or at least it is to me, since I was bitten and then smitten, never recovering from its fatal bite.

"The love bite is so powerful that the chemical flow of dopamine has the same effect on the brain as taking cocaine. No wonder I went around floating on a cloud, feeling nothing but pure happiness and joy like I'd never felt before. I was under the influence of powerful hormones pumping out the same substance as cocaine. No wonder I saw my newfound Romeo, better known as Allen Chance, through 'rose-colored' glasses. Everything he spoke and did was wonderful. Even when he sneezed, I heard musical happiness in my ears. My mind and body were completely distorted by the sudden, oil-struck surge of powerful hormones pumping throughout my brain. I was locked inside a padded latex bubble, flying high and oblivious to his many imperfections.

"Dopamine is the hormone responsible for the 'high' one feels when in love. Interestingly, when consuming addictive substances such as crack, cocaine, nicotine, alcohol, and other various drugs, dopamine is released. Also this amazing hormone creates the feeling of 'cleaving' to another as in clinging as well as jealousy that we experience in love." I hope Annette will get something out of the truths I say to her.

"Stephani, you sound ridiculously insane." Annette flashes another smile toward an olive-kissed man who innocently walks by with a smile. Seconds later, she asks, "Stephani, will you tell me more about ... ah, you know, that serotonin stuff? The love potions that will make me go crazy in love?"

"Yes, certainly," I reply with a slight smile, realizing she didn't understand anything. "Serotonin is the 'magical hormone' that gives you the amazing feeling of love. Serotonin causes your lover to keep popping into your mind and causes the loss of appetite during love. Strangely, serotonin creates the feeling of butterflies in your stomach, the nervousness of awe. And from personal experience, I can say it sends you to a new height of ecstasy, feeling nothing but exhilarating joy and happiness, along with beautiful melodies of sweet nothings in both ears. I was dropping dress sizes like leaves on a windy day.

"Interestingly, a breakthrough experiment in Pisa, Italy, showed that the early stage of love after lust does change the way you think. Dr. Donatella Marazziti, a psychiatrist at the University of Pisa, publically advertised for twenty love-struck couples to participate in her experiment. To participate, the couples had to be 'madly in love' for less than six months. Dr. Donatella wanted to see if the brain chemicals that cause you to constantly think about your lover were related to the brain mechanisms of obsessive-compulsive disorder.

"Amazingly, by analyzing blood samples from the lovers, Dr. Marazitti discovered that serotonin levels of new lovers were surprisingly equivalent to the low serotonin levels of people with obsessive-compulsive disorder," I explain.

"So, the feel-good hormone, serotonin, drops down during the falling-in-love phase, causing you to obsess about your lover and consistently reflect on the romantic times spent with him or her. You actually go crazy, or at least I did. The same thing happens in the brain with people who have obsessive-compulsive disorder. The serotonin is too low. However, research shows that the 'madly in love phase' ends. Try to visualize the mercury in a thermometer rising to the top and then exploding over, but ... in time, the mercury 'love chemicals' dwindle back to their normal level."

"This is unbelievable, Stephani! I want to hear more about this ... What happened to you after the love chemicals dwindled back down?" Annette questions me, now intrigued.

"Annette, it all makes sense now. Let me explain ... I am a girly-type woman. I love everything about being a woman. I love being a mom and a Fluff to my only grand-doll. I love romance, kissing, cuddling, candlelight dinners, the color pink, a home full of beautiful flowers, baking chocolate chip cookies, dinner parties, decorating my home, and much more. And I've never in my entire life liked or enjoyed the one sport my husband absolutely loves: fishing. However, when my Prince Charming, Allen Chance, came into my life, it was magically and completely life changing. Before I knew what hit me, I jetted off with him in a heated moment to wooded acres with a pond. I do not remember much about it or where we were except for the fact that everything he did was so wonderful and magically amazing. In my blissful moment, still floating high in the clouds inside my bubble with my love hormones pumping at full speed, I did something shocking ... I went fishing!

"Well, I can't remember if I actually held a rod and reel or just stood beside Allen while he fished. It's still a fuzzy blur. However, from the photo I have from that very day, I held a live fish! I had never been fishing before in my life, much less held a live fish. It was a moment of insanity. I was floating in a mind-altering space somewhere in the clouds on a different planet. I was under the influence of hormonal chemicals coming straight from the brain. I was floating high—higher than ever before while holding a live fish. And with the magical love potions pumping at full speed, exploding throughout my brain, my own dislikes and fears of a living fish were completely drowned out.

"In my altered state, Allen felt I was the perfect catch. He immediately got the impression that I was intrigued with the fish. Therefore, he was beyond excited to be the first one to introduce me to the fish. And with my altered infatuation with the fish, seeming to be genuine, it excited him to explain the elementary steps of catching various types of fish, along with hundreds of gel-like creatures resembling worms. We spent hours with the fish, so he says. I really don't remember a thing except for his handsome face and lips and, of course, his voice. With every explanation of gel and live fish bait, I only heard his alluring voice echoing in slow motion throughout my brain. I was under the influence of hormones jetting out like a water sprinkler on a hot summertime day.

"Allen was under the hormone-induced influence as well. His brain was pumping at full speed, producing all of the magical, love-connecting chemicals that guarantee the 'in love' sensation of floating on big puffy clouds with angelic music sounding throughout his head—although for Allen, I would say he probably heard more of the lyrics from Bon Jovi singing 'Bed of Roses' than angelic serenading.

"While in this altered, drug-induced euphoria, Allen depicted himself as this perfect, flawless man to me. He jetted me off to Broadway shows in Los Angeles, pretending to love and enjoy the musical shows. Every weekend, he was taking me somewhere magnificently fabulous where we dressed our finest. He possessed the etiquette of a prim and proper gentleman from the royal elite, pedigreed from the finest French and Spanish lineage. He spoke perfect grammar. He posed with self-confidence and irresistible, manly kindness. He eagerly went to church in biblical righteousness, and possessed great intellectual truths. He cooked the finest impromptu, after-work meals and the best cornbread I have ever tasted. He sounded out the most beautiful love songs on his bass guitar while flashing his enticing black eyes into my heart.

"Long after six months, when the liquid hormones dwindled to their normal levels and the serotonin surged back up, the real Allen emerged, and we were happily married. After the magical liquid resumed its normal level, we saw each other for who we really were all along ... total opposites!

"Now after eighteen years of marriage, Allen laughingly jokes and tells everyone he is the 'Tractor Pull' and I am the 'Opera.' We are definitely total opposites. He loves to fish; I hate to fish. I love operas and ballet; he hates operas and ballet. He can't sing and the last pan of cornbread he made was seventeen years ago.

"After making it through the initial phases of love, we are still in love with each other regardless of our many differences. However, let me be honestly clear. Our 'love-bite' levels did dwindle to their normal levels after the first ten months or so. I no longer feel the crazy highs of flying through the air like a bird or hearing angelic music as he speaks. However, he does make my heart skip a beat at times when he flashes his deep black eyes at me. If we had continued in the state we were in at the beginning of our relationship, our hearts would have surely exploded from pure exhaustion.

"Annette, I hope you understand a little more about falling in love— at least how it felt for me. Love is real. Oh yes, love is powerful and causes one to do the strangest things. So please, give yourself time, and don't grab the first man who walks by. Respect yourself. Demand respect, and please, don't flirt and entrap someone else's man. Men are weak when it comes to women flaunting their bare assets or offering free services. You never know what marriage or home you could be destroying. Let me tell you how it works here in Italy and probably most of the world. Please, I'm not judgmental and will never get in your business or that of anyone else that who aboard with us on these tours, unless of course one of them is after my husband. Then ... well, the wrath of hell will come down upon them." I smile and sip my cola with a lemon floating on top.

"You see, Annette, yesterday while you flirted with Antonio, I watched and observed you. Afterward, Antonio told me a very true statement. He said, 'Mamma Mia, Stefania, the Americana women are mad. They come to Italy in the large double-decker buses by the loads, flaunting themselves in front of us—looking for *Italia* love and romance. They think we're all Casanovas—you know, the Italian stallion. They don't care if we're married. Mamma Mia, they don't even ask. Ah, they do not understand this dance of love—the emotions from the heart that consumes our mind and being. They don't understand our wedding vows—they are perpetual, everlasting promises. The Americana women do not understand an affair. What is an affair to you, Stefania?' Antonio asked. Before I could respond, he answered. 'An affair is nothing more than an affair. The Americana women expect much more. What do they want, a marriage license? Ah, they come here and expose themselves, enticing us with nakedness and leaving nothing to our imaginations. They expose everything, begging for our services. Mamma Mia, what is a man to do with this kind of behavior—hide underneath the table or run to the nearest Madonna, praying for restraint?'" Antonio had breathlessly rested his jaws, wiped the sweat from his brow, and kissed the matrimony ring that shields him from the Americana.

29

THE AVVOCATI AND AVOCADOS IN GILMER, TEXAS

One week ago today, I arrived in Italy with another group of Americans. The laughter has not ceased until now. The Americans stare at hundreds of flickering candles and fields of freshly harvested flowers as we stand inside another one of Italy's tucked away churches. We're in a medieval basilica far away from any of the touristy churches. We stand frozen, overwhelmed by the exuberantly ornamented décor of this mind-boggling structure. Before us are countless angels appearing to launch into flight at any moment. There are endless oil paintings of Mary and Jesus with eyes that seem to follow us. To the left are mitred popes in bronze and marble, all gorgeously designed. Within reach of my arm is a wood-carved rostrum rising in the air as though it grew from the marble floor. I see an old leather-worn songbook resting lopsided thereon, waiting for someone to announce the first hymn. My eyes glance toward a lofty perch with a pair of tarnished iron dragons flaming fiercely, not with fire but with oblong lightbulbs.

From above, loving eyes pierce down upon us. They are the eyes of Mary the Madonna holding baby Jesus close to her chest. I feel the holy presence and lower my head to pray and breathe in the fragrance of floral abundance. But before I utter a sound, there is an interrupting echo of leather-strapped feet slapping the marble floor. Surprised to hear such clatter in a world of divine silence, I look up and see a long-robed priest with six monks somberly walking behind him. Their attire, along with toes peeking over the edges of their sandals, sent a message: We are in Italy.

We stand in silence except for the soft music that is now pumping out from the huge pipe organ. One by one they dip their fingers in the holy water, cross themselves, and stroll toward the front. Swiftly they genuflect—they perform a bowlike curtsy to the lifelike statue of Mary and baby Jesus with the holy cross beside them.

"They are showing respect for Christ and their baptism. Catholics crossing themselves and saying aloud, 'The Father, the Son, and the Holy Ghost' are like Protestants saying, 'In Jesus' name, amen,' I whisper to the ones standing close to me who I know are Protestants and have no clue what is happening before them. We stand in awe, and after a few moments, I whisper, "Andiamo, let's go" and turn toward the door.

Outside we hear Tony in an animated conversation with Lucy and Roy, a sweet couple from Louisiana who signed up for this tour with a few things in mind, one being to find a romantic place for their dreamlike wedding in Italy. Hearing their speedy words, I understand it's a chaotic conversation with a lot of *avvocati*.

"Si, si, yes, I understand, but the *avvocato* here in Italy will advise you," Tony explains to them for the hundredth time, telling them the avvocato will handle the details and advise them through the red tape that is surely required for a wedding in Italy.

"But Tony, I want to be married in a small fairy-tale-like town with lots of avocados and pink satin streamers cascading down as if a soft drizzle of rain is pouring upon us," Lucy says. "We will have a beautiful coat of arms with more avocados bursting all around. Yes, my family crest is represented by the avocado symbol and will certainly be at our wedding. Not just one avocado, but many. Do you understand?" Lucy has no idea the word *avvocato* in Italian means "lawyer" until I explain it to her.

"Mamma Mia, Nino. I do not understand where Stefania finds some of these Americanos. Do you understand what this Lucy and Roy explained to me?" Tony asks Nino, rubbing his head as if a sudden illness has come to torment him. "Nino, they say there must be many avvocati [lawyers] at their matrimony. As many as possible, that's what they said. Unbelievable to me. What do they think this country is …? Do they think I control the Roman courts?" Tony walks over to me, his hands swirling in the air. I explain an avvocato versus an avocado.

"Stefania, what is the name of the village that you say are many avvocati—lawyers—in American? You remember, you took me to visit the tall avvocato. The nice one that extends to the ceiling—you know, your former boss. And yes, Peggy lives there and too is an avvocato. The people are very nice in this village because there is no crime with all of the avvocati. And yes they have the thing you like to eat, you know, the long thing that must be baked in the oven," Tony rambles with nonstop speed, making everyone around us ready to escape to this fairy-tale village. And by the time I ponder a response, Tony is ten sentences ahead of me.

"Stefania, this is the village for Lucy and Roy. Si, si, yes. They want a place for good marriage. And yes, do you remember? You said this judge is *bello*—beautiful—you know, she has a nice face, not the face of *brutto*—ugly. She is not in the large building, the *palazzo di giustizia*, the courthouse. No, you pointed to the other place, the one down from Peggy's office. Yes, we must send Lucy and Roy to this signora of a judge. She will marry them and make everything nice for them. They want a fairy-tale place where they will not divorce." Several of our passengers gather around to hear more of Tony's eagerness to rid Lucy and Roy of this storybook dream that they must marry somewhere in Italy.

"Where is this place, Stephani?" Marcy from New Hampshire insists as others chime in as well, all leaning in closer and motioning for more to listen.

"Oh Tony," I laugh at his silly descriptiveness, "you are talking about Gilmer, Texas."

"Si, si, yes, Stefania. They must go to *Gill'imora*—Gilmer. Ah si, yes, that's the place for Lucy and Roy. Mamma Mia Madonna." Tony turns to Nino with both hands twirling through the air as his eyes dilate, causing me to think he's morphed into Rodney Dangerfield. Both of them have the same animated facial features for a Broadway show.

"Where is this wonderful place?" Lucy and Roy say in unison as they draw their faces into wide, happy smiles while shuffling their feet uncontrollably, causing Mary Jo to ask if there is a need for the toilet.

"Oh my, I think I will join Tony with a big *Mamma Mia* right now." I laugh and feel discombobulated with so much confusion but feel the need to explain in detail to the large flock of locals and our group the likes of Gilmer, Texas, and its array of avvocati.

"Yes, I understand how one must surely think a quaint town such as Gilmer, Texas, would be free of crime and have no demand for all the scholarly attorneys who flock to the historical courthouse, or as Tony calls it ... the *palazzo di giustizia*. However, their presence is not limited to that one place. To find more of these legalized power brains bouncing around Gilmer, it would be recommendable to head on down to Titus Street, to which they leisurely maneuver by car or trek at full speed on foot. They arrive at the 115th Judicial District Courtroom, wherein the highly esteemed and natural black-haired beauty, the Honorable Judge Lauren Parish, presides and has for many years. If you're lucky enough to be in her courtroom where she is adorned with a long black robe, you will see her ceremoniously animated when she interprets the law and enjoys the spectacle of a scholarly array of attorneys tap dancing to procedure below her stately bench," I explain, shuffling my own two feet as if I too were dancing with the avvocati.

"Gilmer isn't just a county seat for the many scholarly attorneys floating around town. No. It's also famously known for the annual East Texas Yamboree, as in deliciously, homegrown sweet potatoes we call yams and the highly solicited Yam Queen, who is pedigreed from the aristocrats of Gilmer, Texas, and Upshur County. One lucky lady is annually crowned with the distinguished title of Yamboree Queen and then paraded lavishly on top of a moving ornate float, waving heroically in front of thousands of emotional fans who have traveled from all over the United States to partake in this huge fanfare of traditional pride." I pause and smile at Tony. "Yes, do you have a question, Tony?" I ask, seeing his face of confusion.

"Stefania, did you say 'yams' and 'sweet potatoes'? Ah, Madonna! I do not understand this bloody talk of yams and a floating yam queen." Tony throws his hands in the air once again and mumbles words unfamiliar to the Americans' ears, but I know exactly what he's saying in Italian. The words are not so pleasant when translated to English, but these words are very familiar in Sicilia. I give Tony a slight smile and then continue with my explanation as if he were only a bump in the road.

"I was explaining the Yamboree pageant. Of course, one must not forget the royal court, dressed just as regally as King Louie and Marie Antoinette strutting lavishly around the elected Yam Queen with thousands of fans flashing cameras in their faces. If you're fortunate enough to have purchased your pageant tickets in advance, then surely you will be dazzled by the royal court in all its aristocratic splendor, presenting a pageant equally as prominent as the Oscars on a sizzling movie-star night." I pause for a split second, taking a second breath, and enforce to Tony, "Yes, you could say this is a storybook place.

"With all of this fame and glory and fairy-tale setting amongst the quaintness of Gilmer, Texas, one would surely ask, "Do marriages last forever? Will they, in fact, live happily ever after since this is the Bible Belt of East Texas?' Well, yes; however in reality, there are no towns of any size free of crime or matrimonial splits. It is but a fantasy, a figment of my wishful imagination. I'm sorry, Lucy and Roy.

"Nonetheless, whether it's a crime of passion or a marriage gone bad, rest assured it will be resolved by one of the scholarly attorneys in Gilmer, Texas. They are a tight-knit group of talented minds, and that's probably why certain legendary stars have been known to grace some of their back doors. And of course, on Titus Street they've been known to come through the front doors.

"The majority of great attorneys, though not all of them, started out in Gilmer, practicing law, that is, until somehow, by a lover's magnetic pull or perhaps just needing a change of scenery, they stretched over the county line. I suppose one could say they have one foot in Gilmer—Upshur County, that is—and the other one in ... let's just say the adjacent counties. And with all of their scholarly expertise and skill with the legal system, it's necessary for them to tap dance their way around many of the surrounding cities since their legal knowledge and status far exceeds their small-town population sign.

"However, do not be alarmed, Lucy and Roy. I know you reside in Louisiana, which is the only state in America that still practices law under the old Napoleonic legal system. However, if you are blessed with the wonderful opportunity to call Gilmer, Texas, your home, well, then you will have the best of both worlds. A world within the safety net of the scholarly array of avvocati (lawyers) and an abundance of the delicious green avocado (fruits) as well. Mamma Mia, what a wonderful world."

30

PLEASE TELL US MORE— MIMMO AND GIUSY

"Stefania, please tell us about your next Italy tour. Will you be going to Sicily? Will you go back to Mimmo and Giusy's villa for the harvest of the grapes?" Helen Holland from Henderson, Texas, asks, rummaging for her pen and paper to make note of the dates.

"Yes, Helen. We always go to Sicily for the last harvest of the grapes and of course, the huge feast. We will arrive just in time to see the wagons towering high, loaded down with plump, luscious green and purple grapes. We'll hang over the wagons like little children, taking grapes by the handful and plopping them into our mouths. They are delicious and oh so sweet. You will see how the process starts—you know, the beginning of the wine making. It's exciting to be in Sicily for the last harvest of the grapes, especially with family and friends. And Helen, you already know from our previous tours that every day is a magical adventure.

"Helen, when we take the Americans to Sicily, before we sit at the torch-lit table, we hop into tiny cars and cruise through the vineyards. We trace the vineyard paths to gather chestnuts and succulently plump fruit. Watching the workers wallop the tree limbs as chestnuts rain down upon us is quite the thrilling experience," I explain.

I remember an adorable couple from Dallas—Pat and Jim—who hopped aboard with us on the Southern Italy tour. Arriving in Sicily at the abode of our dear friends Mimmo and Giusy was only the beginning of an unforgettable evening of thrills and exhilaration.

Being ushered through the opened gate, the excitement and animation of family and friends launches us into the most entertaining evening of all in Sicily. Greeted with happy faces and waving hands, Mimmo and Giusy roll out with grace the green carpet for an entrance truly fit for kings and queens. Strolling through the doorway of flowing greenery,

231

we stare in awe at the foreign beauty of their Sicilian home. The wood-burning stove smolders with flaming ambers as the homemade sausages plump and sizzle with an explosive zest within the little fireplace of a stove. To the left, above our heads is a floating honeymoon suite. Freely suspended by no more than flower-laced ribbons, it appears as Aladdin's magical carpet hovering over the plumes of misty smoke. Our eyes dilate as they move downward and encounter an oblong table laced with white linen and flanked with flickering candlesticks in gorgeous candelabras set among mountains of Sicilian gastronomy sprawled all around. We become intoxicated with the abundance of this foreign hospitality and we have merely crossed the threshold into this lively enchantment.

Over to the right, we gasp upon seeing the extravagance of another table, a perfectly orchestrated abundance of beauty and elegance. Giusy blends right in as she shuffles around the table with dancing feet and Sicilian song. Her soprano rolls out in a beautiful Italian operetta, and then, abruptly, like turning a page, she spills out in her Italian words, "Mimmo, the vino!"

Ah, yes, the love affair with the liquid red, the vino, must begin. Within seconds, the liquid red flows out in ceramic decanters, filling wineglasses as Federico, their son, offers freshly baked bread, still steaming with the liquid gold—olive oil—freely doused on top. The pageantry of Sicilian life has begun.

Everyone is placed at the long table with glowing, torch-lit candelabras flickering to the rhythm of the accordion, stretching inward and outward as the captivating procession of Sicilian cuisine begins its spectacle of beauty.

The music pumps out with every squeeze of the accordion, and the laughter spreads like a contagious case of poison ivy. Suddenly, Pat leaps up from her seat like a jack-in-the-box morphed into a kangaroo. Before I can take note of her ascension, two small feet inside leather sandals stand proudly atop the table. With a mouth stuffed with olive-doused bread, I stare as she belts out a strange but funny song—something about Indians—Native Americans—rowing a boat. Thankfully, the dishes remain intact and the table unsoiled as she energetically oscillates her arms as if she were rowing a canoe. Before I swallow my cola with the floating lemon on top, she swings her arms toward her eyebrow, intensely looking for Indians, then switches back to rowing the invisible canoe, all the while singing, "Yackie, Yackie Doodle," a song we Americans have never heard.

"Oh, there is more to tell, Helen, but you already know how we escape to the fairy-tale places off the tourist paths. It would take a hundred lifetimes to see and experience Italy. And you know we have no need for itineraries. We roll with the flow as we please, which is spontaneous and unrehearsed. We get up every morning and welcome the homemade cooking from the day's harvest. We hop aboard our magical coach with Nino at the wheel. We accept each day like a freshly picked grape, peeling away its skin one bite at a time, basking in its pleasure and taste before reaching for another. We etch a path through the rolling hills and over the turquoise-blue Mediterranean. We go where the big tour buses can't go; we eat at the table with family and friends and experience the real Italian life, as you already know from our previous tours." I continue to explain as if she has never been to Italy with us.

"Oh Stefania, per favore—please, tell us how you started this life. Go back to the beginning. Go back as far as you can. Tell us how you live this dream. Oh, please tell us more. Lots more," Helen pleads with a smile on her pink lips, knowing she will be experiencing another fairy-tale tour with us soon.

"We want to know why you left the law office. We want to know the inside scoop of your life, your personal life, that is, if you don't mind sharing it with us. Tell us about your dreams of being a nun and your family. Oh, please, if you don't mind," Laura and Joyce beg, as though they have choreographed a song and dance to expose the naked truths of my life.

I look toward the twelve Americans, all sipping the liquid red except for one, Ann Brogoitti, whose fingers are wrapped about a cup of hot cappuccino that steams toward her angelic face like fog escaping from a genie's bottle. They are shifting their legs on the rich yardage of silk-brocaded seats, eagerly anticipating the entertainment. A few feet away toward the Mediterranean's variegated turquoise waters, I see two lovers kissing and swinging back and forth in each other's arms as though a movie set is playing out before me. They are carrying on right behind the Americans. In fact, the Americans have no idea what my eyes are seeing. Holding them in eagerness, I sip my Italian cola with two floating lemon halves happily bobbing on top and finally nod, agreeing to draw the curtains open—just a little.

I really don't know where to start, I think to myself for a half second, speculating ... swirling my floating lemon on top of my cola. I wonder, *Why do they surround me with such questions when they could be exploring the pages of this storybook of a village?*

"Stephani, you have an attachment to reliquaries, icons, ex votos, and the nuns," Albert says. "I see your eyes light up when talking about them. Tell us about those things. I mean, if you don't mind sharing them with us. Heck, your store Decorate Ornate is floor to ceiling with all sorts of religious antiques you find here in Italy. In fact, I've never seen such a store as yours. Your life is far from normal. Well, I mean you have an interesting life, gallivanting all over Italy, going off the tourist paths with Tony and Nino by your side. Now come on, give us some insight to your life before now. And oh, Michael said something about you were a nun or didn't make the cut." He laughs and raises his glass toward the waiter. "Fill it up," he says, giving his wife a wink and then drawing his eyes back to mine.

"Ah, it's rather difficult to explain my impulsiveness, such as plunging in deep with the things I love. What seems to be normal for me, well, is rather craziness to others. As a child, for some strange reason I pretended to be a nun. I pulled my turtleneck blouse up over my head, shifted it perfectly around my olive face, and instantly I was a nun with a shoulder-length habit."

I laugh as Marty Sue from Galveston slides into the conversation by saying, "Yes, I did the same thing as a child, but I pretended to be a rock star. I was never a nun. Why in the world would you want to be a nun? Nuns have no fun at all."

"Ha, well I did. I used to sing along with Diana Ross and the Supremes with my habit and the brush being my microphone. They were one of my mother's favorite singers," I confess, watching Michael from the short distance.

"Michael," I holler on impulse, interrupting his conversation with Tony and Nino, who are devouring my favorite antipasti, caponata, along with the freshly baked bread sliced into one-inch rounds. "Can you hop over here for a second?" I sense the momentum of questions starting to roll and feel as though I'm being stripped, invaded, and possibly must expose more than I care to show even though I am a talker. At this moment, I feel a restlessness consuming my thoughts. I want to wander the narrow medieval streets of this amazing village and stroll through the tiny shops where local artisans still labor with their hands. I want to watch the shoemaker cut strips of leather, creating the latest fashion with his own hands. But to be respectful of my friends, my passengers, I oblige their wishes.

"Okay, my friends, if you want to hear more of my life then brace yourselves, because as you know, my cousin Michael is quite a talker. He talks more than I do." I flash a big smile, giving Michael an exaggerated wink, knowing good and well we'll both talk as if two cars are gearing up for the racetrack, bypassing the other when given the chance. But also I know that Michael will take the lead and allow me to visit with cousins Bruno and Willie who just arrived, bellowing in Italian, "Ciao, ciao."

31

LEAVING THE LEGAL WORLD
FOR A DIFFERENT WORLD

What's happening over here?" Michael asks while dragging up a chair to our table with a big grin stretching his olive face. "So you want to hear the inside scoop, a little genealogy on my cousin? Ah, this will be fun and quite entertaining." Michael rests his nose on the edge of his wineglass, inhaling the floral bouquet of wild flowers and citrus fruits into his nasal passage. He slowly inhales the fruity fragrance as though he'd forgotten the inquisitiveness of our American friends.

"Well, I can sure tell you a few things about my cousin. But if you want to know the full story, then I'd suggest we watch the interview on my iPad. I recorded it with Mrs. Adams, a writer outside of Austin," Michael explains with a wink, knowing I've already heard the full story of her rigorous interrogation.

The liquid red is flowing around the table, and within minutes we are watching Michael and Mrs. Adams on the small screen of an iPad as if we are looking through a crystal ball, seeing and hearing them converse from the outside looking in.

"I want to know everything you can tell me about Stephani Chance, or do you call her Stefania?" Mrs. Adams inquires in a pleasant voice while rejecting a glass of liquid red with a slight nod resting atop of her elongated neck.

"Neither," Michael says. "The family calls her Stevi except for her husband, Allen, and he refuses to utter such a name. He says the name Stevi does not fit her image and whoever came up with such a nickname is really, well, never mind ... I'll not go into that right now, but Allen is rather blunt with his words at times.

"Oh, I see. And what does he call his wife? Stefania, I presume?"

"No, he calls her Stephani, her name, without the ending *e*, which should be added since it's on her birth certificate. But her mother thought it would be cute, I suppose, to omit the ending *e* from her name so she would be different. However, I can guarantee you that Stephani doesn't need a vowel deleted from her name to be different. Ha, my cousin was born different," Michael says with a lively chuckle as the woman scribbles down his every word and then reaches for a bottled water inside her designer leather bag.

"Oh, I understand. Can you tell me about the fire within her that burns so fiercely? You know, her love for the unusual and her spontaneous decisions. Can you start from the beginning of her career?" Mrs. Adams asks, stretching her arm to press the button on her tiny recorder.

"Well, you see Mrs. Adams, if Stevi, I mean Stephani had known her profession required a sharp ear to hysterical folks chattering on and on about their personal escapades along with refereeing muddled debates over countless situations throughout the workday, not to mention metamorphosing herself into an invisible detective, then she would have probably reconsidered her life's career choice. She would have joined a nun's convent in the rolling Tuscan hills of her beloved Italy. Then again probably not, since the life of a nun is so reclusive and requires absolute celibacy along with a natural face. Not to mention, a body tightly wrapped with black-and-white fabric from top to bottom, with her unmanageable chestnut hair forever forced underneath the required fabric that engulfs her entire head," Michael continues to ramble and Mrs. Adams, who already looks confused, jots down a few words.

"Choosing the path of a nun would be a far cry from her colorful image of style and her love for the unusual—such as her possession of a Russian fur hat purchased at the Arezzo, Italy, market on a chilly fall morning with her Sicilian papa Tony Filaci, and the adorable Nino, who was tagged long ago 'Nino, the little bambino.' Not to mention, her Italian chinchilla designed and created by the famous celebrity designer Franco Veroli in Roma, who is married to Luisa, the beautiful celebrity model for the famous designer line Armani. Both of these wonderful people are knitted tightly into her life by certain Italian threads."

Pausing for a mere second, Mrs. Adams reaches for her tape recorder and adjusts its position with a slight nudge in an obvious attempt to reassure herself the recording mechanism captures his every word.

"So she actually wanted to be a nun? And she wanted to live in Italy with the sisters, as in saintly sisters?" Mrs. Adams asks.

"Yes, that's correct. Picturing Stephani strolling down the cobblestone streets in the beautiful regions of Italy along with the saintly sisters concealed in their black-and-white attire is hard to imagine without, of course, a gigantic grin stretching across one's face. And renouncing her sparkling red lips along with confronting the world with a monotonous face, not to mention leaving Franco Veroli's Italian designs behind, was far more than enough reason to prevent her life's stay in a secluded convent even though it was in her beloved Italy."

"Ah, I'm getting the picture now. Bless her heart. She wanted to be a nun but was way too worldly for the cause. Yes, okay, please carry on," Mrs. Adams says with a smiling approval.

"Well, the thought of depriving her face from such needed color redirected her toward the journey she is now traveling, a life that is remarkably similar to the convent when it comes to strong values and her devout faith in God. However, the saintly sisters would highly reprimand her flamboyant style and her love for the unusual such as her red-painted lips and her passion to love and marry a tall olive man with thick black hair. Not to mention giving birth to a son Shane and a daughter Naiches along with excessively spoiling her only grand-doll, Kaitlyn Paige, with too many earthly goods. Also, her playing hostess in an overly embellished home that's filled with too many religious relics she's found in Italy and doting over two manicured black poodles that tiptoe around in Parisian style with dazzling rhinestone collars fitted perfectly around their furry little necks. Oh, there is more to be said, trust me, but we'd be here all night with the laundry list of debaucheries my cousin calls essentials."

With an awkward, half laugh, Michael continues. "Do you get the picture now? No, I'm sure you can't imagine such a life until you've actually met her. Stephani has never been plain; in fact, she's just the opposite. She goes over the top on just about everything she does and that includes ... well, this is veering off the subject a little, but when it comes to decorating ... I'll just say, stepping inside her home during our family Christmas parties will send your hair straight up with shock, and that's putting it mildly. Calling the inside of her home 'excessive' would be considered an insult to most, but the adjective brings a big smile to her olive-toned face. Come to think of it, *excessive* is an understatement for her. Oh yes, she loves to decorate, and I will leave it at that."

"Oh my, she does sound like … well, she certainly has no place in a convent. No, she would probably try to convert the faithful sisters over to her sinful nature of worldly pleasures. Oh yes, most definitely, she would indeed," Mrs. Adams chimes as she scribbled frantically on her pad.

"Stephani is a comical, outgoing Protestant born at Saint Paul's Hospital in Dallas, with European genes stretching far across the deep blue pond. She's an enormous splash of French 'ooh la la' with a little dash of Italian spice, and a whole lot of New Orleans jazz blended with a strong helping of good old East Texas baked right in. And thanks to her mother, God bless her soul, she wouldn't be complete without a flavorful sprinkle of hot, jalapeno peppers inflaming her thermostat every now and then." Michael laughs, reaching for a sip of his liquid red.

"Ah, so you say she is an outgoing Protestant? Hmm, I would assume her to be Catholic because of her love for Italy and desire to be a nun and all," Mrs. Adams comments to Michael with a gigantic question mark in her eyes.

"No, well, perhaps, but no, she is … but she wholeheartedly believes and loves the biblical truths," Michael says, and then stops. We presume that Michael is pondering his own thoughts and leaving her in debatable suspense as we lean in closer to the iPad and watch this entertaining interview.

"Giving up the sisterhood in her beloved Italy idea was a decision she made long ago for another choice, a career choice. A career spinning around the judicial system for sixteen adventurous years in a long, boxed building with thousands of legal documents and a tall scholarly attorney by her side. The years went by swiftly inside the long box and, *BAM!* With one flip of a magazine page, her world changed, everything changed."

"Hold up, Michael. What do you mean Stephani's world changed with a flip of a magazine page?" Mrs. Adams demands with an engaging sternness.

"Well, I haven't finished my sentence yet, Mrs. Adams. Please allow me to continue before I lose my train of thought," Michael replies curtly with a slight roll of his eyes.

"Oh yes, excuse me. Yes please continue on," Mrs. Adams leans back in the overstuffed sofa with Mattie Kay, a gorgeous Himalayan cat, curled beside her.

"Are you sure?" Michael asks, displaying drawn eyebrows pressed together and appearing to be in pain. But in reality, we can see he's just annoyed by too many interruptions. "Hmm, well, I've forgotten where I was going with this. Oh yes, I remember.

"Stephani was flipping through the pages of a magazine one day and with a flip of the page, a glossy photo of an old Italian castle jumped out at her. The photo magically slapped her inner spirit, awakening it from a long siesta and refueling old memories woven together from her past."

Snatching her ink pen again, Mrs. Adams jots down a few more words and totally disregards the tape recorder that is capturing his every word.

"Like a lightning bolt flashing across the East Texas sky, in a moment's notice her world changed. Old family connections were roused from sleep to take her from a legal world to an old Italian world—a world that is bound tightly together with family that refuses to conference with the disconnected. And like an animated Sicilian marionette that's magically activated, she dances through scenes as though the stages were set just for her. She dances in many directions mysteriously set in motion that are maneuvering, working, and controlling her every move." Michael relates all of this with a swirl of his liquid red, watching it whirl around and around in the crystal glass.

"I need clarification of what you just said. Ah, never mind. I get it. You are surely talking about God orchestrating her life and destination. Oh, yes, certainly ... Please continue on," Mrs. Adams says with excitement, portraying a satisfied look of a job well done as though she were a detective.

Michael gazes at Mrs. Adams with raised eyebrows. Not saying a word, he pauses and waits for her to interrupt him again. Then, dabbing his lips with a lavender napkin, Michael continues.

"Leaving the legal world for a different world caused many locals to assume the worse and ask too many ridiculous questions, such as Is she suffering from a dreaded illness? Is she going through a divorce? Did she find a new love? Did she inherit considerable fortune from her wealthy uncles, giving her financial freedom from the legal box?"

"Hmm, well, what happened? Did her uncles …?" Mrs. Adams tries to ask, but the dynamics of the conversation changes as Michael swiftly cuts her off like a fast race car before she finishes her sentence.

"Oh, the ridiculous chatter continued much too long. You know how people think and assume the worse. However, she took a leap of faith, you could say. She jumped out of the box and away she flew. Ha! That's how she rolls … My cousin is very spontaneous. She prays first and then leaps out running, never walking. Nevertheless, they finally heard the big news, and it went like this: 'She's finally out of the box and Mamma Mia, Italy will never be the same.'" Michael chuckles while reaching for his liquid red.

"Well, Mrs. Adams, I hope you have a better understanding of my cousin," he concludes as Mrs. Adams reaches for her tape recorder, pressing the button off.

"Oh, yes, indeed, but I want to go back to the long box, you know, the legal box. You said she worked with a tall scholarly attorney, and I would like to hear more about him and of course Stephani as well, if that's possible."

"I'm sorry, but I have no more time allotted for today. However, Stephani is writing a book, a memoir and true stories of what the Americans do on her Italy tour groups. Perhaps you should wait for the book," Michael suggests.

With a loud clap of hands, Michael pretends to slowly bring the Americans out of the crystal ball as he pushes the iPad to off, leaving them in anticipation of hearing more. But before they speak, Michael springs from his seat and treks toward the towering plate of pasta. Feeling déjà vu, as if exhausted from the interview once again, he rejoins Tony, Nino, Willie, and Bruno, all of whom are having their own celebration with the hefty platters of pasta.

"Now wait just one minute. Stephani, you have left us in great desire to hear more of this life. We cannot wait until you have published a book. No. You must tell us about this box and this attorney. What did Michael mean when he said you 'jumped out of the box'? I want to know about the old castle of a house too. Please, Stephani, tell us everything."

32

THE LAW OFFICE

The empty wineglasses are whisked away, and before I respond to their questions, tiny glasses of limoncello are placed before them along with baskets of biscotti. Excitement soars when Tony prompts his local friend to draw the cork from his favorite vino of all, the famous Brunello. A chorus of handclaps applauds as more of the liquid red flows beside the little glasses of limoncello, and before I take another sip of my cola with the floating lemons on top, another local friend brings out towering platters of creamy chocolate cannoli. The parade of food will go on for another hour or so, and before it gets any later, I keep my promise.

"Okay, my friends, follow along with me as I take you to the long box, the law office—my life before this life. But please, you must follow along with me in your mind. You must visualize as I take you inside. And yes, I will tell you about Dwight Brannon and his special brain circuits." I take a deep breath and watch as the Americans giggle with excitement as if I were preparing them for a bedtime story.

I begin my story. "The weather outside is deceivingly dark. At seven thirty or so, heavy drops of cool rain from dense black clouds transform the horizon into a dreary scene of midnight, chasing me back toward the barred door. It's only been an hour or so since I was inside the long box meticulously working, but time ran out. Did the clock strike five or was it six? It doesn't really matter, because time means nothing in this profession. There is always a deadline, an emergency, a death, a prenuptial, a divorce, a crime, a transaction, a dispute, and of course the telephone.

"Returning to the law office on this dreary, wet night gives me hope of reducing the high stacks of legal files down to eye level. Before heading out of the office this evening, Dwight generously added a few more files on my desk with his attached notes. There is so much to do before the highly publicized murder trial begins next week, but who am I kidding?

Catching up is utterly impossible in this law office. No sooner do I complete one task than another one is added.

"Being alone here tonight, it feels a little eerie in this long, rectangular box on Titus Street. The entire building completely lacks windows except for one, and it's guarded by iron bars. From the two door exits, my office seems miles away. It's just about midstream from the front and back door exits to the outside world of daylight, which in my case would be night light. This tightly sealed building at night is the ideal work environment, excluding the mysterious echoes heard from the far back room chilling my spine. And no, I will not go in to the mysterious sounds this night. I will save that for another late night," I say, springing back into the story line.

"The walls of this long building are thick—many layers of brick, I'm told. Once inside the elongated box, you never know whether it's raining, snowing, thundering with a tornado spinning toward you or bright rays of sunlight are piercing down against the painted brick. It doesn't really matter, though, since it's all experienced in the same way from inside. On the front of the long brick box, which has been my home for these last sixteen adventurous years, professional letters proudly proclaim 'Dwight A. Brannon, Attorney at Law,'"

"Entering my office, I am engulfed by legal files stacked everywhere, literally knee-deep in the rainbow colors of blue, yellow, brown, and manila. Each color represents a certain area of law, such as civil, criminal, family law, wills and probate, real estate, and so on. I feel compelled to flip on every light switch in the building as I continue down the long hallway, which surrounds me with a dead silence.

"At the end of this rectangular building reminiscent of a bowling alley is the bleakest and gloomiest room of all. The room is filled with thousands of case files that have already been settled or otherwise have met their fate of judgment in the courtroom. All of them rest peacefully, lying dormant by the hundreds in black, metallic, fireproof filing cabinets, one after the other, from floor to ceiling.

"Entering this dreary room is like walking into a cold dusky morgue, full of closed chapters in so many lives. Many of these files rest in peace, knowing they have prevailed in total victory before the courts of law. There are other files lurking in tightly sealed cabinets, full of secrets from their destructive and murderous pasts, which are way too painful to reminisce, especially tonight.

"Glancing over to the left wall of this cold morgue, I spot a towering stack of boxes. Printed in black ink on the outside of these boxes, I see the names of past clients. I remember the horrific details that now send chills down my spine. One particular case, the one I'm looking at now, made national headlines in a certain acclaimed tabloid that surely left people thinking, *This can't be true!*

"I see hundreds of sleeping files and wonder how many of them returned to this dungeon-of-a-room in tearful remorse, sorry for ending their once picture-perfect fairy-tale marriages. *They are guilty as charged, thinking the pastures were greener on the other side,* I speculate for a brief second.

"I gaze at many divorce files sealed in total darkness back here, locked away by final judgment. Many rest peacefully, enjoying their peace and quiet and relishing the total victory. Turning my eyes to the other side of the filing cabinets, I can't help but think of the many lives, rich and poor, represented in this dead air room, laid to rest or perhaps heavily burdened from the humiliation that forever looms within these closed metal filing cabinets.

"My mind wanders in this illuminated paper cemetery, bringing me a sense of pride and gratitude in knowing each of these cases, regardless of status, was indeed represented by one of the finest legal minds I have ever known. Working beside Dwight Brannon for so many years underneath his 'straight and narrow' veil, reassures me that each case resting here tonight did indeed receive the best legal counsel that the State Bar of Texas has to offer. Victoriously representing the innocent is no problem for Dwight because he is fully equipped with what I describe as unique brain circuits and an IQ privileged by most geniuses. He's blessed with a special gift from God, an exceptional brain wired for a perpetual remembrance of details. I would avoid this room, if possible; however, on many occasions, there is a need to return and revisit a sleeping file for various reasons.

"Tonight, there's no telephone ringing, no soft music floating throughout the building, no hysterical clients begging for miracles, and no Dwight Brannon performing such miracles. I am alone. And not tonight of course, but in Dwight's office, the four of us congregate behind closed doors. Three chairs directly in front of Dwight's huge, stately desk hold Ondra Lee Gilbert, Tish Jenkins, and me, Stephani Chance, also known as Stevi by the inner circle, sitting with pad and pen clenched in hand. We are waiting attentively as Dwight opens the mountainous bundle of mail, discussing the most urgent pieces, and if the mood is calm, hearing a few of his stories from long ago. Some might say—but probably not, because of the differences in hair color and slight body shapes—that we three ladies resemble the original, illustrious movie stars on *Charlie's Angels*. All three of us are perched comfortably with pen and pad, hanging on to Charlie's—well, in our case, Dwight's—every word, but not tonight."

33

DWIGHT A. BRANNON,
ATTORNEY AT LAW

"Dwight is a handsome, towering attorney who stands at a monumental height of six foot five— or more. He is tremendously blessed with the brain of Einstein, not to mention a photographic memory that retains every single event of the last sixteen adventurous years in the long box. He recalls information as though his brain were a computer chip, downloaded with his entire legal practice stored in tact, detail to detail.

"Working day after day with someone for so long, you become well acquainted. I possess a deep respect for him as a very intense, morally upright man who practices law with such fervent passion to help people. Not only that, but Dwight cherishes his wife, Brenda, with a respect and love that is refreshing in our contemporary world. He possesses many delightful qualities. In particular, he allows me to learn from his inexhaustible, scholarly mind. From his towering height to his storytelling events, by his burning seriousness of practicing law, I was molded, smashed down, and molded again. In Dwight's world of legal perfection, it's safe to say that perfection is obtained by the potter's own hand, and in my case, it was his left hand.

"When observing Dwight Brannon, the absolute confidence in his demeanor is evident along with a head full of thick, grayish-brown hair that's always styled to movie-star perfection. Never a hair out of place— no, never. Each strand is heavily coated with fresh-smelling shimmering gel that leaves a hint of alluring masculinity. His thick, straight hair is neatly parted to the right, giving off a lustrous style of intelligence and a hint of city-style glamour, which is rare behind the old 'Pine Curtain.' Pine Curtain is just another name for our particular area here in beautiful East Texas. Legend has it that once you maneuver within the Pine Curtain, you have absorbed an experience like no other in the great state of Texas, which to me is undisputable. East Texas is a wonderland of pine trees and rolling hills nestled with massive lakes and a vast array of oil wells pumping to the beat of gold—black gold, that is, which sadly to report, I have none.

"After sixteen plus years of working underneath Dwight's rigorous leadership as a paralegal, trying to understand his computerized brain circuits, equivalent to the congressional law library and a mathematical computer, I must say, he meticulously molded me to his high standards of acute impeccability.

"Many times I've wavered, swaying on wobbly legs inches below his straight and narrow towering canopy. I've been enfeebled by his continuous legal jargon switching from one case to another in an attempt to remember every minute detail. In Dwight's electronically wired brain, each case is filed alphabetically with all the facts singing loudly. Dwight commands a fierce respect with his powerful brain circuits and his overshadowing height. Nonetheless, I choose to overlook him, in my mind, that is, and never allow him to intimidate my challenged soul. A few times, only a few, I've threaded on the brink of collapse, contemplating tossing in the towel. However, just before calling in the 'expert relief team' of Ondra Lee Gilbert and Tish Jenkins, the perpetual legal assistants who would no doubt rescue me, I miraculously bounced back, landing on top of the never-ending spinning wheel inside this legal box."

34

The Old Castle of a House in DeKalb, Texas

Others have now gathered around our table along with the Americans. The liquid red is still flowing, and the music is pumping in the distant background. The little shops are reopening after being closed for the ritual siesta. To the Italians, the evening hasn't even started, and to the Americans, well … it's time to prepare for bed. I've been talking for what seems to be an hour or so, but in reality it's only been minutes, save the interruptions of more food being piled upon our table.

Nonetheless, I've gone into great detail describing the long boxed law office and Dwight Brannon. But from the countless questions still bombarding me and the fact that Michael shared a few things about my grandparents' old castle of a house and the dangling marionettes to some of them on the coach, I must carry on or they will accompany me to my room tonight for the rest of the story.

"Stephani, you bounced back on the never-ending spinning wheel, but tell us about the magical moment when lightning hit. You know, the moment the lights went off in your head, causing you to leap from the long box. What caused your mind to drift into a total different direction? Was it your grandparents? I do not understand what Michael said about a magazine—something about a castle. Also, if you don't mind, please tell us about the chocolate pies and the great room," Mary Jo plows deeper into the questions, leaving no way out but to explain.

"Sixteen plus years have come and gone in the long, narrow law office and with one flip of a magazine page right before my eyes I see the most magnificent photo of a medieval castle with red flags flapping gracefully through the Toscana air in Italy. At that very moment, I find myself taken back in time—only a few years ago it seems—to a small, wonderful, southern town called DeKalb, Texas, the home of my Grandmother and

Granddaddy Prestridge and eventually mine as well after leaving our home in Dallas."

"Staring at the glossy Italian magazine now clenched in my hands, I see an old Tuscan castle looking back at me. It's hauntingly beautiful and very enticing. The longer I stare at the castle, the more it slowly fades into my grandparents' old southern-style castle of a house. It is inspiring emotions of exhilaration topped with memories of a southern world I grew up in as a child. The red flags waving on the Italian castle slowly fade into red-velvet fabric, exploding from the high vaulted ceilings and crashing down hard onto the dark polished wood floors in my grandparents' home.

"My memory recalls the massive great-room with mahogany furniture and yards of damask fabric enveloping the gorgeous divans. My favorite of all was the enormous, circular divan, highlighting the massive great-room with exquisite, towering statues of marble and bronze. The room possessed a welcoming presence for everyone who entered. A welcoming to sit upon its velvety, Parisian divans with endless supplies of cashmere throws. A welcoming to accept a tall glass of iced tea with fresh lemons pierced around the rim of the glass. And always, a welcoming to enjoy a fresh fried pie, or if the timing is right, a thick slice of homemade chocolate pie with towering meringue bronzed perfectly on top.

"Slowing slipping back into my grandparents' home, I lift my eyes toward the heavenly realm of the blue-clouded ceiling. *Surely airplanes fly above, surely they do,* I thought as a child. The splendor of such wonderment draws sighs of breathtaking beauty and a feeling of adoration for the magnificent blue heavens painted on the rapturous ceilings. Stepping inside the great-room is magically enticing, instantly engulfing me in a heavenly world of creamy antiquities and feathery-winged angels holding bounteous flowers in lustrous shades of reds, purples, honey gold, and soft pinks. I am surrounded by the mesmerizing Murano chandelier that is exploding high above my head with dazzling crystals of iridescent brilliancy cascading down like a slow drizzle of springtime droplets. This magnificent room refreshes the weary soul with heavenly jubilation and creates a sense of happiness as the huge flock of angels smile down upon me from the endless-journey sky.

"Over three stories high, able to meander in so many directions, spiral endlessly up three winding stories with no hope of ever stopping ... making the long journey up and down, day after day, step after step, perpetually lifting one shoe at a time as I bypass one landing and then another was my life for a long time, it seems.

"Living on the top story of the old castle of a house was like living on a mountaintop. Way down below existed another world, a world of unusual things. In my eyes, it was an enchanting world that compares to a life in the fairy-tale storybook of *Alice in Wonderland*, except it's not Alice in this world, it's me, a child mesmerized by stupendous people, tall, fascinating, bronze people who are extremely cold to the touch and tower way above me. Some of these people have heads, some are without heads, and some have no arms. An extremely strange thing to see as a child but it was normal for me, normal to see the unusual decor from a different world.

"Standing in front of the massive stairs, with my right hand clenched tightly to the mahogany wood baluster, I look up and swallow hard. Miles above me, I see more of the blue-clouded skies, angels descending out of large, puffy clouds, and endless steps leading to the scary world above. My heart beats faster and faster the farther I step up the soaring staircase. This staircase is not like the modern-day staircases in the multimillion dollar mansions. Oh no, it's nothing like them at all. This endless, yellow-brick-road of a staircase leads me around and around, swirling and bypassing each massive landing.

"Adjusting my eyes downward, I see miles of endless, twisting stairs leading up to the world above that is now my home. It is a big and massive world with tall castle doors on each landing opening up to more massive rooms that meander in many directions to another fairy-tale world of strange things.

"Way down on the first floor, I peek inside the music room and see Granddaddy Prestridge sitting at his grand piano, his fingers rolling off the keys in a fast motion, zipping left to right, sounding out harmonizing tunes from the Old World of New Orleans jazz. He is surrounded by endless yards of heavy Old World, damask fabric in the traditional colors of ruby reds and antique gold.

"'It's the old rendezvous of ruby reds,' My mother would explain in splendid detail, as though I actually cared to know such things as a small child, but according to her, one must know the various hues of color coordination and especially the touch of fabrics.

"I see the explosion of fabrics erupting down the creamy meringue walls, resembling a massive volcano spewing and pouring from the stained-glass windows high above. Patriarch saints are hovering way above the massive furniture, appearing victorious in the clouded heavens. I see grandeur and European magnificence from ceiling to floor as flavors of enticement arouse my senses.

"Escaping the great-room in haste and drawn toward the maid's kitchen, I follow the alluring aromas of fresh fried okra, or a simmering pot of garden crowder peas from last night's shelling. Arriving inside the kitchen, I see bubbly thick, new potatoes absorbing large scoops of real yellow butter, simmering perfectly on the stovetop. Over to the right I see hot peppered cornbread resting in a black iron skillet, too hot to touch, and mountains of garden-picked tomatoes, cantaloupes, and hot peppers, not to mentioned the smothered roast festooned with bright orange carrots, chopped onions, garlic, and many other seasonings that Granddaddy says are critically necessary for the perfect southern meal.

"Arriving in haste, Granddaddy Prestridge slides into the kitchen like a baseball runner arriving to home plate and quickly wraps his white apron around his waist as though he's now heading for a fire escape. Without thought, he reaches for the liquid gold—olive oil—to freely douse the diced tomatoes, along with piles of diced jalapenos. Within minutes, Granddaddy is pouring creamy, warm chocolate batter into two steaming pie shells that were rolled and pressed perfectly into two glass pie plates earlier this morning by Grandmother Prestridge. Just a few minutes before the creamy egg whites were beaten to stiff peaks with an abundant pour of the liquid vanilla, along with a pinch of cream of tartar and splashes of white sugar. All of this completed the golden-brown meringue piled high on the best chocolate pies in Texas.

"Thinking of homemade chocolate pies coming out of my grandparents' oven has absolutely nothing to do with the glossy magazine page before me right now. However, the medieval castle captured by the click of a photographer's hand in the Tuscany hills of Italy did. Thankfully, though, I've not taken up too much time sitting here daydreaming and allowing my mind to steal the delightful memories from long ago in the old castle of a house.

"In a blink's notice, my black flocked lashes crash, causing my eyes to refocus on the magazine page. It's almost like a dream or a magical wand swirling quickly above my mesmerized head, bringing me the realization that a vast array of opportunities, in fact, do await me.

"*What about bringing the Old World to East Texas?* I think to myself as I allow my mind to keep rolling. It was Granddaddy Prestridge's old smokehouse filled with treasures from the Old World that enticed me as a child. It was filled with strange things, such as his wood-carved Sicilian marionettes dangling from the ceiling, appearing as little people hanging from their necks. Demijohns rested high up in the old, musky smokehouse, along with massive trunks overflowing with strange things he called treasures.

"Thoughts of driving throughout Italy and France in search of medieval castle doors and old religious relics are racing through my head, and I clearly see myself zigzagging around the tiny curves in Tuscany and zooming upward to the fairy-tale, walled villages.

"I see myself entering the medieval walls protecting the hidden villages, spiraling around and around and ascending high into the clouds. I feel my heart pounding, thinking about searching the many forgotten wine cellars from long ago, hoping to find beautiful, carved doors and stained-glass windows from the early crusades of long ago.

"I allow my mind to slip back to the day my dearest cousin, Denton Bundy, and I followed Granddaddy out to his old smokehouse.

"I can still see Granddaddy reaching for his shovel just a few feet inside, as Denton and I climb to the top shelf. We are trying our best to open one of the many large trunks, but it's difficult to open in the position we're in right now. Me being the larger one and without doubt the bossier one, I instruct Denton to pull as hard as he can while I pry a large tool behind the rusty latch. Within seconds, the old rusty latch flies open, and out pops little people with large, smiling faces and beautiful little outfits covered with forged iron. Not realizing what's before us, assuming they're alive and surely out to harm us, we scream with fear and jump to our possible deaths. Surprisingly, we survive without broken legs or giving

Granddaddy a massive heart attack. Afterward, Granddaddy tells us the mesmerizing story of the little people.

"'They come from Sicily, and they are handmade marionettes. You know, as in puppets but not just any puppets,' Granddaddy explains in long detail."

MAMMA MIA, SHE'S OUT OF THE BOX!

"At some point, I realize I'm still staring at the glossy magazine page, the Italian castle photographed so majestically. Lost within this page and staring deep into the castle, my mind shifts into second gear, and I'm on a roll that will not stop. I'm seeing beautiful castle doors, iron-forged balconies and an endless arrays of architectural treasures showcased in new homes being built right here in East Texas. *Why not bring these rare beauties to East Texas? Why not launch an antiques store filled to the ceiling with gorgeous, hand-carved castle doors and rare relics that are found only in Italy?*

"Decorating is my passion—at least one of them—and I adore ornate, hand-carved wood, not to mention, beautiful religious relics. Would people come to a store such as this and purchase old castle doors? Would they buy the iron-forged balconies and beautiful home decor from the southern parts of Italy? And, oh, what about the beautifully hand-painted ceramics found throughout Italy, especially the Moorish Head urns made in Caltagirone, Sicily?

"Thinking of leaving the law office is surely ridiculous, I know. Nonetheless, within weeks, I've signed my name on the necessary legal documents and handed over a substantial check to the sellers for their long commercial building, and within a year's time, a new chapter has been written. I'm a full-time business owner of an import shop, Decorate Ornate, and more, as in taking two fun-loving groups of Americans to Italy twice a year with a hilariously funny Sicilian, Tony Filaci.

****

I hope you have enjoyed our rendezvous, zigzagging throughout Italy. As of right now, this is my fourteenth year taking two groups of

Americans to Italy and beyond twice a year. There are many more true and unbelievable stories to tell of the Americans in Italy and beyond. If you have enjoyed traveling with us, reading about our escapades, then let me hear from you via email, ALNCHANCE@AOL.COM, and visit the website DecorateOrnate.com.

If you want to join in the fun, hop aboard with us. Who knows, you might just make the next book! To be continued.

ACKNOWLEDGMENTS

Thank God for the Americans' adventurous spirit and the ones who faithfully hop aboard my Italy tours twice a year and the ones who toss their money across the counter saying, "Sign me up," never asking where we're going just as long as it's Italy, along with those who call from afar, asking when we depart. With a humorous laugh, I thank God for the Americans who ask Tony the hair-raising questions and comments that repeatedly cause animated facial gestures of disbelief on his olive-kissed face.

"Why do you have so many rolling hills in Tuscany? Why not level them down and make the drive faster? It's ridiculous to have so many sharp curves. Haven't you heard of a bulldozer? Why must you eat pasta every day? Where do we get the hamburgers and hot dogs? Where is the salad bar? Why are so many of you Italians Catholic? Have you ever heard of Baptist or Methodist? Why do you say Mamma Mia?"

And yes, I'm even thankful for the Americans who refuse to walk inside the famous basilicas where the relics of biblical saints reside, saying they would rather lick the gelato and browse the couture shops, insisting they've seen plenty of churches in America. "They all look alike," they say, never peeking inside the towering doors to see the magnificent creations. And there are the Americans who do enter the ancient churches—talking too loudly, giggling, and touching everything in sight while disregarding the praying saints who are fingering one bead at a time of their sacred rosary, while asking why there are so many fresh flowers. "Is there a funeral or wedding starting soon?" they ask in bellowing voices. I'm even thankful for the Americans who wear their long cowboy boots and big Stetson cowboy hats, shaking their heads in disbelief at the colorful hues of the tightly fitted pants on the Italian men. And God bless the Americans who bring their luggage packed full of power bars, insisting they will stay slim and trim while on holiday, never touching those fattening pastas and garlicky breads saturated with the liquid-gold olive oil. And too, the Americans who turn their nose up at the liquid red, the sacred wine, preferring Coca-Cola, gulping them down as if they're in the hot desert. And the Americans who insist on French fries and cups of ketchup with their pizzas and those who demand instant service when knowing the mamma is in the kitchen preparing a homemade meal fit for a king or queen, even the Americans who ask why the windows in the Coliseum have not been replaced, or why the Coliseum is still standing, suggesting, "You should demolish this old spectacle! It's taking up too much of your prime property here in Rome." Mamma Mia, I love the Americans!

On a personal note, I thank God for my olive-kissed Romeo, Allen Chance, my devoted husband who loves me more than I deserve and tolerates my countless escapes across the pond. Thank you for stealing my heart and sending me on a whirlwind journey that I'd never experienced—the fatal love bite with the repercussions of "falling in love" as I'd never known. I love you!

Thank you, God, for my treasured possessions, my son, Shane and his adorable wife, Amy, and my daughter, Naiches. Thank you for loving me beyond comprehension and serving God with a servant's heart. My only grand-doll, Kaitlyn Paige, who is a gift from God and brings our family and me so much happiness. It's true, grandchildren are the best. They light up your world.

Thank you, Dwight Brannon, attorney at law, for showing me the true meaning of an attorney: a godly man with morals that uses his God-given talents to help those in need, day after day, and puts himself last. Thank you for being my mentor in the career of law. Thank you for setting the standards high, causing me to never accept anything lower.

How can I say thank you to Tony Filaci, my extended papa, my mentor and best friend. I love you dearly. We have shared a lifetime of fun and laughter, along with our beloved Nino, who drives us all over Europe, zigzagging up and down and around the rolling hills. My Italian family and friends, I am forever grateful for your love and devotion and open arms.